J

THE

BIG

BOOK

◆ OF ◆

WAR

BOOK
GUY

VOLKANO

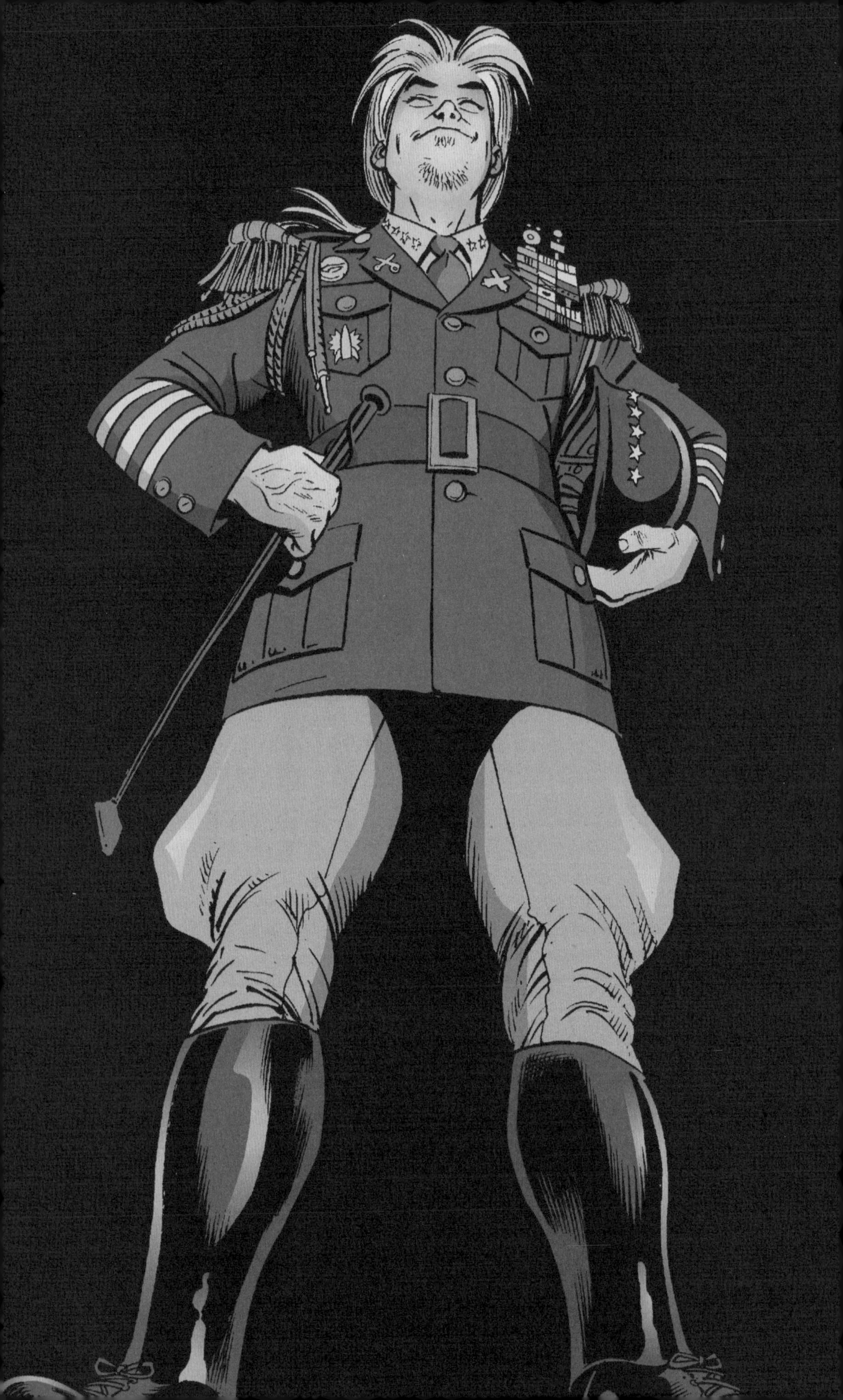

JACK of FABLES

THE

BIG BOOK OF WAR

BILL WILLINGHAM
MATTHEW STURGES
WRITERS

TONY AKINS
RUSS BRAUN
PENCILLERS

JOSÉ MARZÁN, JR.
DAN GREEN
INKERS

DANIEL VOZZO
COLORIST

TODD KLEIN
LETTERER

BRIAN BOLLAND
ORIGINAL SERIES COVERS

Jack of Fables created by **BILL WILLINGHAM**

KAREN BERGER
SVP-Executive Editor

ANGELA RUFINO
Editor-original series

GEORG BREWER
VP-Design & DC Direct Creative

BOB HARRAS
Group Editor-Collected Editions

SCOTT NYBAKKEN
Editor

ROBBIN BROSTERMAN
Design Director-Books

CURTIS KING JR.
Senior Art Director

DC COMICS

PAUL LEVITZ
President & Publisher

RICHARD BRUNING
SVP-Creative Director

PATRICK CALDON
EVP-Finance & Operations

AMY GENKINS
SVP-Business & Legal Affairs

JIM LEE
Editorial Director-WildStorm

GREGORY NOVECK
SVP-Creative Affairs

STEVE ROTTERDAM
SVP-Sales & Marketing

CHERYL RUBIN
SVP-Brand Management

Cover illustration by BRIAN BOLLAND
Logo design by JAMES JEAN

JACK OF FABLES: THE BIG BOOK OF WAR

Published by DC Comics. Cover and compilation Copyright © 2009 DC Comics. All Rights Reserved.
Originally published in single magazine form as JACK OF FABLES 28-32.
Copyright © 2009 Bill Willingham and DC Comics. All Rights Reserved.
All characters, their distinctive likenesses and related elements featured in this publication
are trademarks of Bill Willingham. VERTIGO is a trademark of DC Comics.
The stories, characters and incidents featured in this publication are entirely fictional.
DC Comics does not read or accept unsolicited submissions of ideas, stories or artwork.

DC Comics, 1700 Broadway, New York, NY 10019
A Warner Bros. Entertainment Company.
Printed in Canada. First Printing.
ISBN: 978-1-4012-2500-1

 SFI CERTIFIED SOURCING — Fiber used in this product line meets the sourcing requirements of the SFI program. www.sfiprogram.org PWC-SFICOC-260

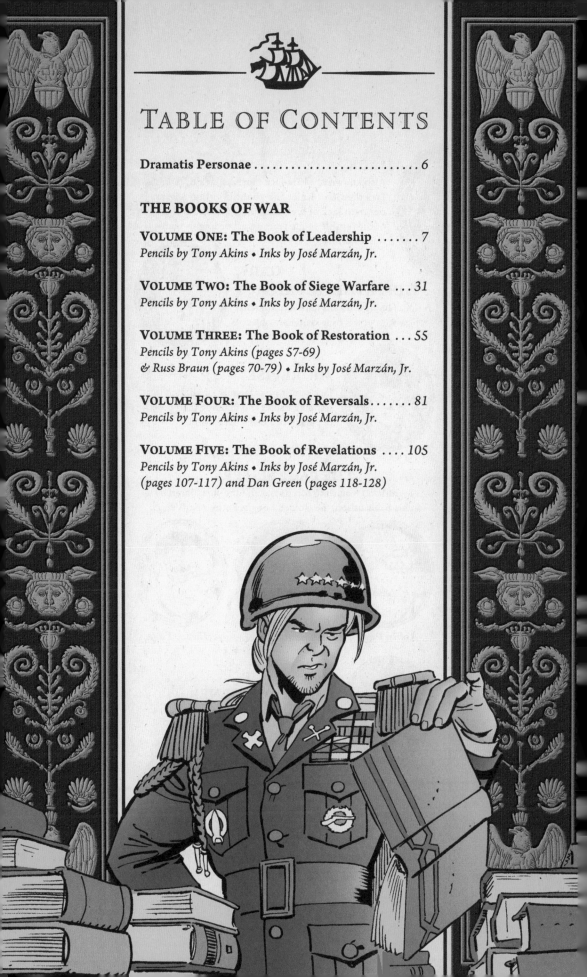

TABLE OF CONTENTS

Dramatis Personae 6

THE BOOKS OF WAR

VOLUME ONE: The Book of Leadership 7
Pencils by Tony Akins • Inks by José Marzán, Jr.

VOLUME TWO: The Book of Siege Warfare . . . 31
Pencils by Tony Akins • Inks by José Marzán, Jr.

VOLUME THREE: The Book of Restoration . . . 55
Pencils by Tony Akins (pages 57-69)
& Russ Braun (pages 70-79) • Inks by José Marzán, Jr.

VOLUME FOUR: The Book of Reversals 81
Pencils by Tony Akins • Inks by José Marzán, Jr.

VOLUME FIVE: The Book of Revelations 105
Pencils by Tony Akins • Inks by José Marzán, Jr.
(pages 107-117) and Dan Green (pages 118-128)

DRAMATIS PERSONAE

JACK

Also known as Little Jack Horner, Jack B. Nimble, Jack the Giant Killer and countless other aliases, our hero Jack of the Tales embodies the archetype of the lovable rogue (minus, according to many, the lovability).

GARY, THE PATHETIC FALLACY

A timid, impressionable and warm-hearted fellow with power over inanimate objects.

MR. REVISE

Jack's untiring antagonist, dedicated to trapping Fables and draining their power in pursuit of a magic-free world.

THE PAGE SISTERS

Right-hand women to Mr. Revise and the chief librarians at his Fable prison, the Golden Boughs Retirement Village.

Robin Page   *Priscilla Page*   *Hillary Page*

THE BOOKBURNER

The head librarian of Americana, and the Fables' worst nightmare.

KEVIN THORNE

The father of Mr. Revise and the son of the Pathetic Fallacy, he is one of the most powerful Literals in all existence.

BABE

A blue ox with a gift for self-invention.

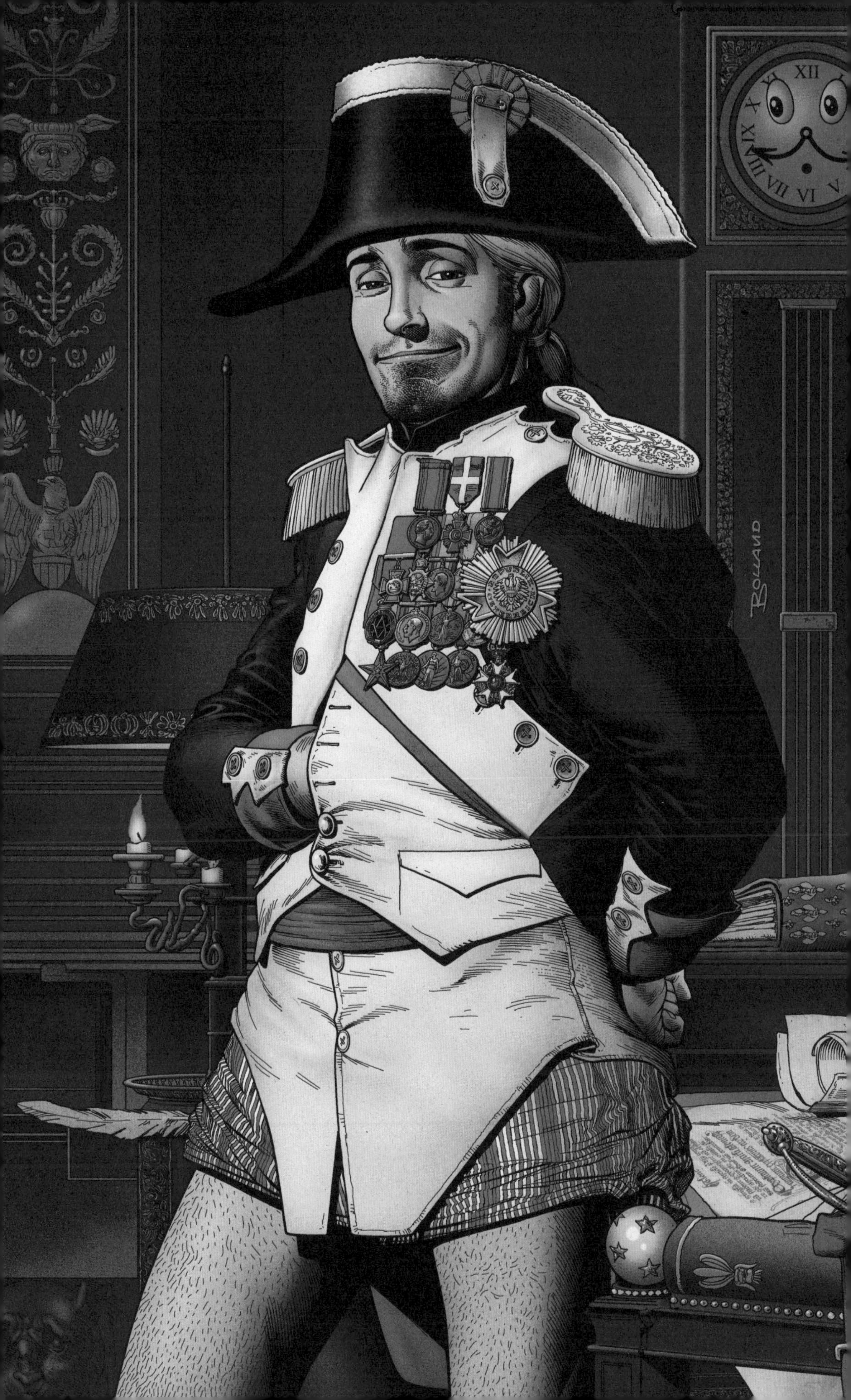
BOLLAND

*"Step aside and let a bona fide **war hero**
show you how this is done."*

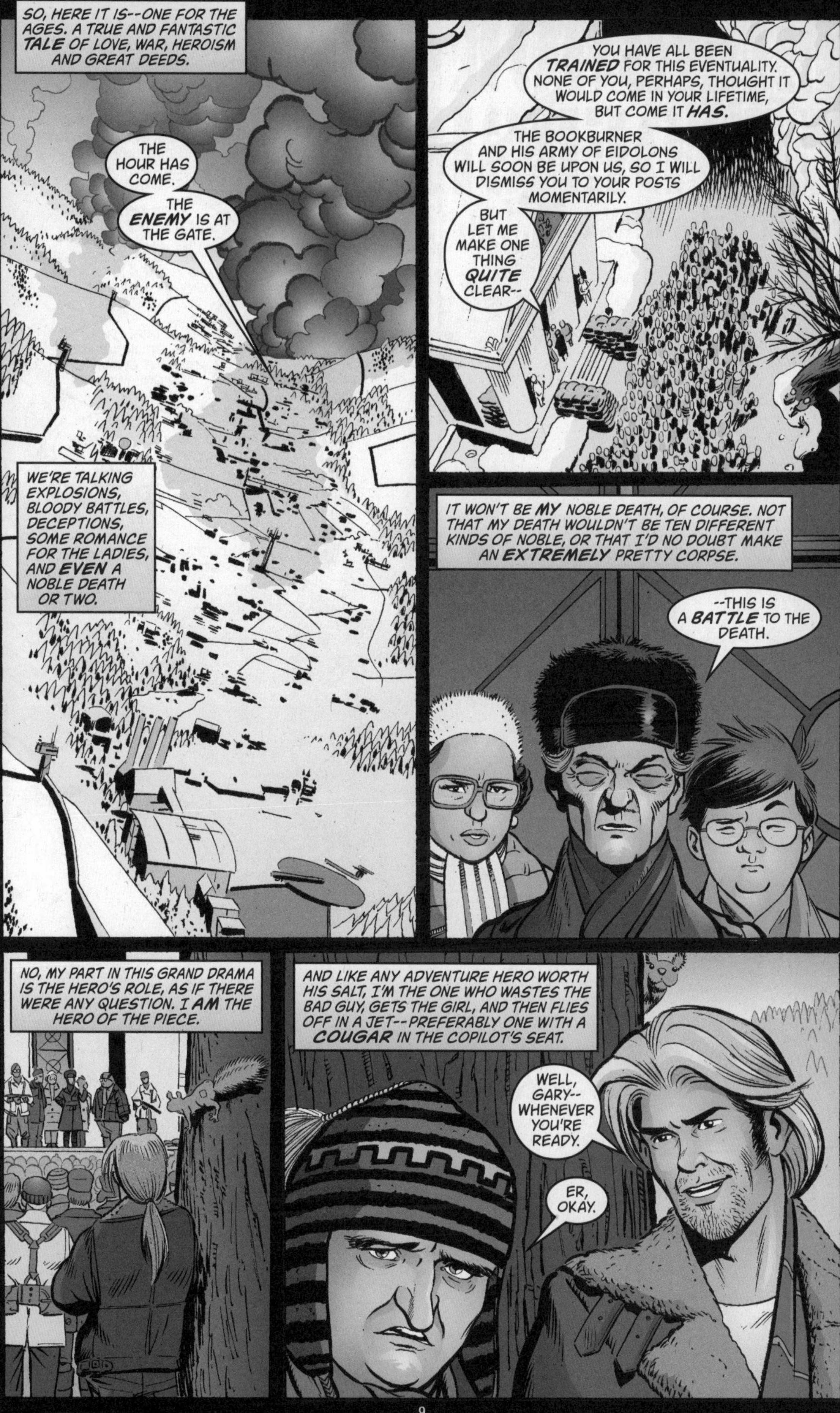
SO, HERE IT IS--ONE FOR THE AGES. A TRUE AND FANTASTIC TALE OF LOVE, WAR, HEROISM AND GREAT DEEDS.
THE HOUR HAS COME.
THE ENEMY IS AT THE GATE.
WE'RE TALKING EXPLOSIONS, BLOODY BATTLES, DECEPTIONS, SOME ROMANCE FOR THE LADIES, AND EVEN A NOBLE DEATH OR TWO.
YOU HAVE ALL BEEN TRAINED FOR THIS EVENTUALITY. NONE OF YOU, PERHAPS, THOUGHT IT WOULD COME IN YOUR LIFETIME, BUT COME IT HAS.
THE BOOKBURNER AND HIS ARMY OF EIDOLONS WILL SOON BE UPON US, SO I WILL DISMISS YOU TO YOUR POSTS MOMENTARILY.
BUT LET ME MAKE ONE THING QUITE CLEAR--
IT WON'T BE MY NOBLE DEATH, OF COURSE. NOT THAT MY DEATH WOULDN'T BE TEN DIFFERENT KINDS OF NOBLE, OR THAT I'D NO DOUBT MAKE AN EXTREMELY PRETTY CORPSE.
--THIS IS A BATTLE TO THE DEATH.
NO, MY PART IN THIS GRAND DRAMA IS THE HERO'S ROLE, AS IF THERE WERE ANY QUESTION. I AM THE HERO OF THE PIECE.
AND LIKE ANY ADVENTURE HERO WORTH HIS SALT, I'M THE ONE WHO WASTES THE BAD GUY, GETS THE GIRL, AND THEN FLIES OFF IN A JET--PREFERABLY ONE WITH A COUGAR IN THE COPILOT'S SEAT.
WELL, GARY--WHENEVER YOU'RE READY.
ER, OKAY.

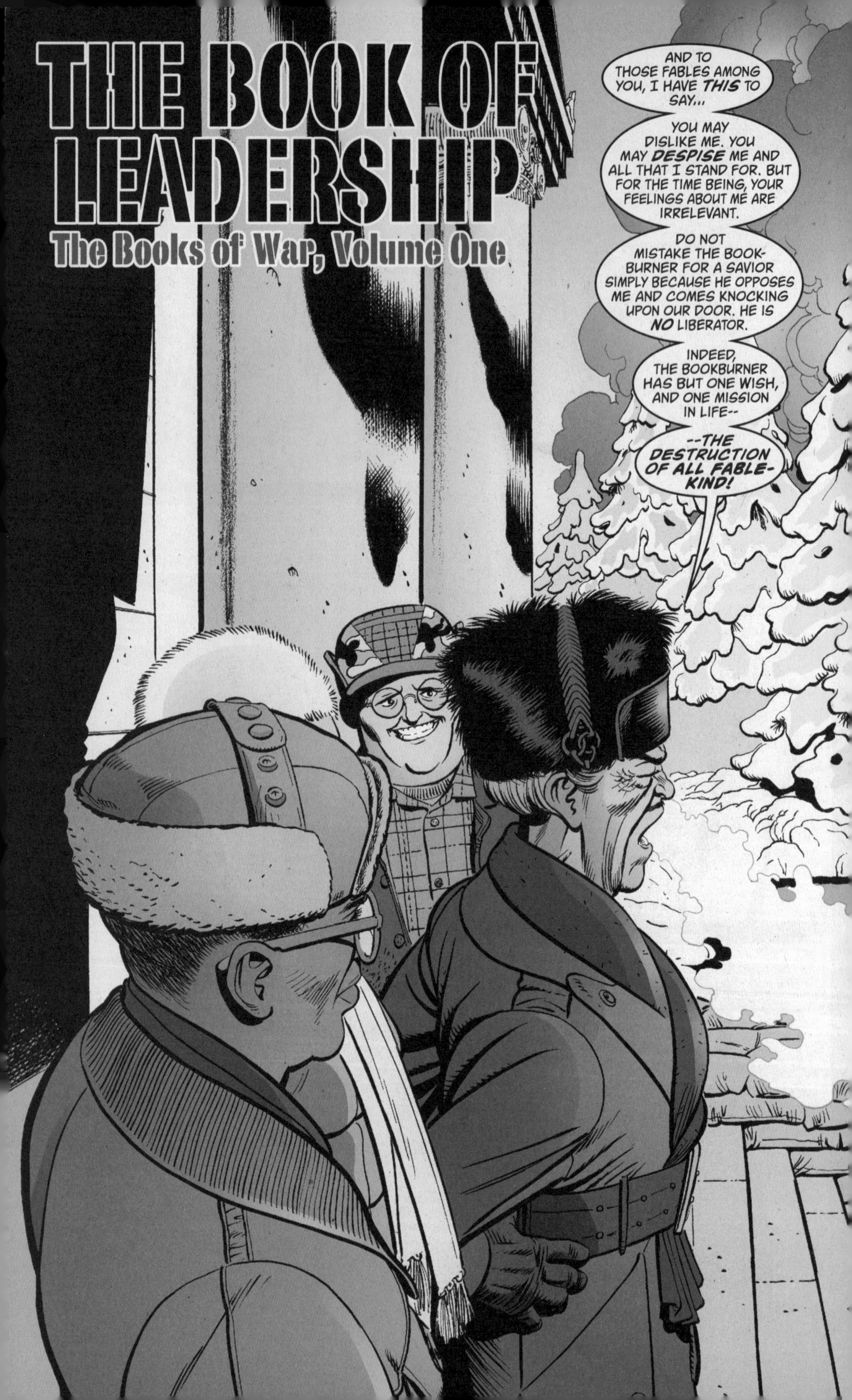
THE BOOK OF LEADERSHIP
The Books of War, Volume One
AND TO THOSE FABLES AMONG YOU, I HAVE THIS TO SAY...
YOU MAY DISLIKE ME. YOU MAY DESPISE ME AND ALL THAT I STAND FOR. BUT FOR THE TIME BEING, YOUR FEELINGS ABOUT ME ARE IRRELEVANT.
DO NOT MISTAKE THE BOOK-BURNER FOR A SAVIOR SIMPLY BECAUSE HE OPPOSES ME AND COMES KNOCKING UPON OUR DOOR. HE IS NO LIBERATOR.
INDEED, THE BOOKBURNER HAS BUT ONE WISH, AND ONE MISSION IN LIFE--
--THE DESTRUCTION OF ALL FABLE-KIND!

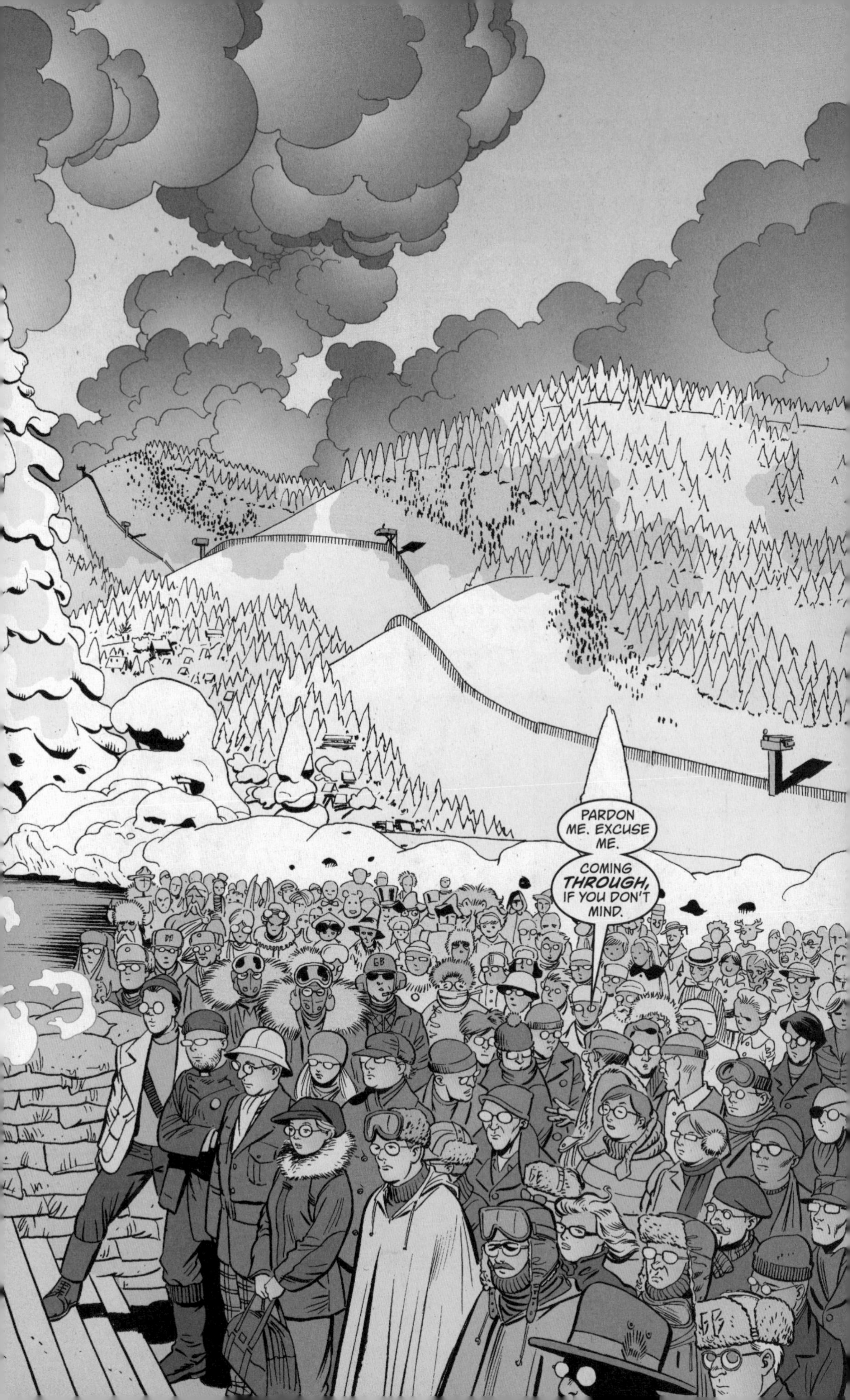
PARDON ME. EXCUSE ME.
COMING THROUGH, IF YOU DON'T MIND.

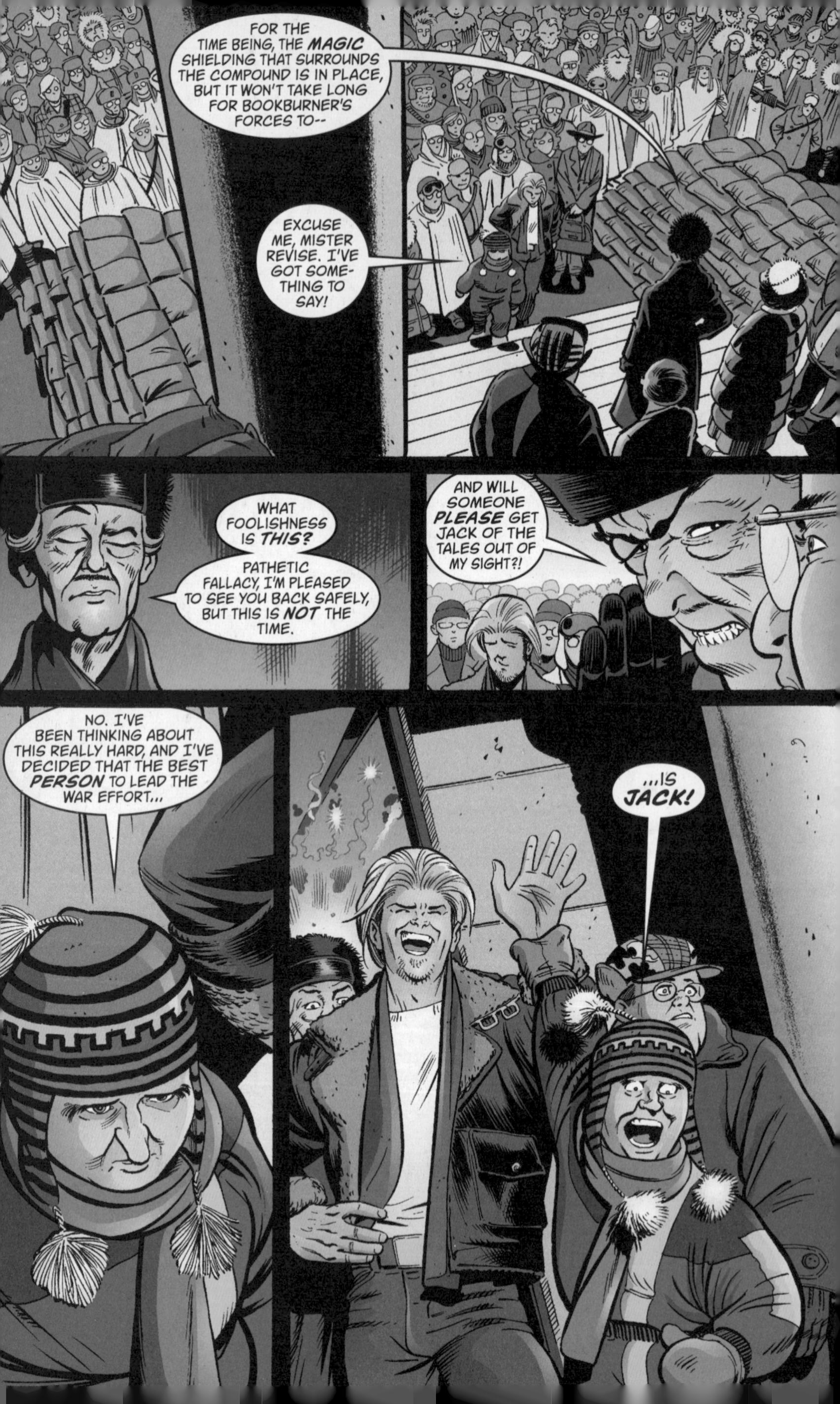
FOR THE TIME BEING, THE MAGIC SHIELDING THAT SURROUNDS THE COMPOUND IS IN PLACE, BUT IT WON'T TAKE LONG FOR BOOKBURNER'S FORCES TO--
EXCUSE ME, MISTER REVISE. I'VE GOT SOMETHING TO SAY!
WHAT FOOLISHNESS IS THIS?
PATHETIC FALLACY, I'M PLEASED TO SEE YOU BACK SAFELY, BUT THIS IS NOT THE TIME.
AND WILL SOMEONE PLEASE GET JACK OF THE TALES OUT OF MY SIGHT?!
NO. I'VE BEEN THINKING ABOUT THIS REALLY HARD, AND I'VE DECIDED THAT THE BEST PERSON TO LEAD THE WAR EFFORT...
...IS JACK!

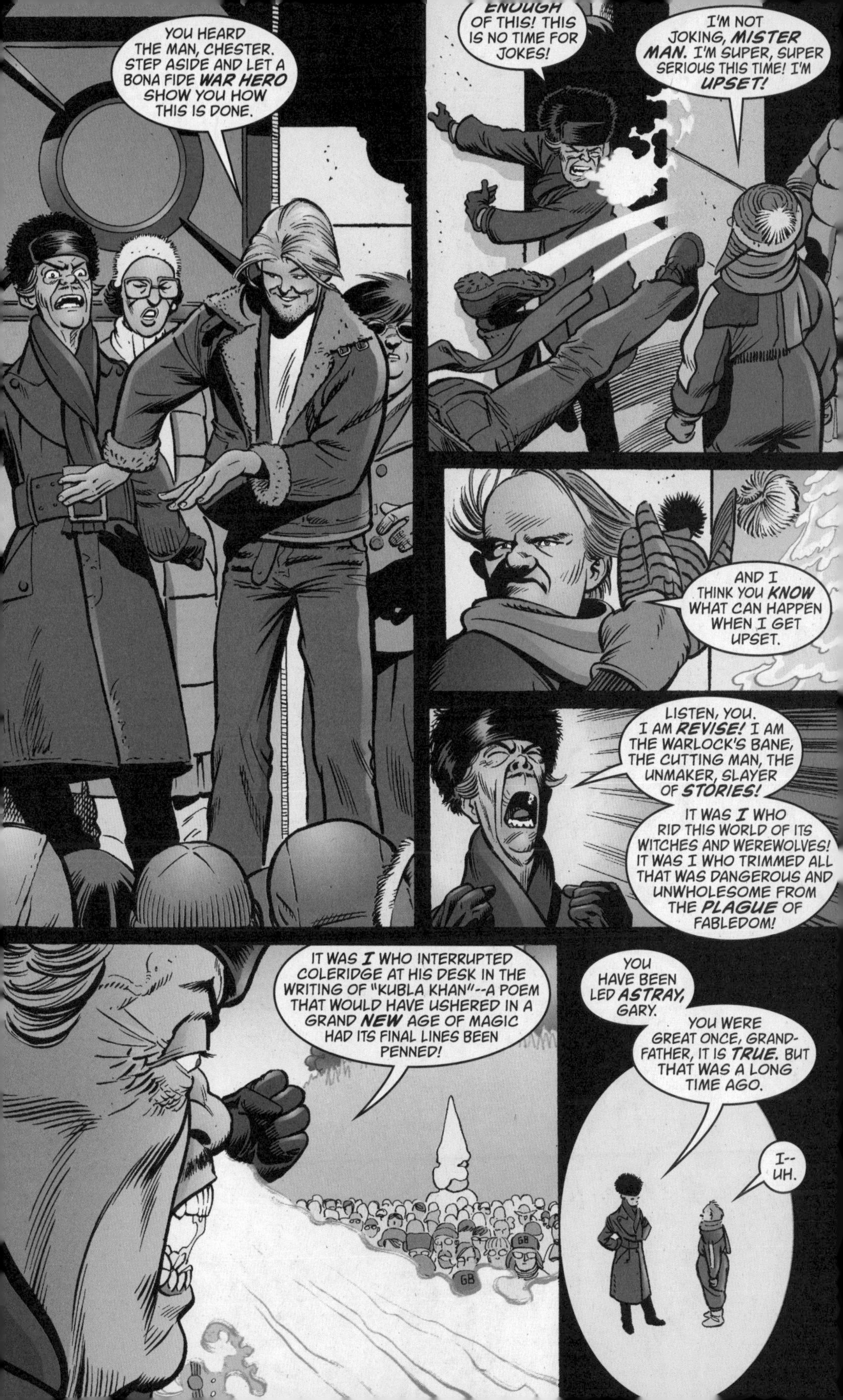
YOU HEARD THE MAN, CHESTER. STEP ASIDE AND LET A BONA FIDE WAR HERO SHOW YOU HOW THIS IS DONE.
ENOUGH OF THIS! THIS IS NO TIME FOR JOKES!
I'M NOT JOKING, MISTER MAN. I'M SUPER, SUPER SERIOUS THIS TIME! I'M UPSET!
AND I THINK YOU KNOW WHAT CAN HAPPEN WHEN I GET UPSET.
LISTEN, YOU. I AM REVISE! I AM THE WARLOCK'S BANE, THE CUTTING MAN, THE UNMAKER, SLAYER OF STORIES!
IT WAS I WHO RID THIS WORLD OF ITS WITCHES AND WEREWOLVES! IT WAS I WHO TRIMMED ALL THAT WAS DANGEROUS AND UNWHOLESOME FROM THE PLAGUE OF FABLEDOM!
IT WAS I WHO INTERRUPTED COLERIDGE AT HIS DESK IN THE WRITING OF "KUBLA KHAN"--A POEM THAT WOULD HAVE USHERED IN A GRAND NEW AGE OF MAGIC HAD ITS FINAL LINES BEEN PENNED!
YOU HAVE BEEN LED ASTRAY, GARY.
YOU WERE GREAT ONCE, GRAND-FATHER, IT IS TRUE. BUT THAT WAS A LONG TIME AGO.
I-- UH.
GB
GB

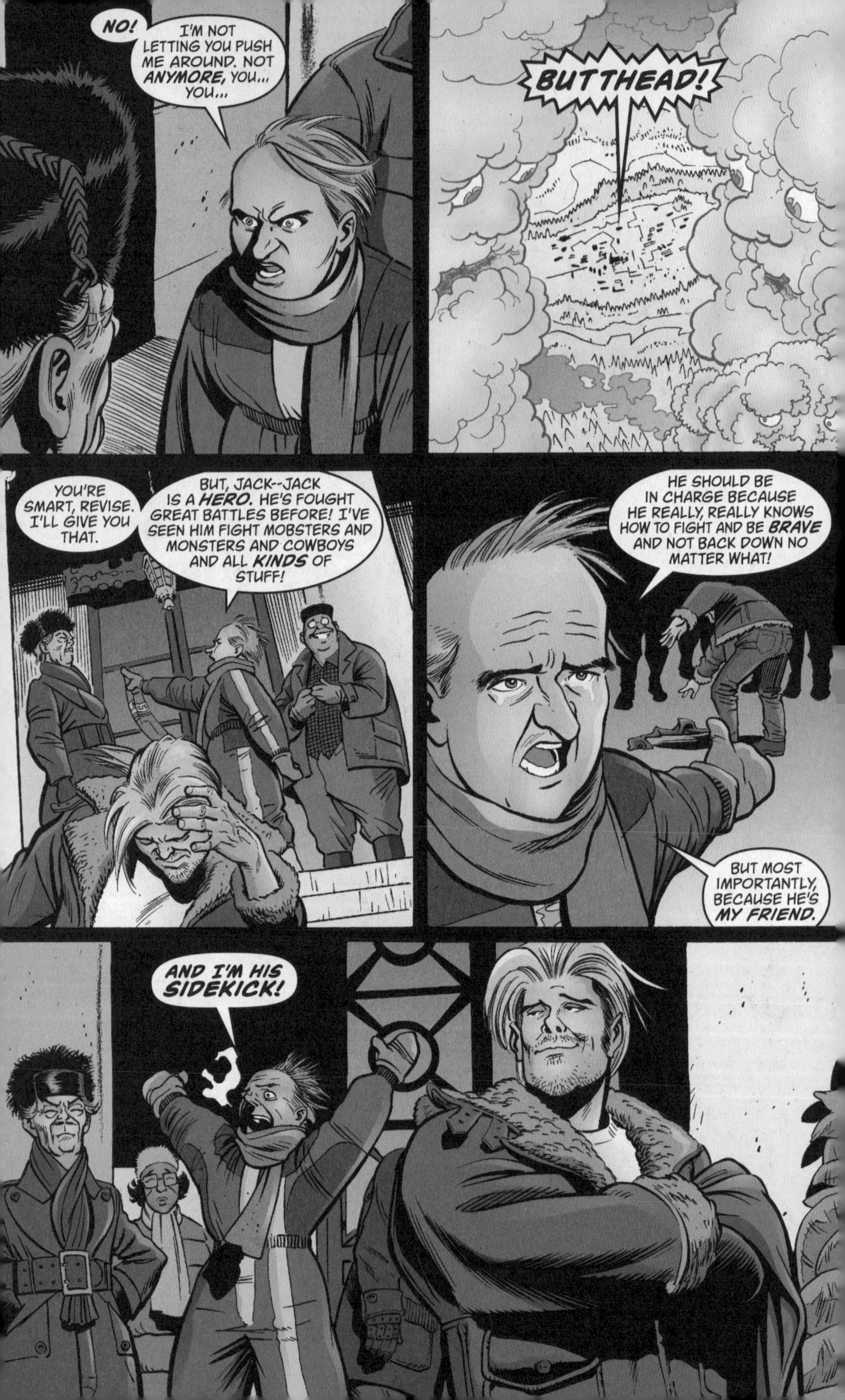
NO!
I'M NOT LETTING YOU PUSH ME AROUND. NOT ANYMORE, YOU... YOU...
BUTTHEAD!
YOU'RE SMART, REVISE. I'LL GIVE YOU THAT.
BUT, JACK--JACK IS A HERO. HE'S FOUGHT GREAT BATTLES BEFORE! I'VE SEEN HIM FIGHT MOBSTERS AND MONSTERS AND COWBOYS AND ALL KINDS OF STUFF!
HE SHOULD BE IN CHARGE BECAUSE HE REALLY, REALLY KNOWS HOW TO FIGHT AND BE BRAVE AND NOT BACK DOWN NO MATTER WHAT!
BUT MOST IMPORTANTLY, BECAUSE HE'S MY FRIEND.
AND I'M HIS SIDEKICK!

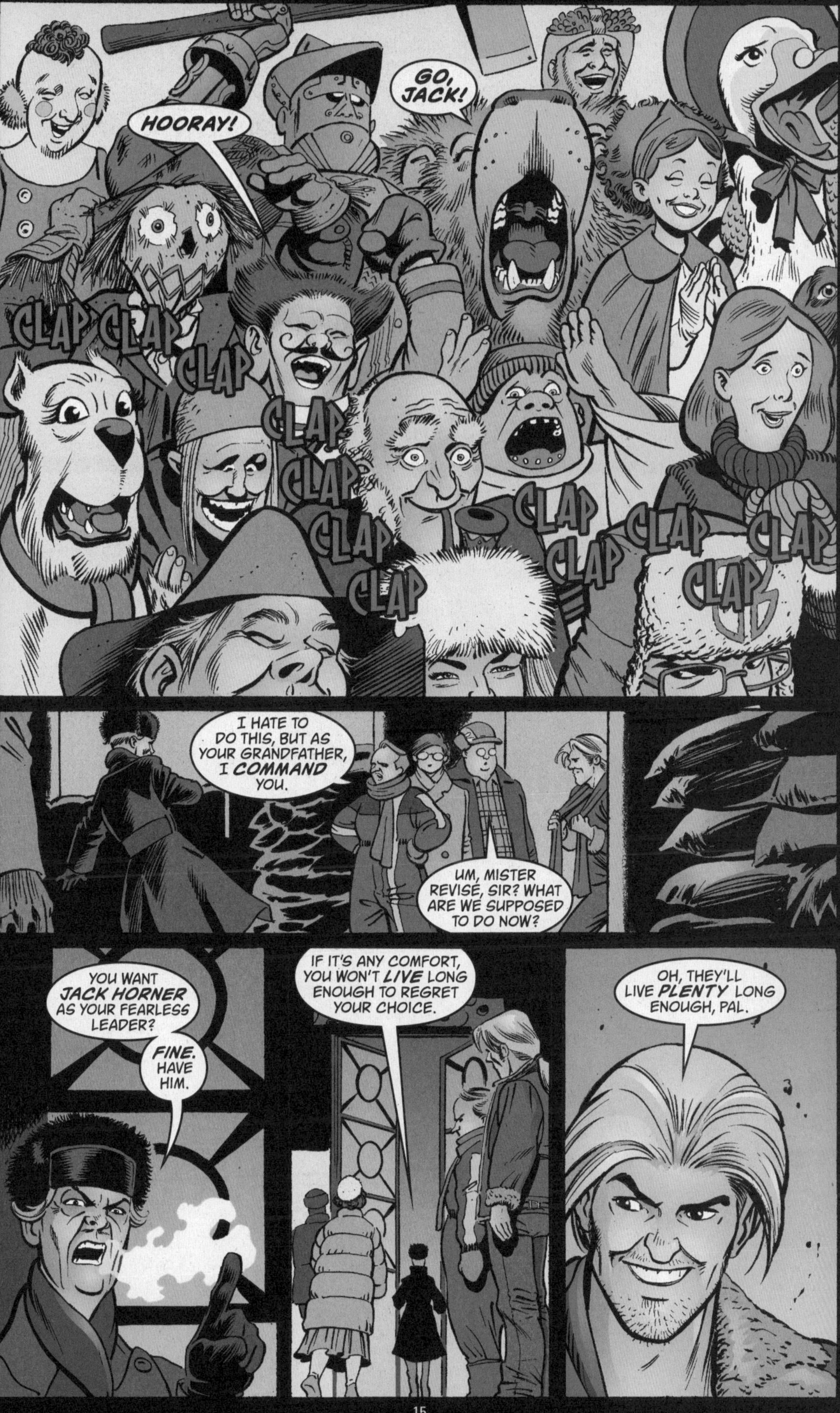
HOORAY!
GO, JACK!
CLAP CLAP CLAP CLAP CLAP CLAP CLAP
CLAP CLAP CLAP CLAP CLAP
I HATE TO DO THIS, BUT AS YOUR GRANDFATHER, I *COMMAND* YOU.
UM, MISTER REVISE, SIR? WHAT ARE WE SUPPOSED TO DO NOW?
YOU WANT *JACK HORNER* AS YOUR FEARLESS LEADER?
FINE. HAVE HIM.
IF IT'S ANY COMFORT, YOU WON'T *LIVE* LONG ENOUGH TO REGRET YOUR CHOICE.
OH, THEY'LL LIVE *PLENTY* LONG ENOUGH, PAL.

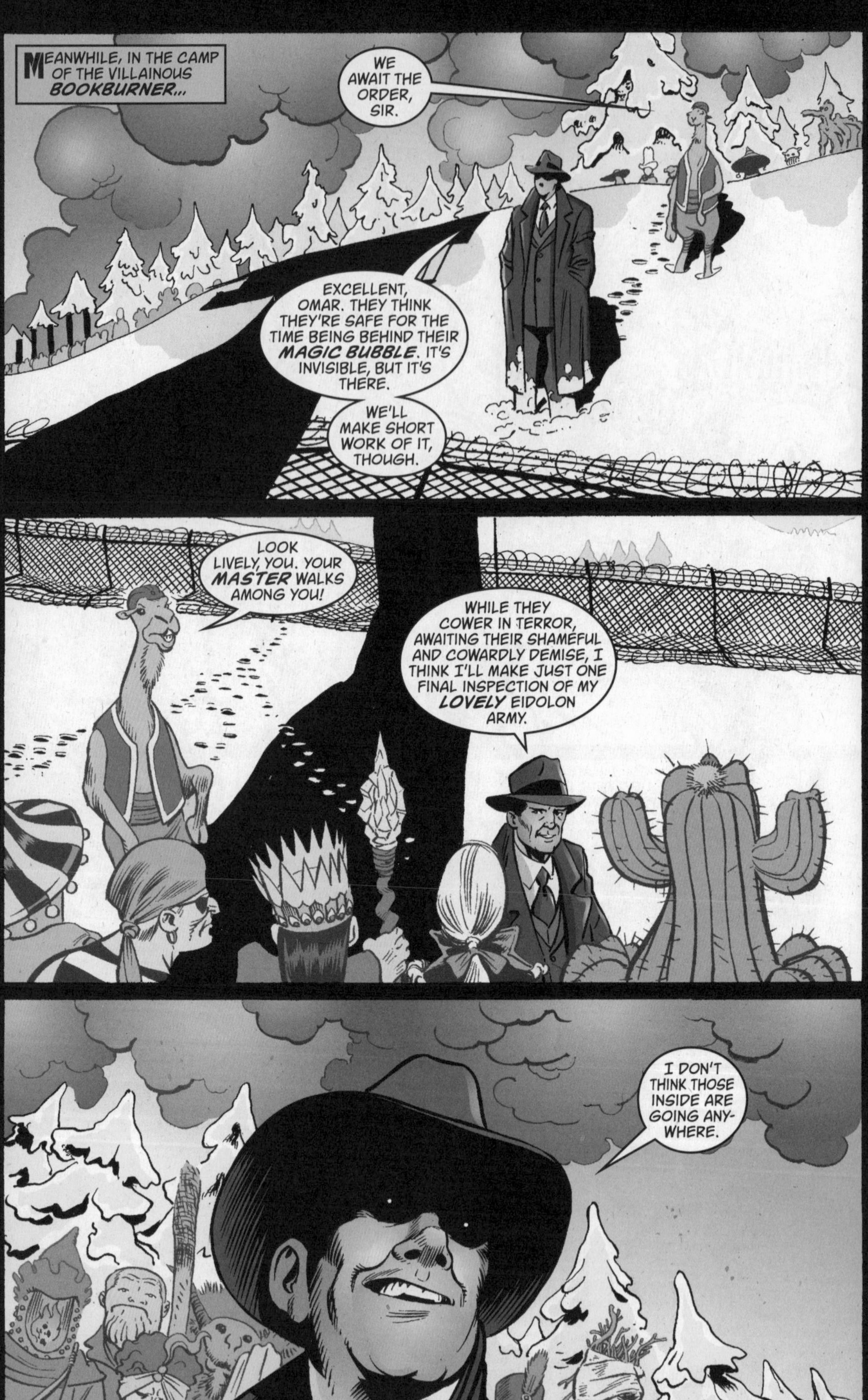

MEANWHILE, IN THE CAMP OF THE VILLAINOUS BOOKBURNER...
WE AWAIT THE ORDER, SIR.
EXCELLENT, OMAR. THEY THINK THEY'RE SAFE FOR THE TIME BEING BEHIND THEIR MAGIC BUBBLE. IT'S INVISIBLE, BUT IT'S THERE.
WE'LL MAKE SHORT WORK OF IT, THOUGH.
LOOK LIVELY, YOU. YOUR MASTER WALKS AMONG YOU!
WHILE THEY COWER IN TERROR, AWAITING THEIR SHAMEFUL AND COWARDLY DEMISE, I THINK I'LL MAKE JUST ONE FINAL INSPECTION OF MY LOVELY EIDOLON ARMY.
I DON'T THINK THOSE INSIDE ARE GOING ANYWHERE.

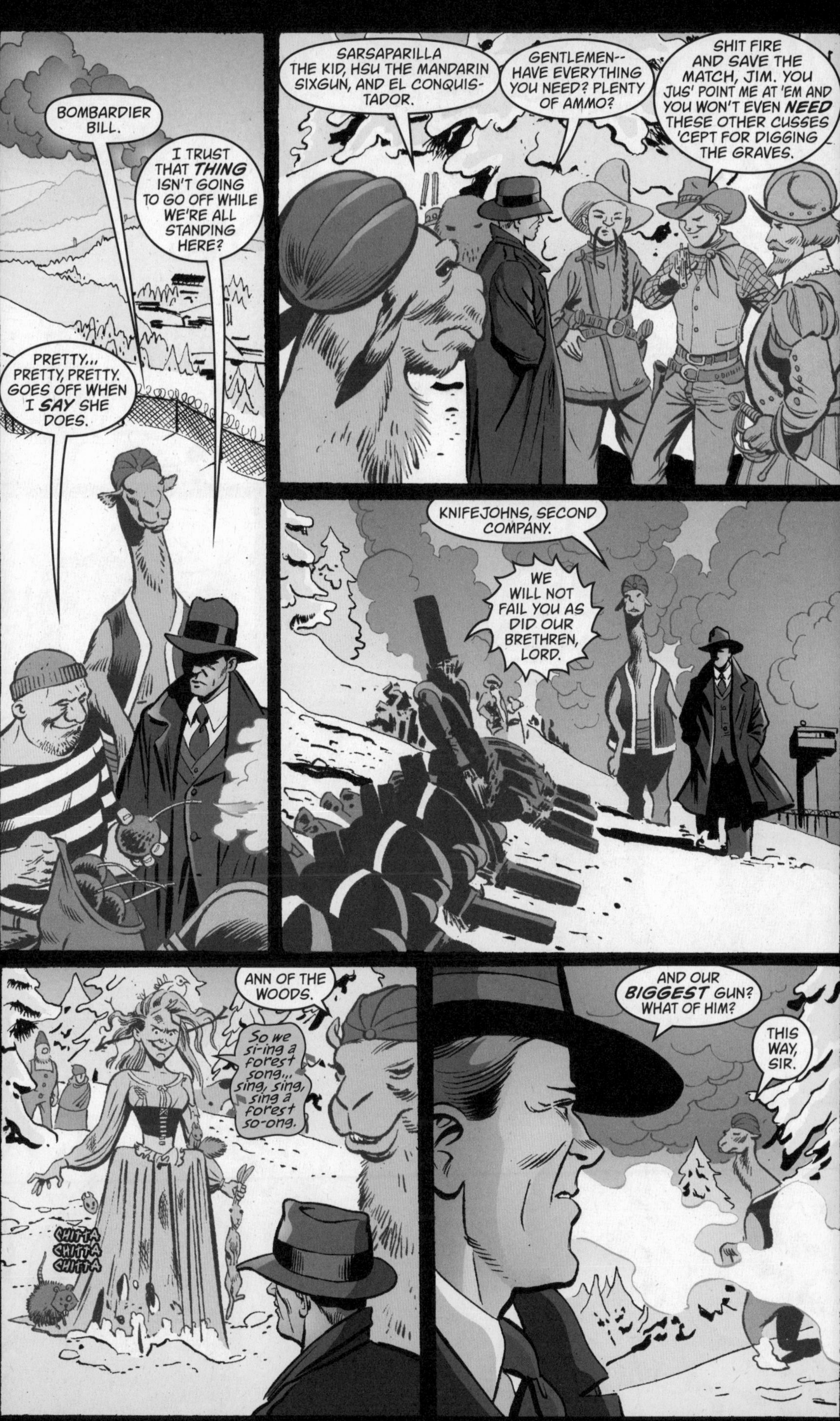
BOMBARDIER BILL.
I TRUST THAT THING ISN'T GOING TO GO OFF WHILE WE'RE ALL STANDING HERE?
PRETTY... PRETTY, PRETTY. GOES OFF WHEN I SAY SHE DOES.
SARSAPARILLA THE KID, HSU THE MANDARIN SIXGUN, AND EL CONQUISTADOR.
GENTLEMEN-- HAVE EVERYTHING YOU NEED? PLENTY OF AMMO?
SHIT FIRE AND SAVE THE MATCH, JIM. YOU JUS' POINT ME AT 'EM AND YOU WON'T EVEN NEED THESE OTHER CUSSES 'CEPT FOR DIGGING THE GRAVES.
KNIFEJOHNS, SECOND COMPANY.
WE WILL NOT FAIL YOU AS DID OUR BRETHREN, LORD.
ANN OF THE WOODS.
So we si-ing a forest song... sing, sing, sing a forest so-ong.
CHITTA CHITTA CHITTA
AND OUR BIGGEST GUN? WHAT OF HIM?
THIS WAY, SIR.

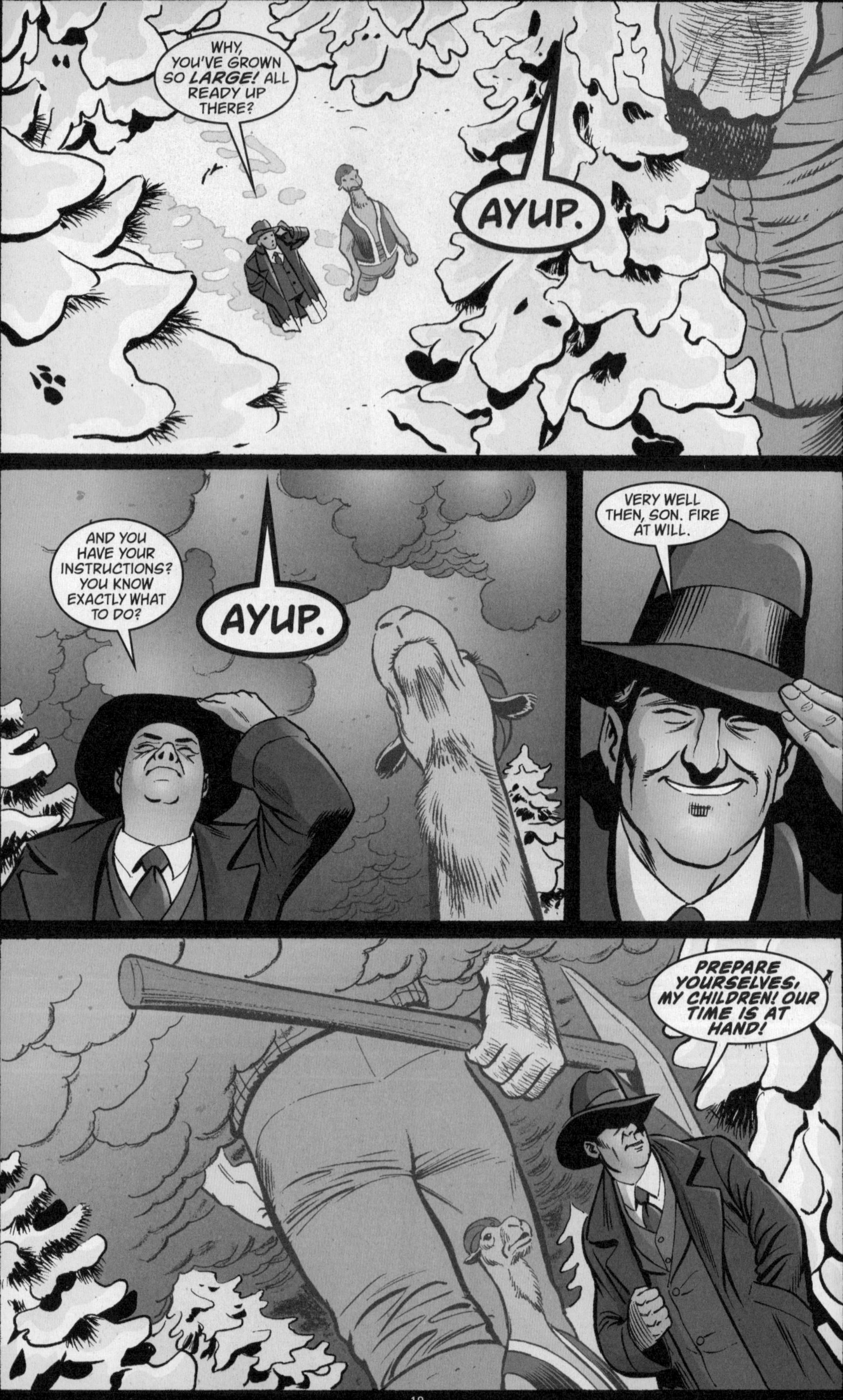
WHY, YOU'VE GROWN SO *LARGE!* ALL READY UP THERE?
AYUP.
AND YOU HAVE YOUR INSTRUCTIONS? YOU KNOW EXACTLY WHAT TO DO?
AYUP.
VERY WELL THEN, SON. FIRE AT WILL.
PREPARE YOURSELVES, MY CHILDREN! OUR TIME IS AT HAND!

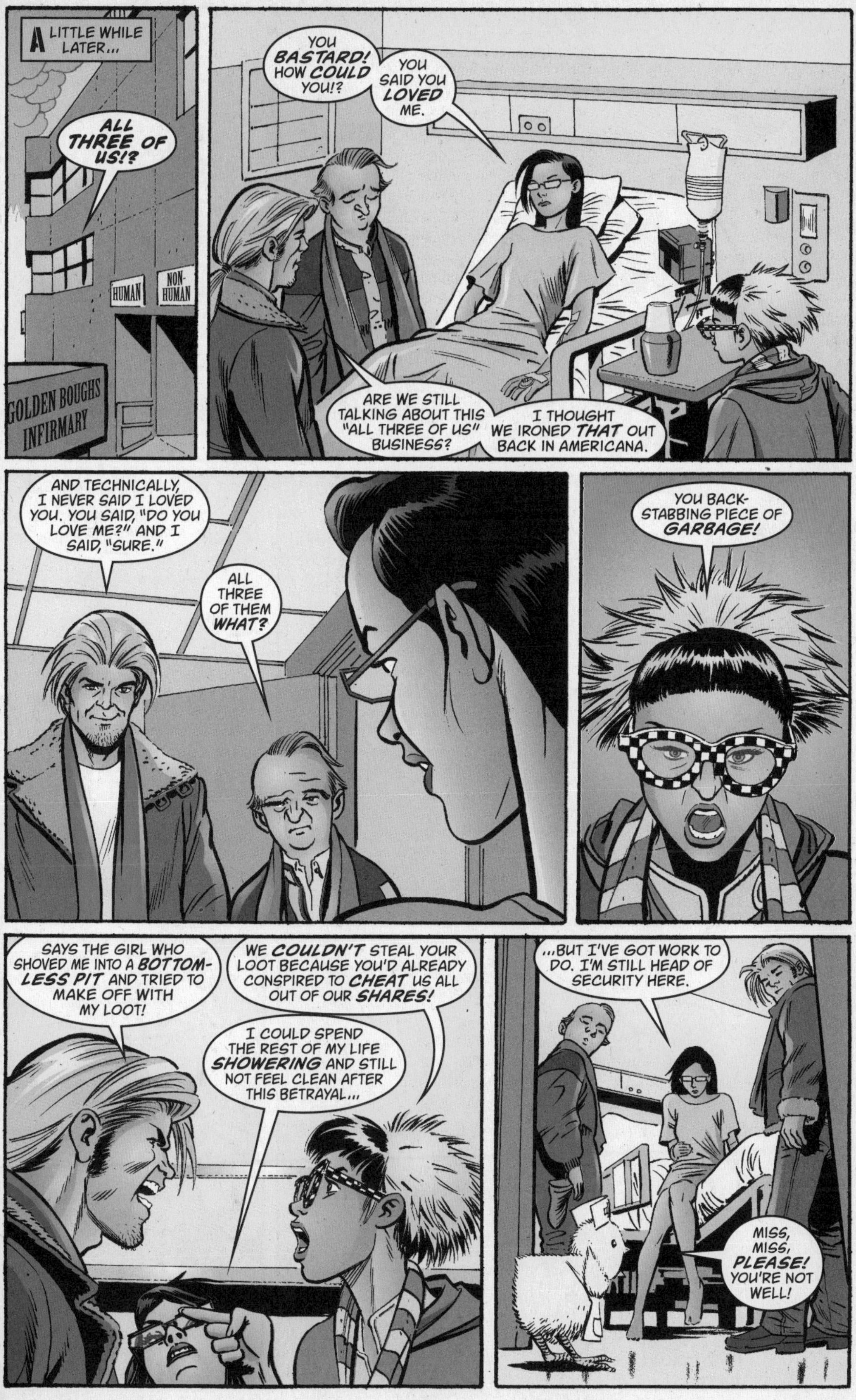
A LITTLE WHILE LATER...
ALL THREE OF US!?
HUMAN
NON-HUMAN
GOLDEN BOUGHS INFIRMARY
YOU BASTARD! HOW COULD YOU!?
YOU SAID YOU LOVED ME.
ARE WE STILL TALKING ABOUT THIS "ALL THREE OF US" BUSINESS?
I THOUGHT WE IRONED THAT OUT BACK IN AMERICANA.
AND TECHNICALLY, I NEVER SAID I LOVED YOU. YOU SAID, "DO YOU LOVE ME?" AND I SAID, "SURE."
ALL THREE OF THEM WHAT?
YOU BACK-STABBING PIECE OF GARBAGE!
SAYS THE GIRL WHO SHOVED ME INTO A BOTTOMLESS PIT AND TRIED TO MAKE OFF WITH MY LOOT!
WE COULDN'T STEAL YOUR LOOT BECAUSE YOU'D ALREADY CONSPIRED TO CHEAT US ALL OUT OF OUR SHARES!
I COULD SPEND THE REST OF MY LIFE SHOWERING AND STILL NOT FEEL CLEAN AFTER THIS BETRAYAL...
...BUT I'VE GOT WORK TO DO. I'M STILL HEAD OF SECURITY HERE.
MISS, MISS, PLEASE! YOU'RE NOT WELL!

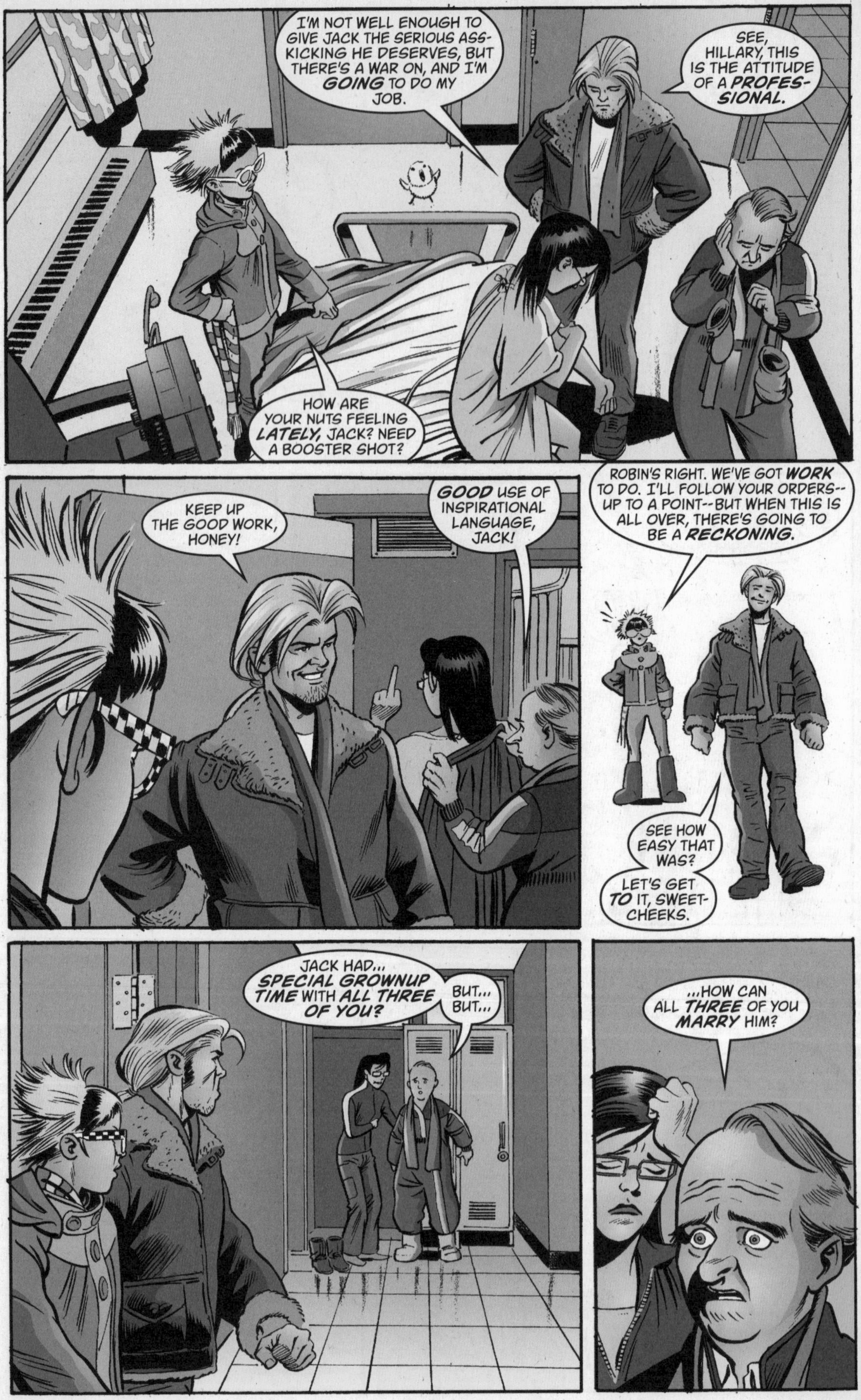
I'M NOT WELL ENOUGH TO GIVE JACK THE SERIOUS ASS-KICKING HE DESERVES, BUT THERE'S A WAR ON, AND I'M GOING TO DO MY JOB.
SEE, HILLARY, THIS IS THE ATTITUDE OF A PROFES-SIONAL.
HOW ARE YOUR NUTS FEELING LATELY, JACK? NEED A BOOSTER SHOT?
KEEP UP THE GOOD WORK, HONEY!
GOOD USE OF INSPIRATIONAL LANGUAGE, JACK!
ROBIN'S RIGHT. WE'VE GOT WORK TO DO. I'LL FOLLOW YOUR ORDERS--UP TO A POINT--BUT WHEN THIS IS ALL OVER, THERE'S GOING TO BE A RECKONING.
SEE HOW EASY THAT WAS?
LET'S GET TO IT, SWEET-CHEEKS.
JACK HAD... SPECIAL GROWNUP TIME WITH ALL THREE OF YOU?
BUT... BUT...
...HOW CAN ALL THREE OF YOU MARRY HIM?

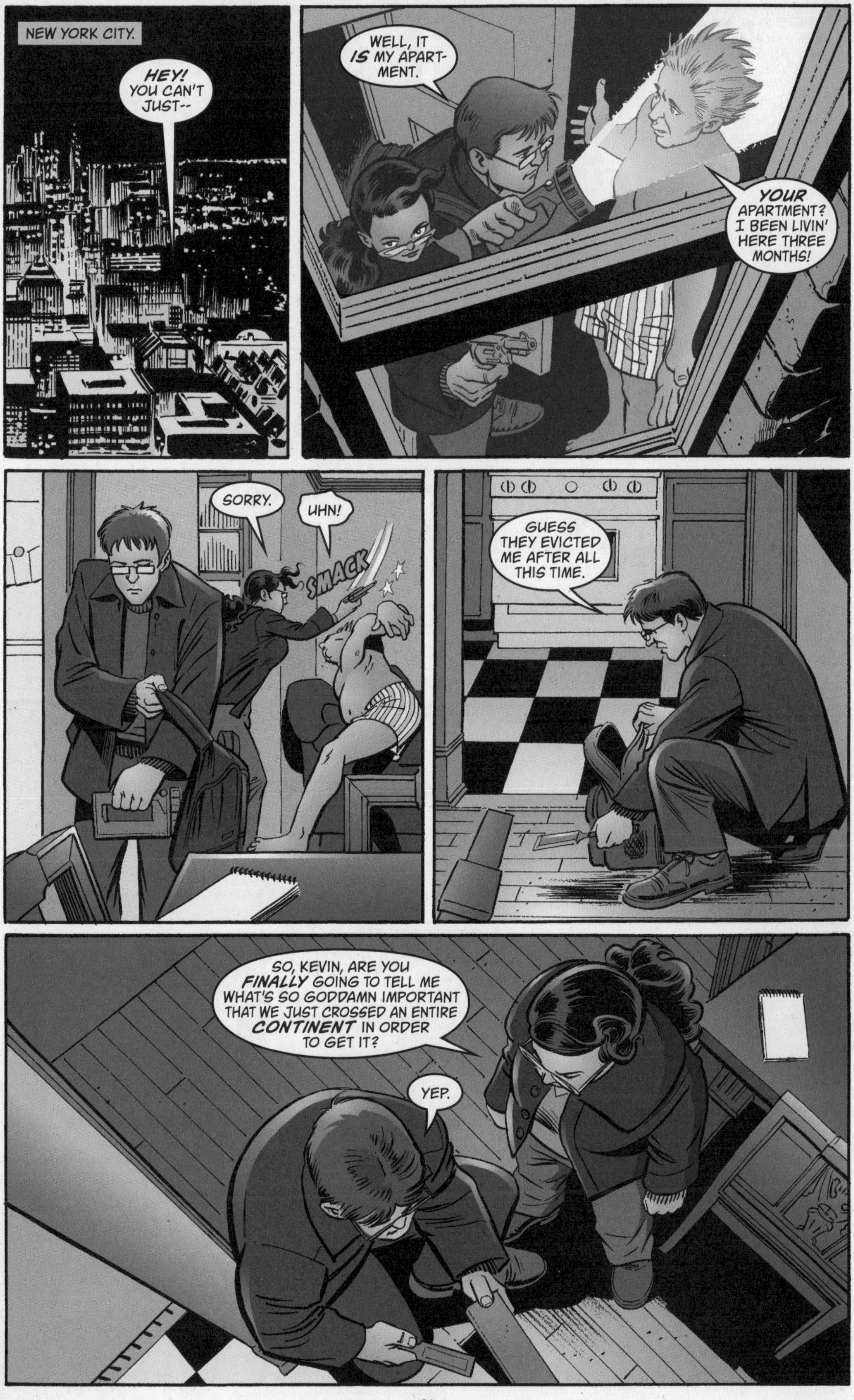
NEW YORK CITY.
HEY! YOU CAN'T JUST--
WELL, IT IS MY APARTMENT.
YOUR APARTMENT? I BEEN LIVIN' HERE THREE MONTHS!
SORRY.
UHN!
SMACK
GUESS THEY EVICTED ME AFTER ALL THIS TIME.
SO, KEVIN, ARE YOU FINALLY GOING TO TELL ME WHAT'S SO GODDAMN IMPORTANT THAT WE JUST CROSSED AN ENTIRE CONTINENT IN ORDER TO GET IT?
YEP.

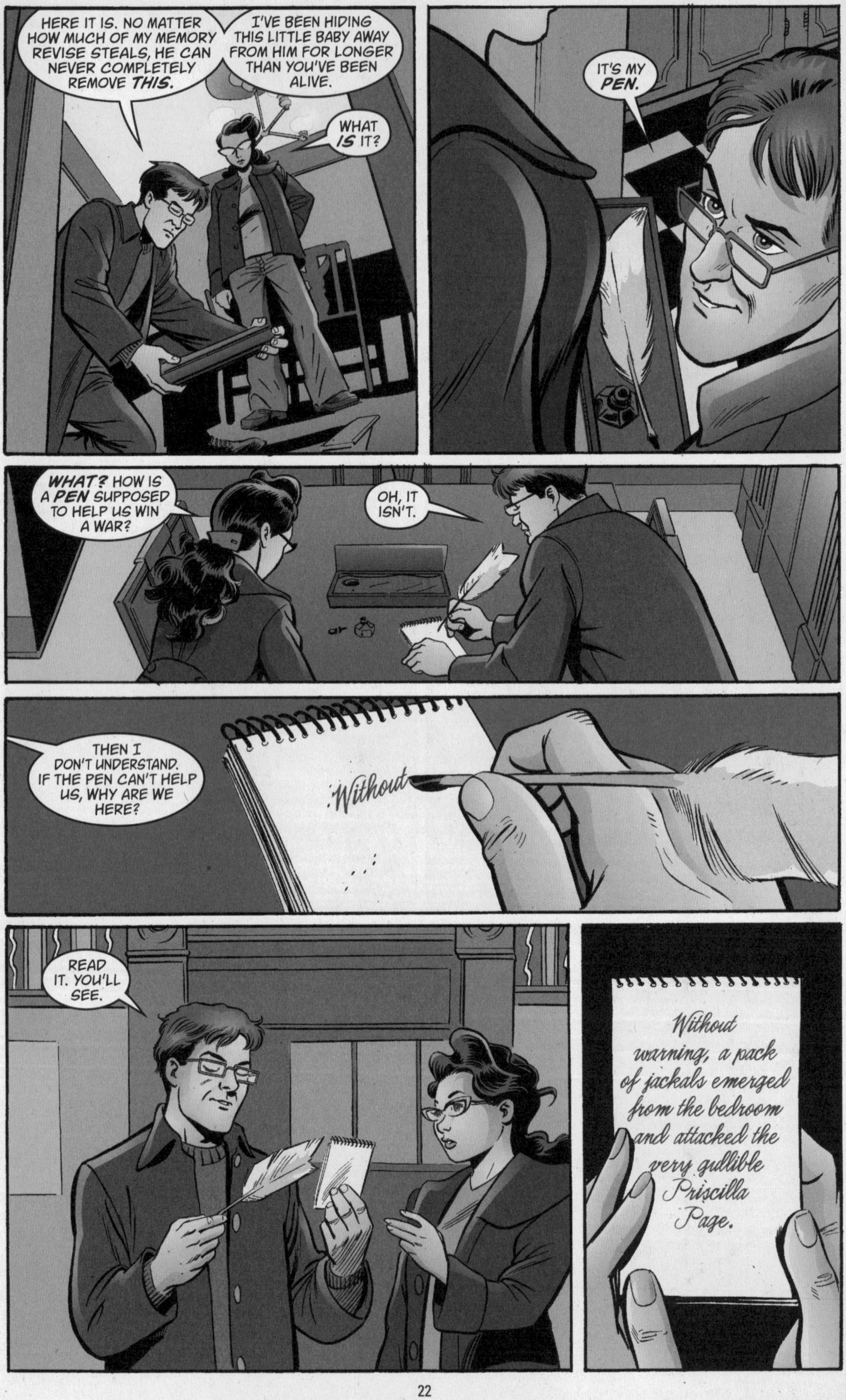
HERE IT IS. NO MATTER HOW MUCH OF MY MEMORY REVISE STEALS, HE CAN NEVER COMPLETELY REMOVE THIS.
I'VE BEEN HIDING THIS LITTLE BABY AWAY FROM HIM FOR LONGER THAN YOU'VE BEEN ALIVE.
WHAT IS IT?
IT'S MY PEN.
WHAT? HOW IS A PEN SUPPOSED TO HELP US WIN A WAR?
OH, IT ISN'T.
THEN I DON'T UNDERSTAND. IF THE PEN CAN'T HELP US, WHY ARE WE HERE?
Without
READ IT. YOU'LL SEE.
Without warning, a pack of jackals emerged from the bedroom and attacked the very gullible Priscilla Page.

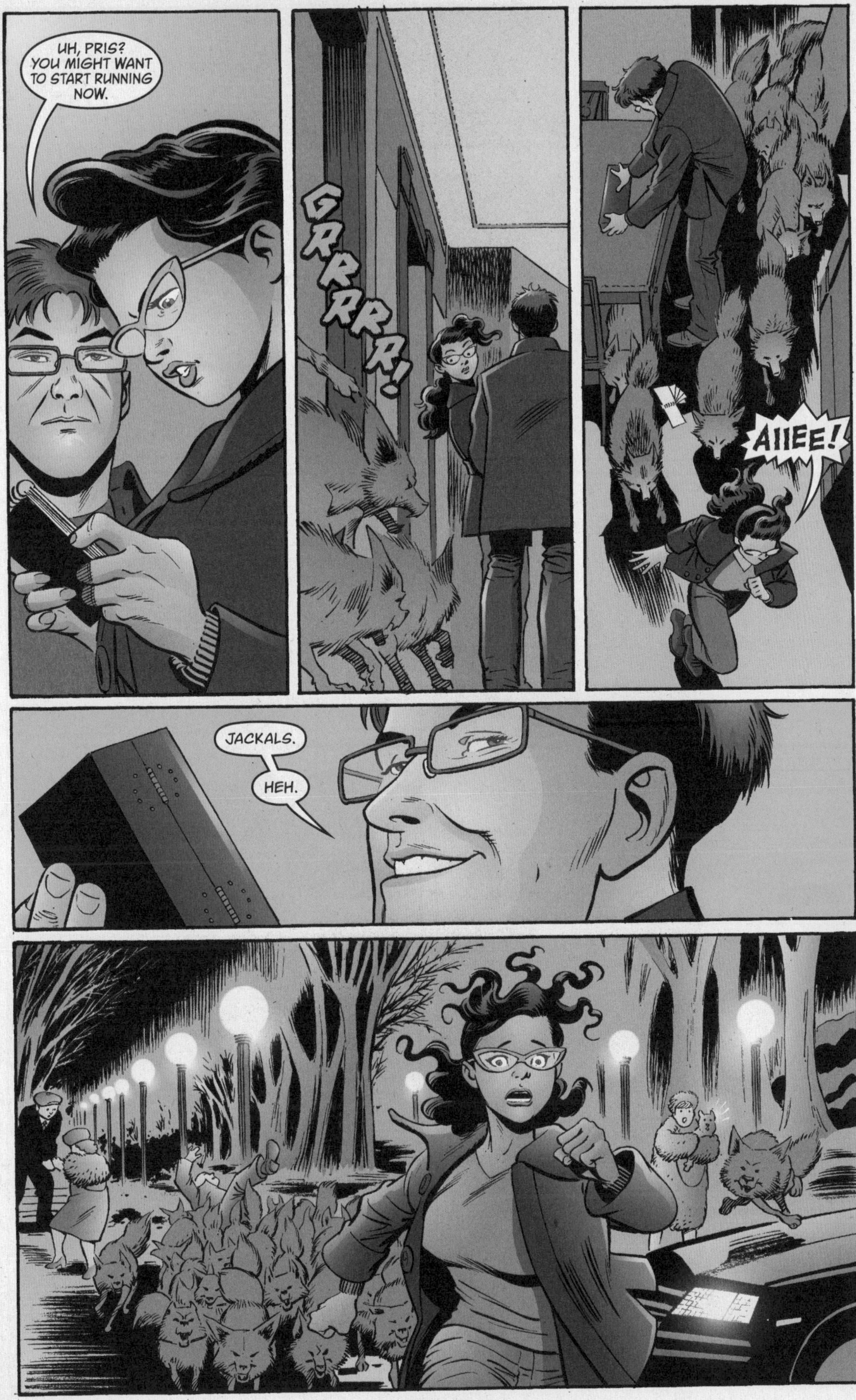
UH, PRIS? YOU MIGHT WANT TO START RUNNING NOW.
GRRRRR!
AIIEE!
JACKALS.
HEH.

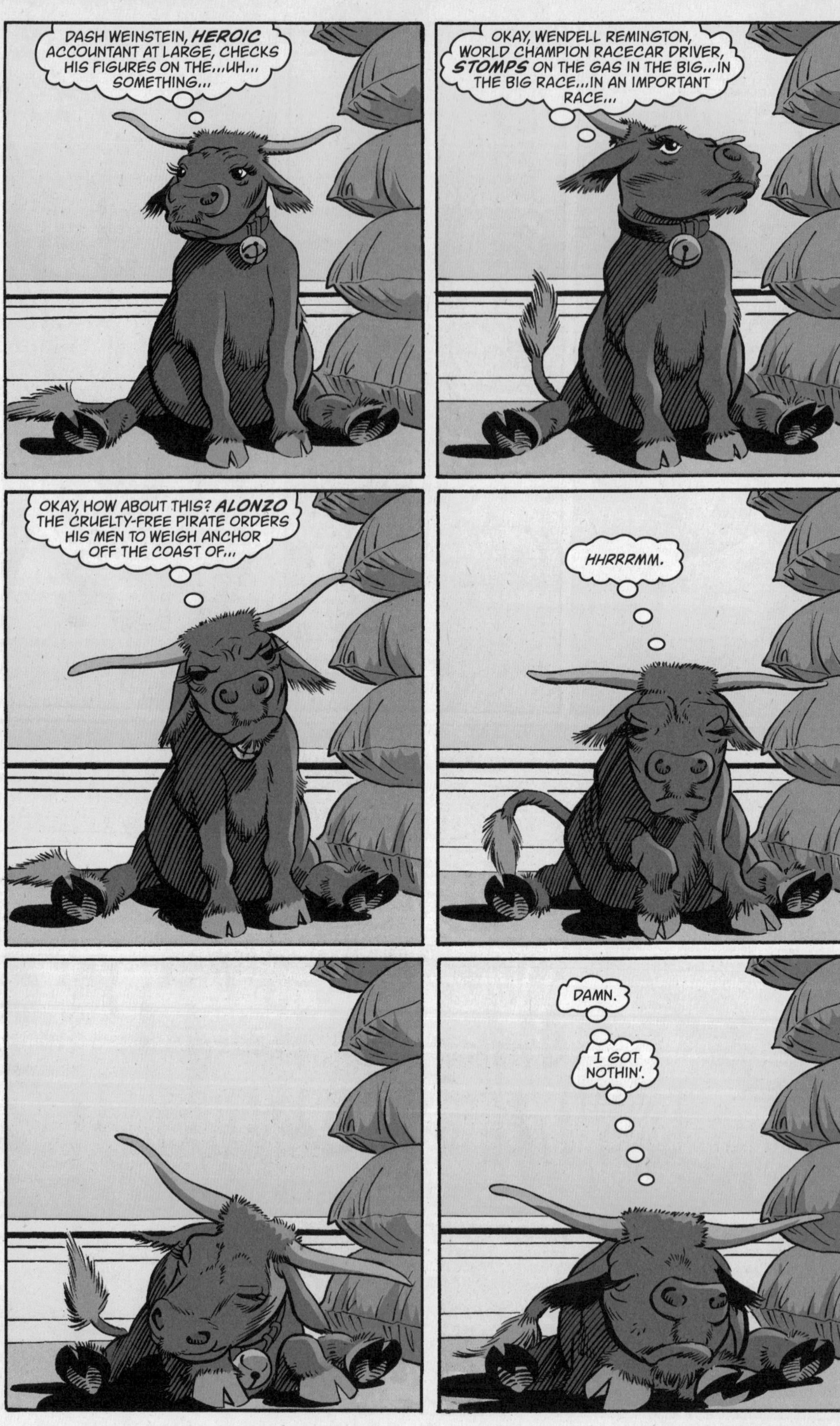
DASH WEINSTEIN, HEROIC ACCOUNTANT AT LARGE, CHECKS HIS FIGURES ON THE...UH... SOMETHING...
OKAY, WENDELL REMINGTON, WORLD CHAMPION RACECAR DRIVER, STOMPS ON THE GAS IN THE BIG...IN THE BIG RACE...IN AN IMPORTANT RACE...
OKAY, HOW ABOUT THIS? ALONZO THE CRUELTY-FREE PIRATE ORDERS HIS MEN TO WEIGH ANCHOR OFF THE COAST OF...
HHRRRMM.
DAMN.
I GOT NOTHIN'.

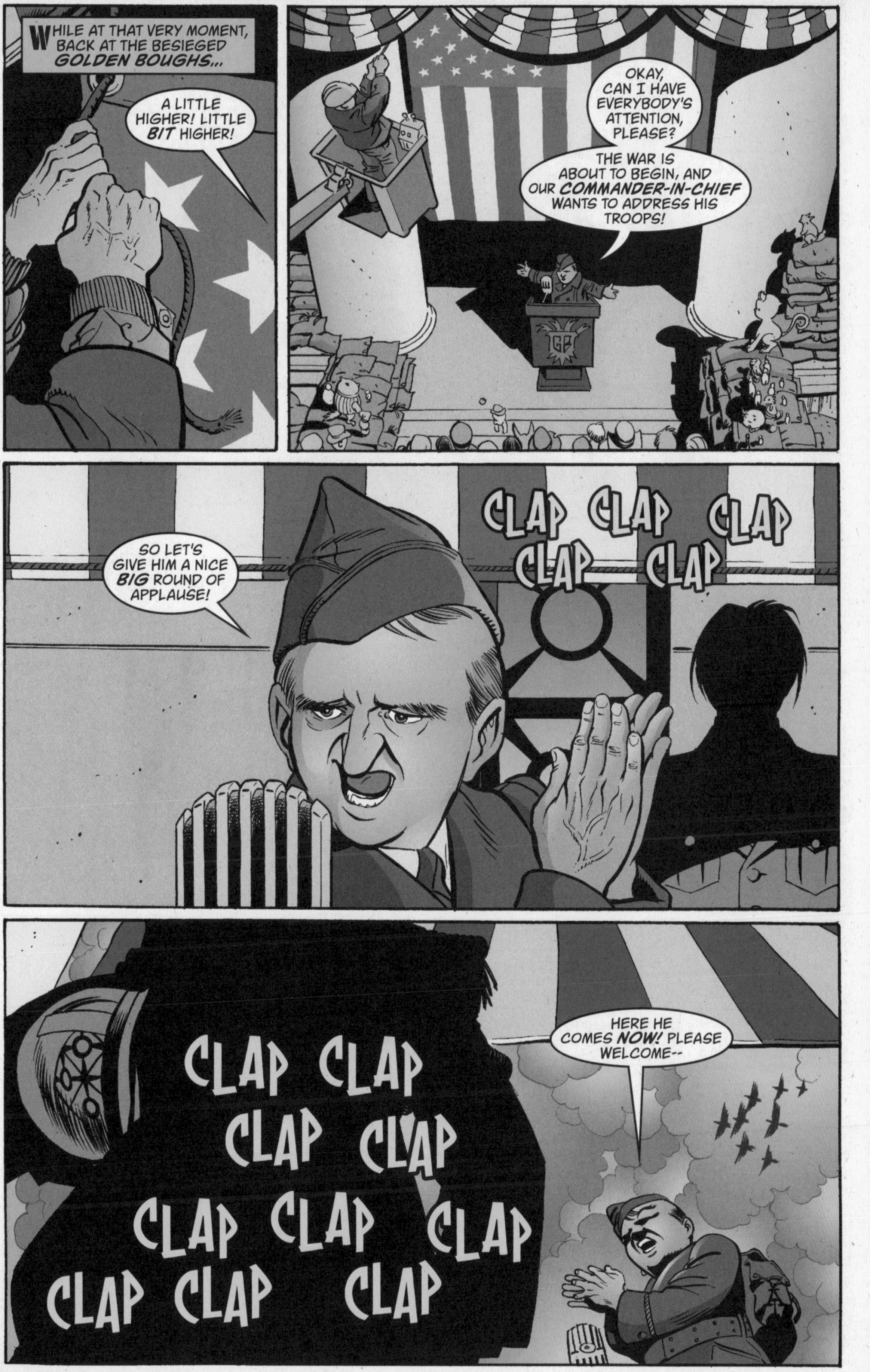
WHILE AT THAT VERY MOMENT, BACK AT THE BESIEGED GOLDEN BOUGHS...
A LITTLE HIGHER! LITTLE BIT HIGHER!
OKAY, CAN I HAVE EVERYBODY'S ATTENTION, PLEASE?
THE WAR IS ABOUT TO BEGIN, AND OUR COMMANDER-IN-CHIEF WANTS TO ADDRESS HIS TROOPS!
SO LET'S GIVE HIM A NICE BIG ROUND OF APPLAUSE!
CLAP CLAP CLAP CLAP CLAP
CLAP CLAP CLAP CLAP CLAP CLAP CLAP CLAP CLAP CLAP
HERE HE COMES NOW! PLEASE WELCOME--

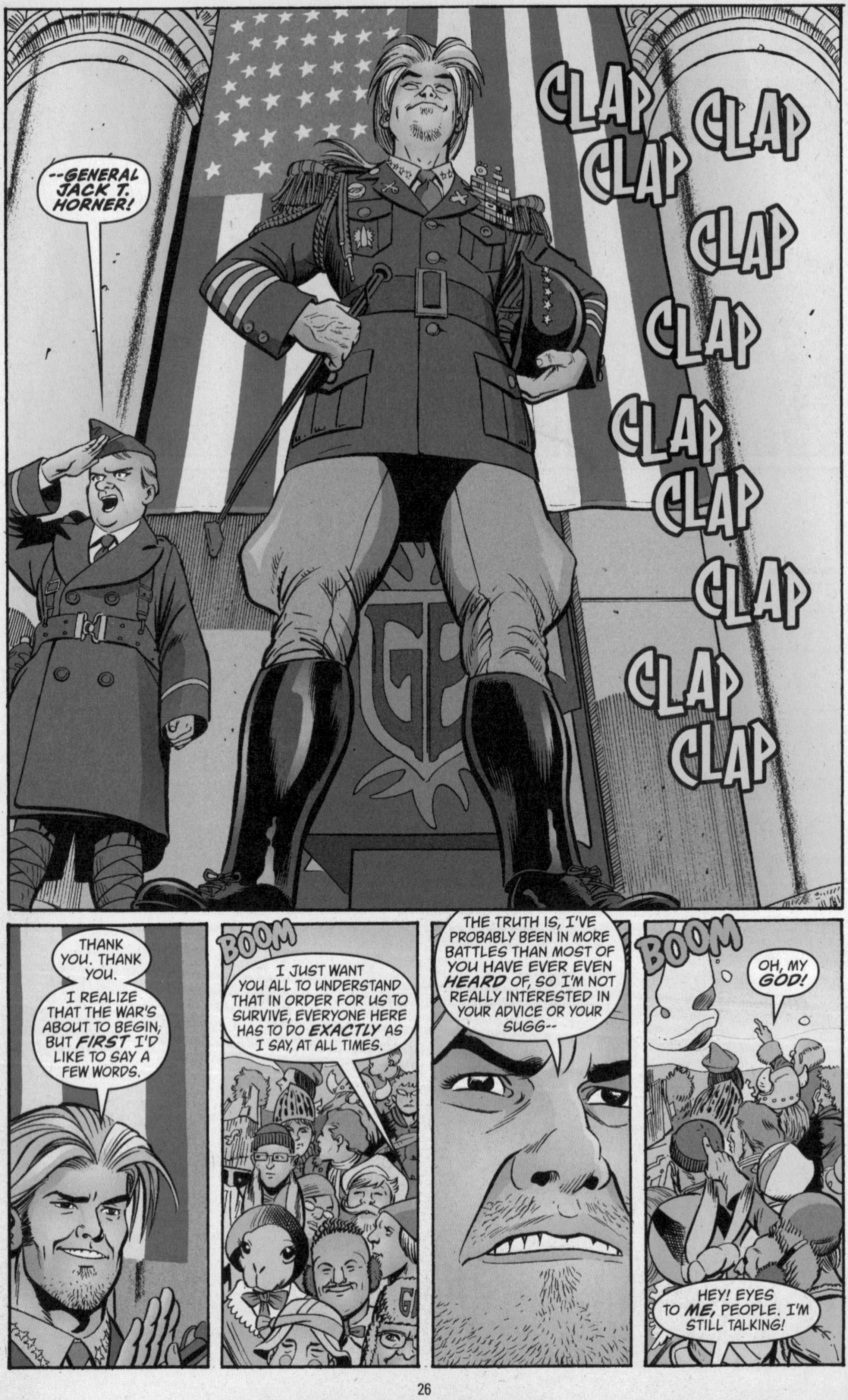
--GENERAL JACK T. HORNER!
CLAP CLAP CLAP CLAP CLAP CLAP CLAP CLAP CLAP CLAP
THANK YOU. THANK YOU.
I REALIZE THAT THE WAR'S ABOUT TO BEGIN, BUT FIRST I'D LIKE TO SAY A FEW WORDS.
BOOM
I JUST WANT YOU ALL TO UNDERSTAND THAT IN ORDER FOR US TO SURVIVE, EVERYONE HERE HAS TO DO EXACTLY AS I SAY, AT ALL TIMES.
THE TRUTH IS, I'VE PROBABLY BEEN IN MORE BATTLES THAN MOST OF YOU HAVE EVER EVEN HEARD OF, SO I'M NOT REALLY INTERESTED IN YOUR ADVICE OR YOUR SUGG--
BOOM
OH, MY GOD!
HEY! EYES TO ME, PEOPLE. I'M STILL TALKING!

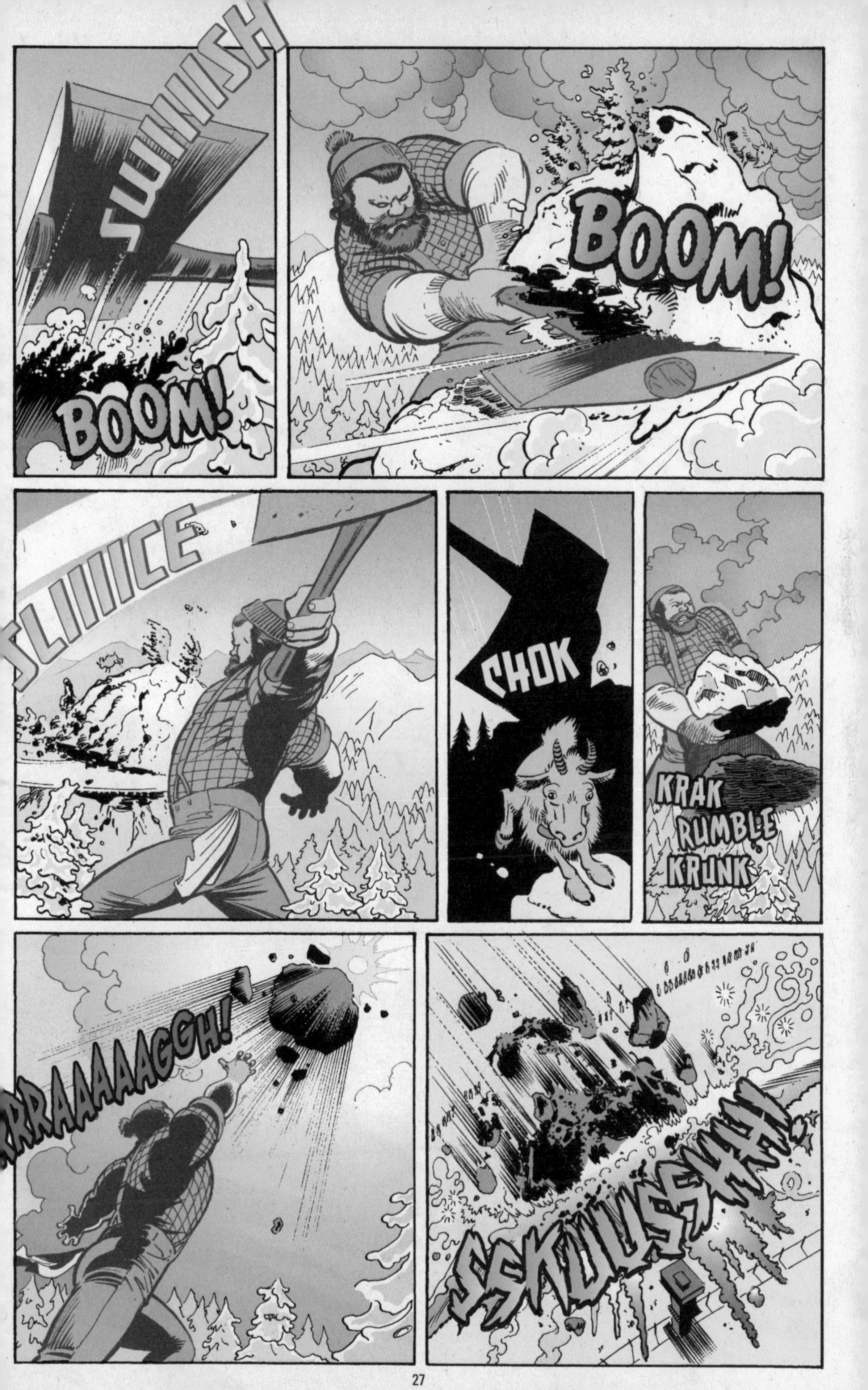
SWIIISH
BOOM!
BOOM!
SLIIIICE
CHOK
KRAK
RUMBLE
KRUNK
RRAAAAAGGH!
SSKUUSHH!

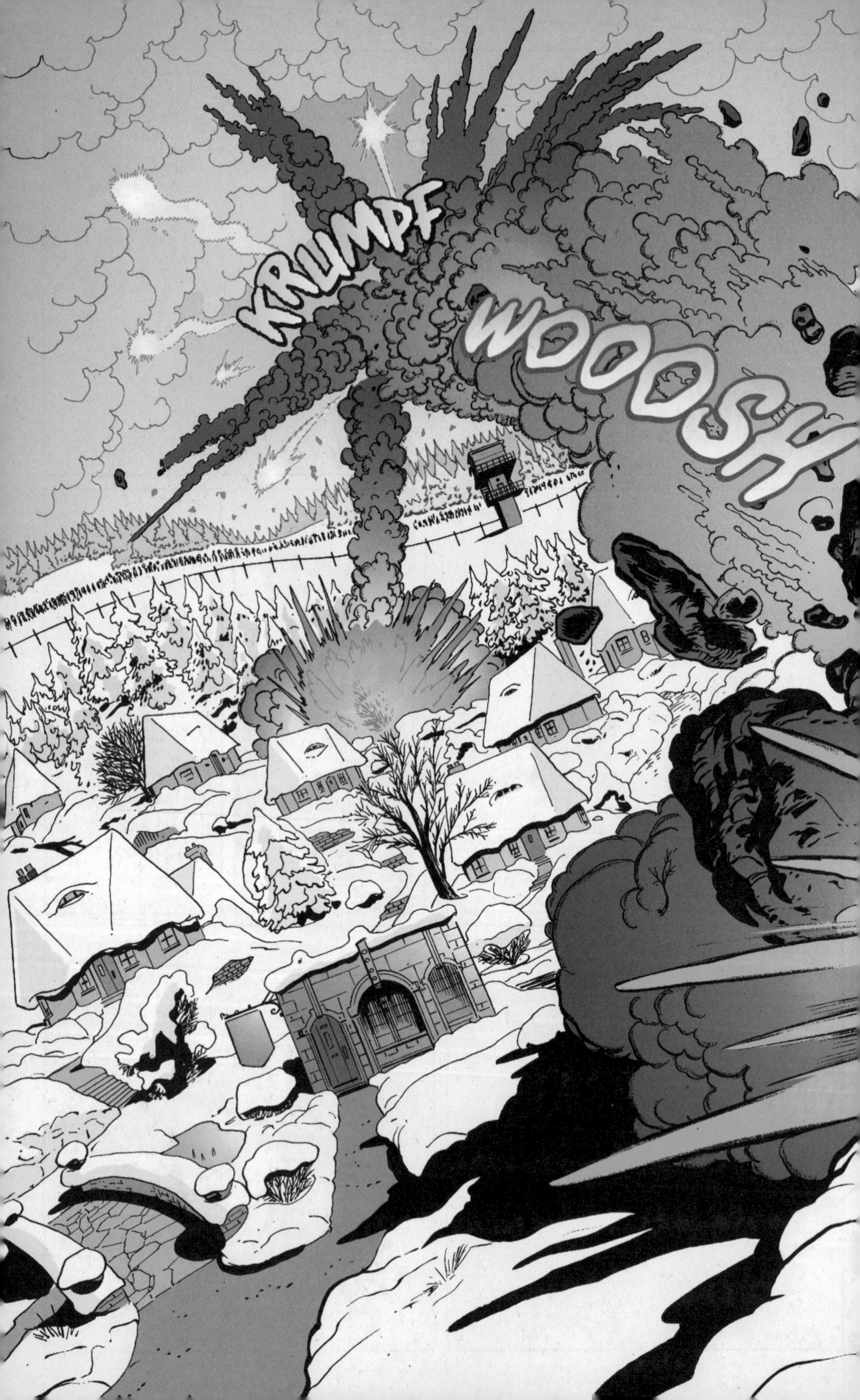
KRUMPF
WOOOSH

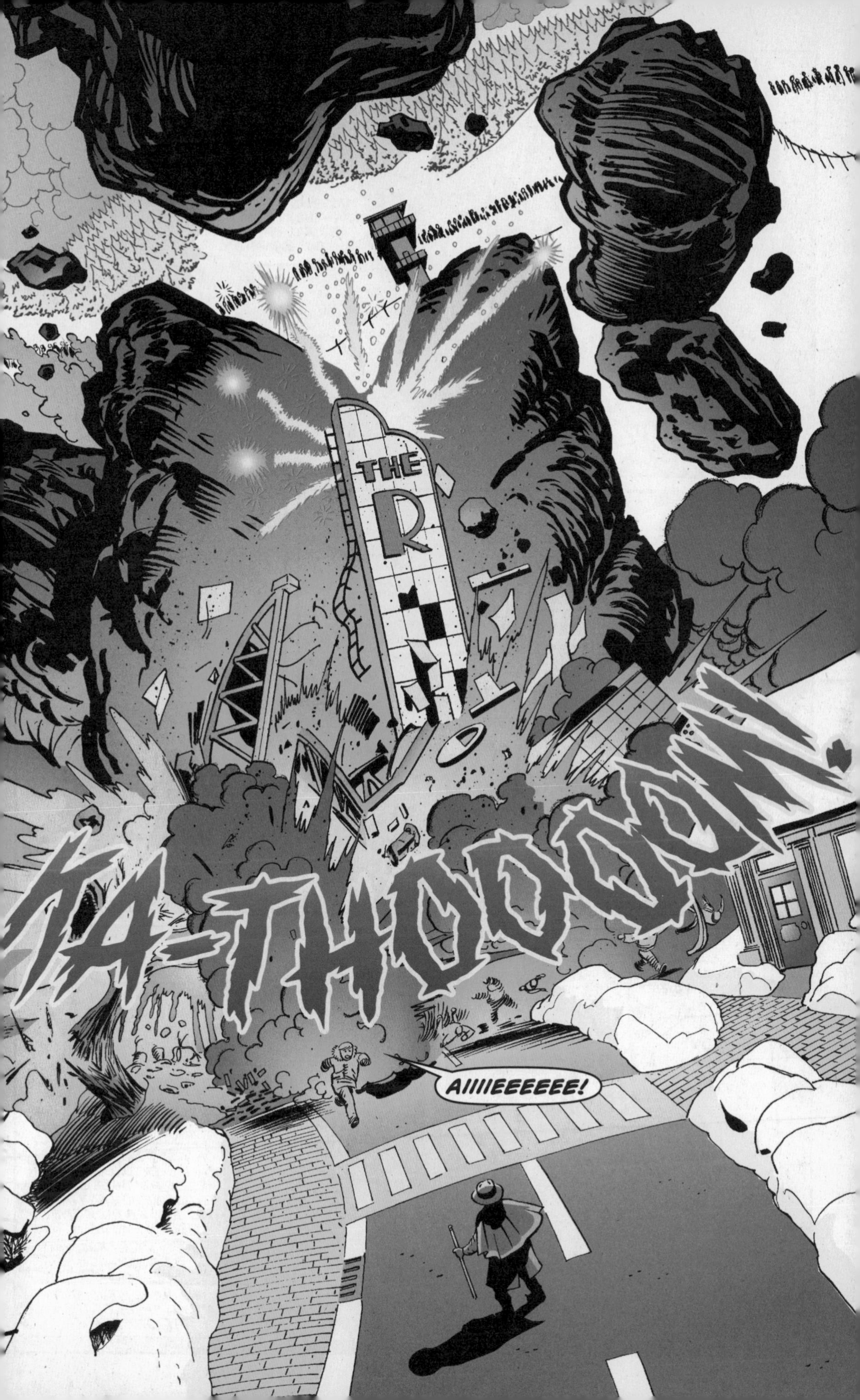
THE R
KA-THOOOOM!
AIIIIEEEEEE!

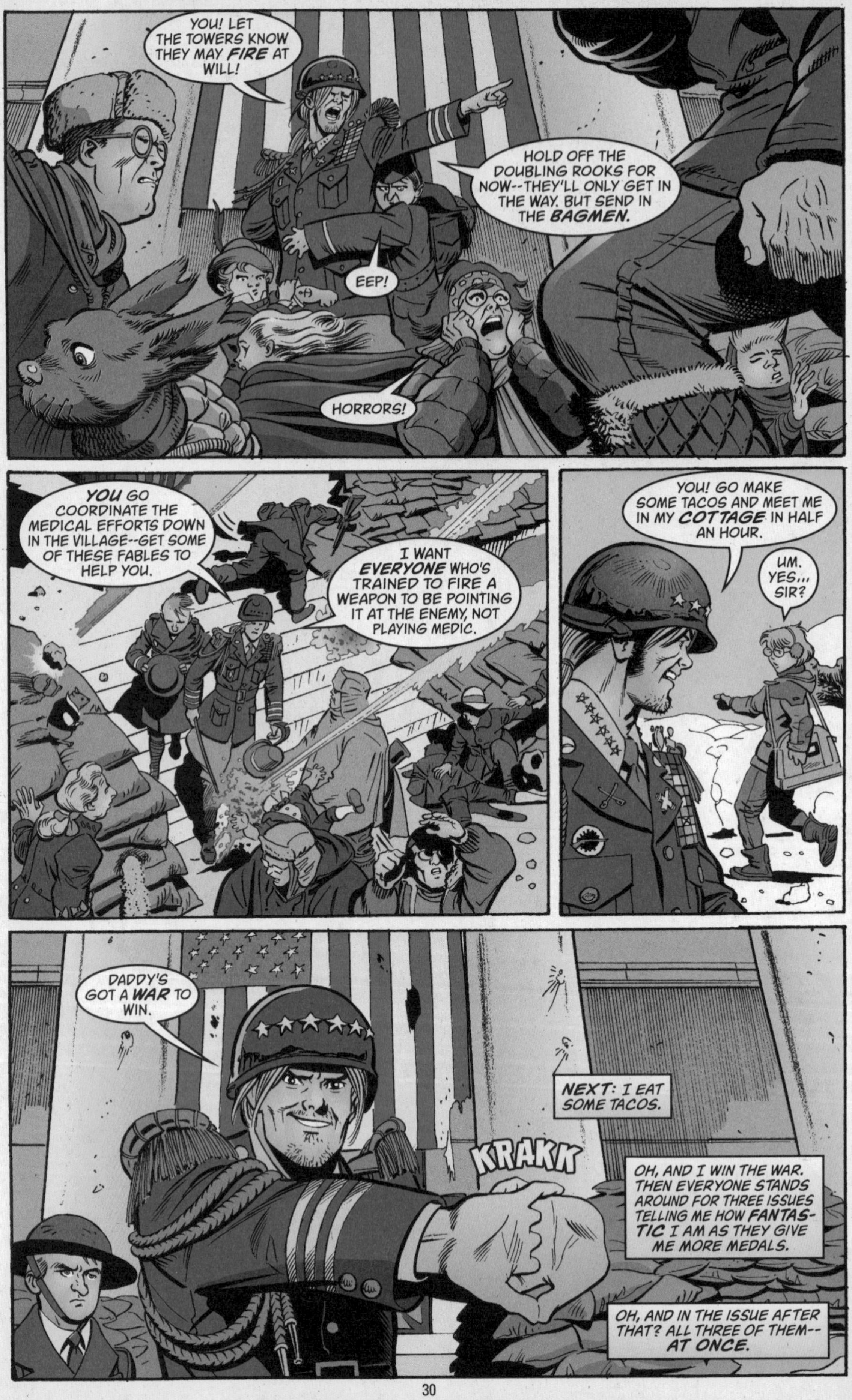
YOU! LET THE TOWERS KNOW THEY MAY FIRE AT WILL!
HOLD OFF THE DOUBLING ROOKS FOR NOW--THEY'LL ONLY GET IN THE WAY. BUT SEND IN THE BAGMEN.
EEP!
HORRORS!
YOU GO COORDINATE THE MEDICAL EFFORTS DOWN IN THE VILLAGE--GET SOME OF THESE FABLES TO HELP YOU.
I WANT EVERYONE WHO'S TRAINED TO FIRE A WEAPON TO BE POINTING IT AT THE ENEMY, NOT PLAYING MEDIC.
YOU! GO MAKE SOME TACOS AND MEET ME IN MY COTTAGE IN HALF AN HOUR.
UM. YES... SIR?
DADDY'S GOT A WAR TO WIN.
NEXT: I EAT SOME TACOS.
KRAKK
OH, AND I WIN THE WAR. THEN EVERYONE STANDS AROUND FOR THREE ISSUES TELLING ME HOW FANTASTIC I AM AS THEY GIVE ME MORE MEDALS.
OH, AND IN THE ISSUE AFTER THAT? ALL THREE OF THEM--AT ONCE.

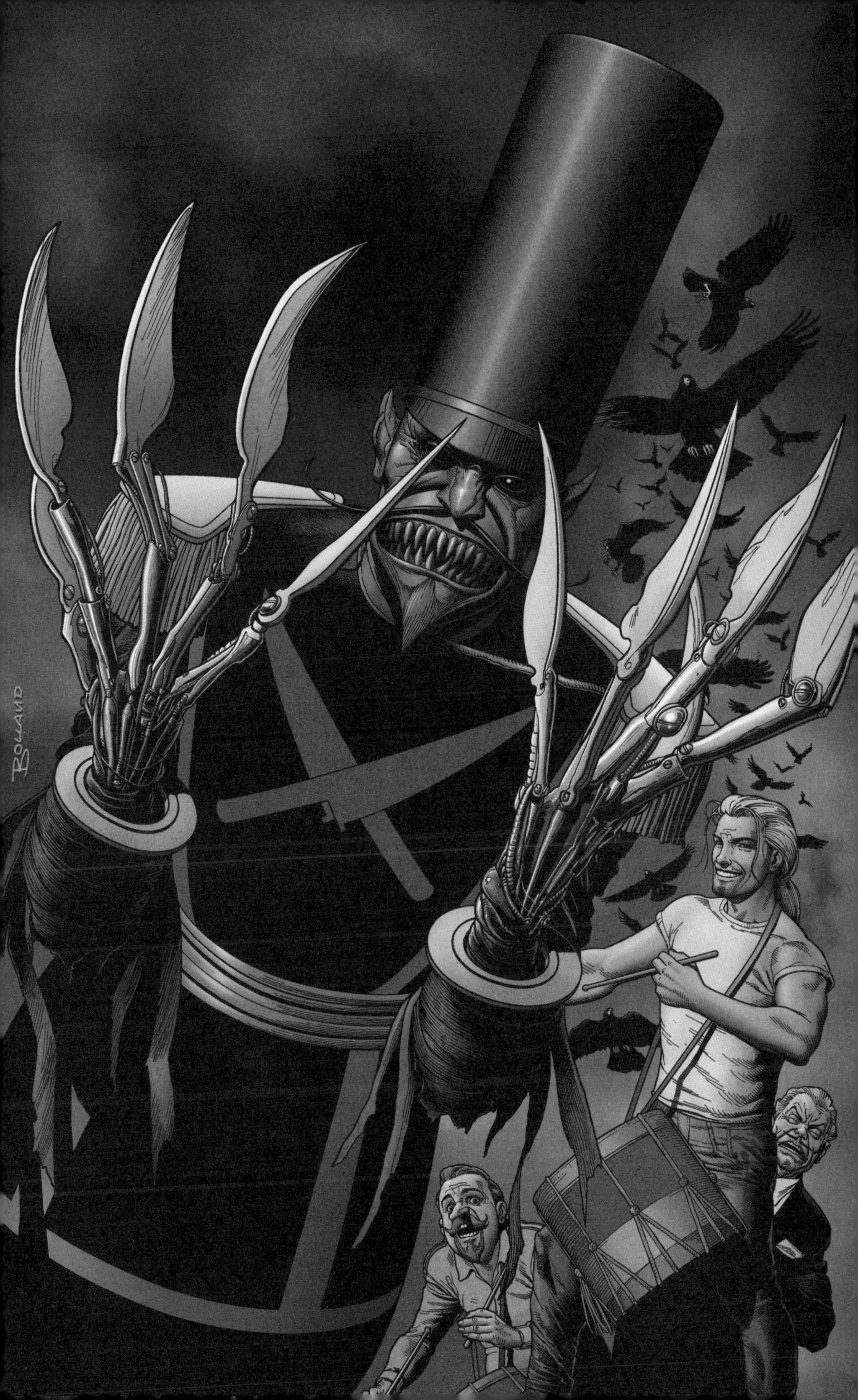
BOLLAND

*"I can't believe I fell for that slimy bastard's **bullshit**."*

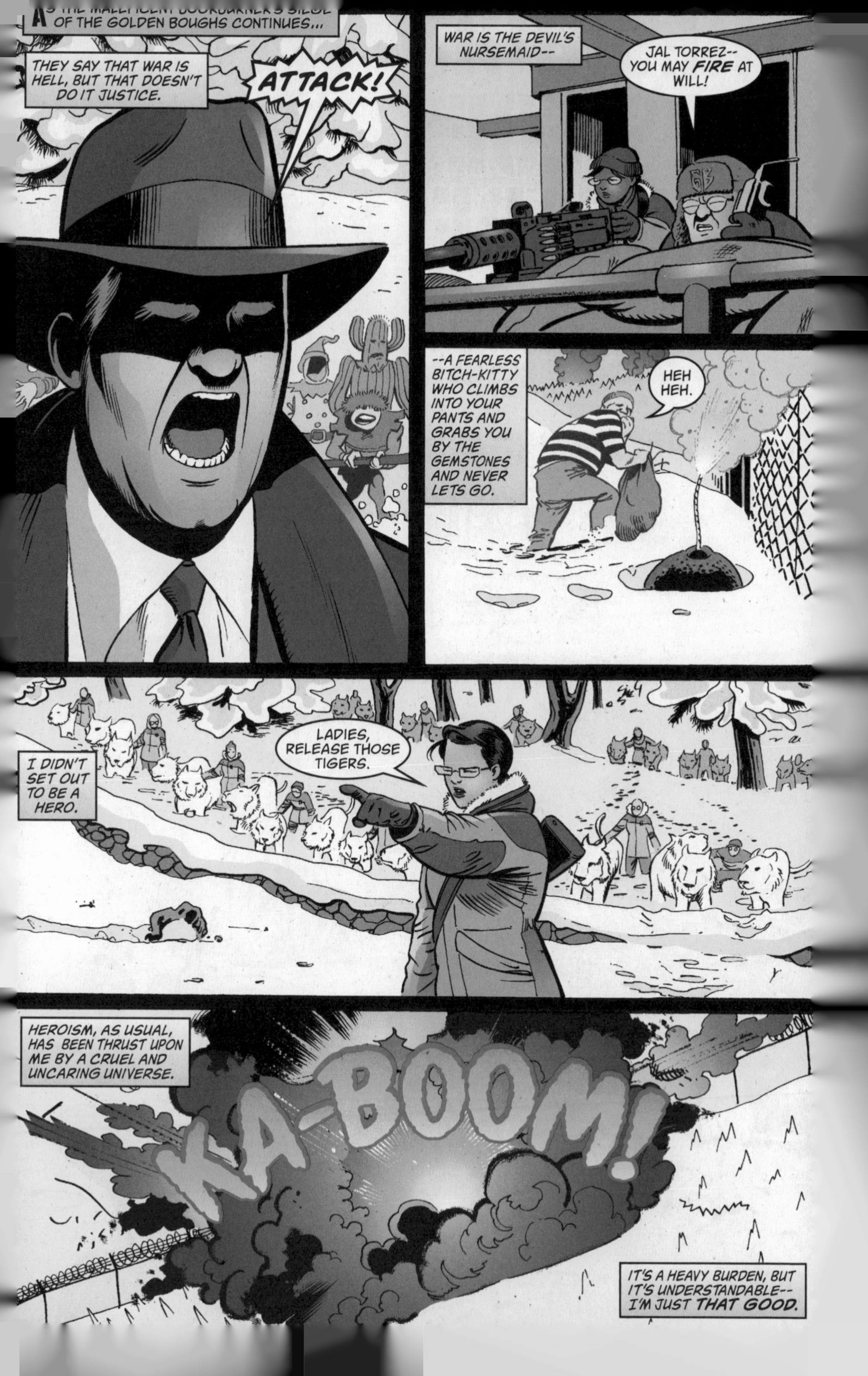

OF THE GOLDEN BOUGHS CONTINUES...
THEY SAY THAT WAR IS HELL, BUT THAT DOESN'T DO IT JUSTICE.
ATTACK!
WAR IS THE DEVIL'S NURSEMAID--
JAL TORREZ-- YOU MAY FIRE AT WILL!
--A FEARLESS BITCH-KITTY WHO CLIMBS INTO YOUR PANTS AND GRABS YOU BY THE GEMSTONES AND NEVER LETS GO.
HEH HEH.
I DIDN'T SET OUT TO BE A HERO.
LADIES, RELEASE THOSE TIGERS.
HEROISM, AS USUAL, HAS BEEN THRUST UPON ME BY A CRUEL AND UNCARING UNIVERSE.
KA-BOOM!
IT'S A HEAVY BURDEN, BUT IT'S UNDERSTANDABLE-- I'M JUST THAT GOOD.

THE BOOK OF SIEGE WARFARE

The Books of War, Volume Two

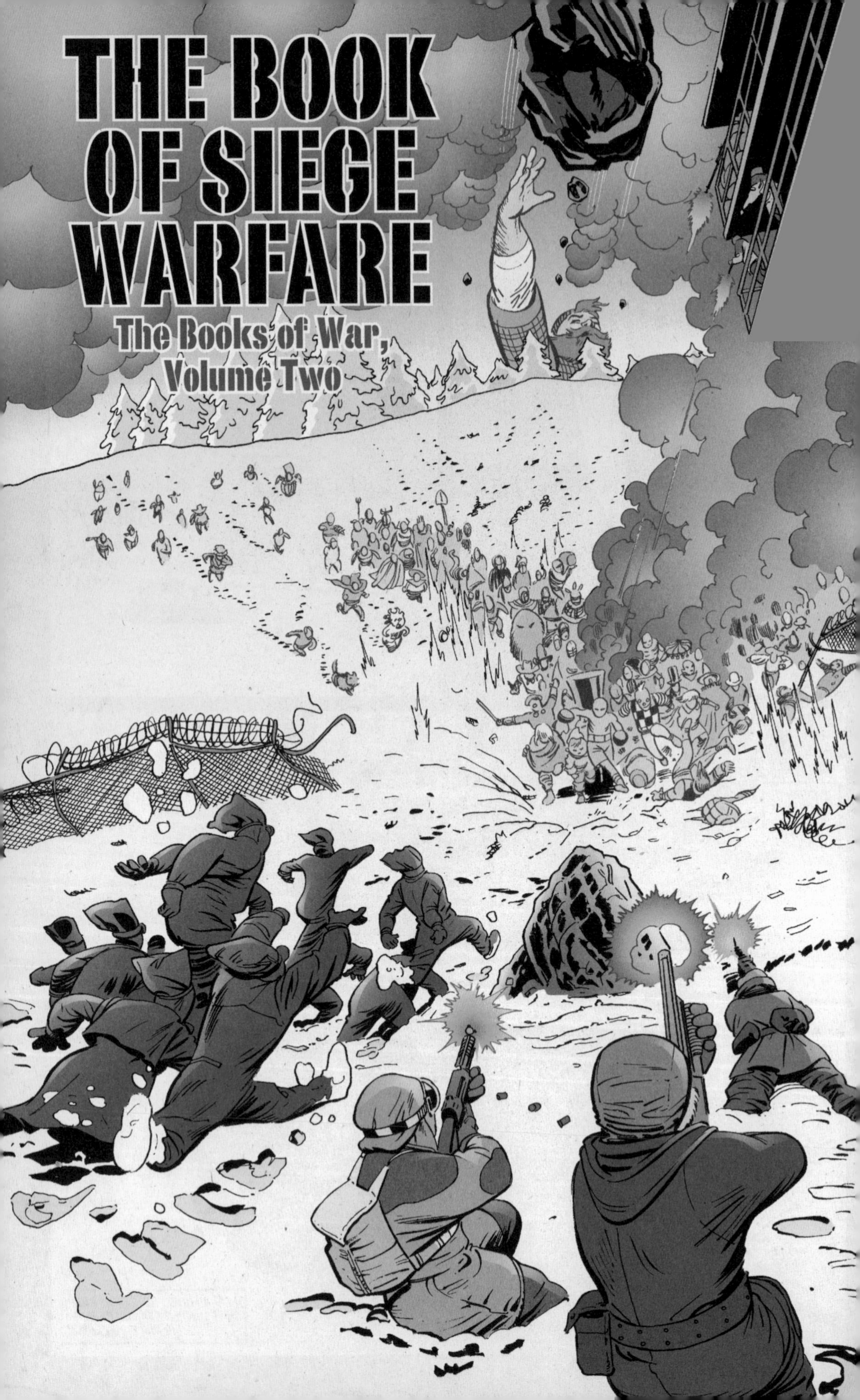

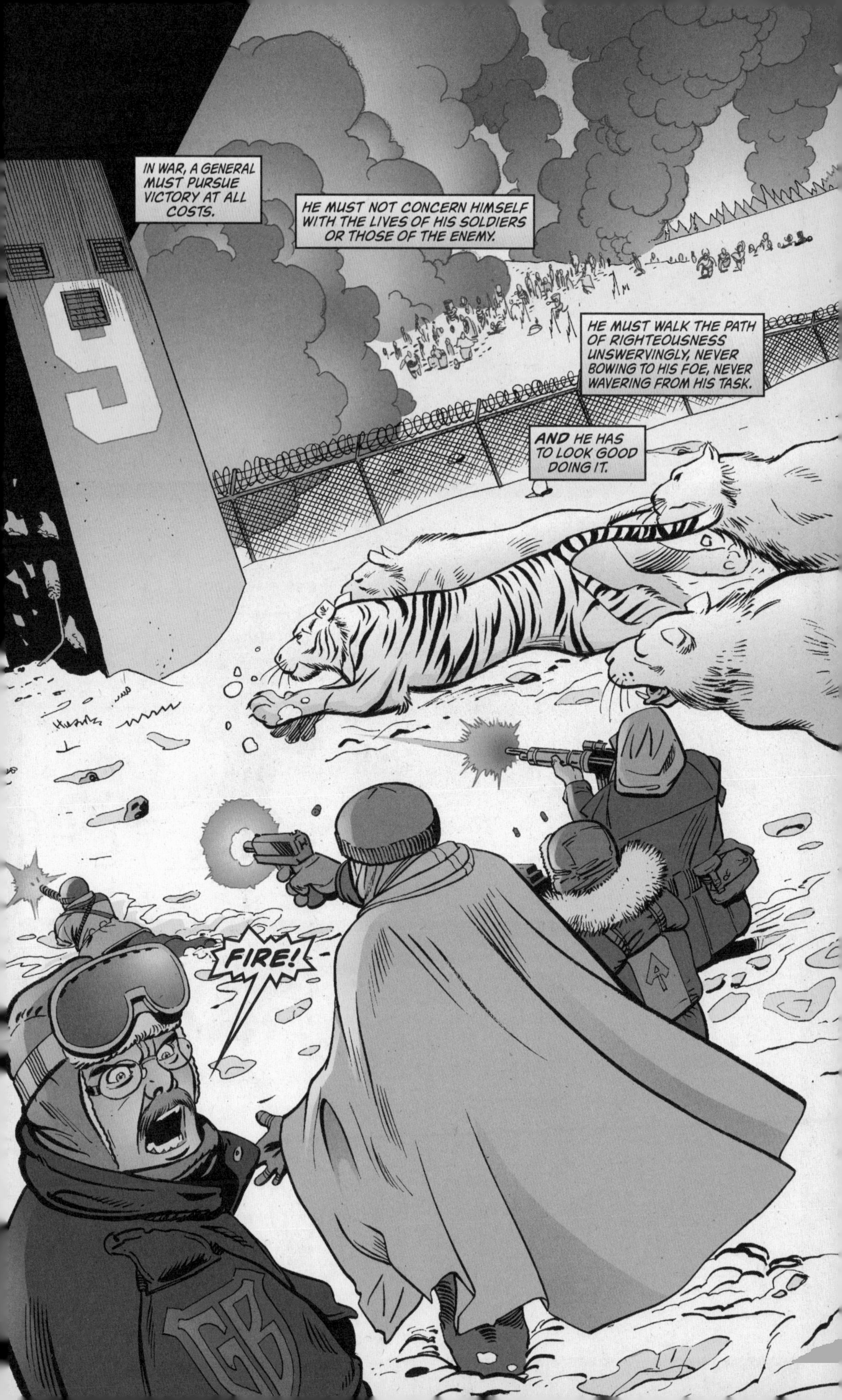

IN WAR, A GENERAL MUST PURSUE VICTORY AT ALL COSTS.
HE MUST NOT CONCERN HIMSELF WITH THE LIVES OF HIS SOLDIERS OR THOSE OF THE ENEMY.
HE MUST WALK THE PATH OF RIGHTEOUSNESS UNSWERVINGLY, NEVER BOWING TO HIS FOE, NEVER WAVERING FROM HIS TASK.
AND HE HAS TO LOOK GOOD DOING IT.
FIRE!

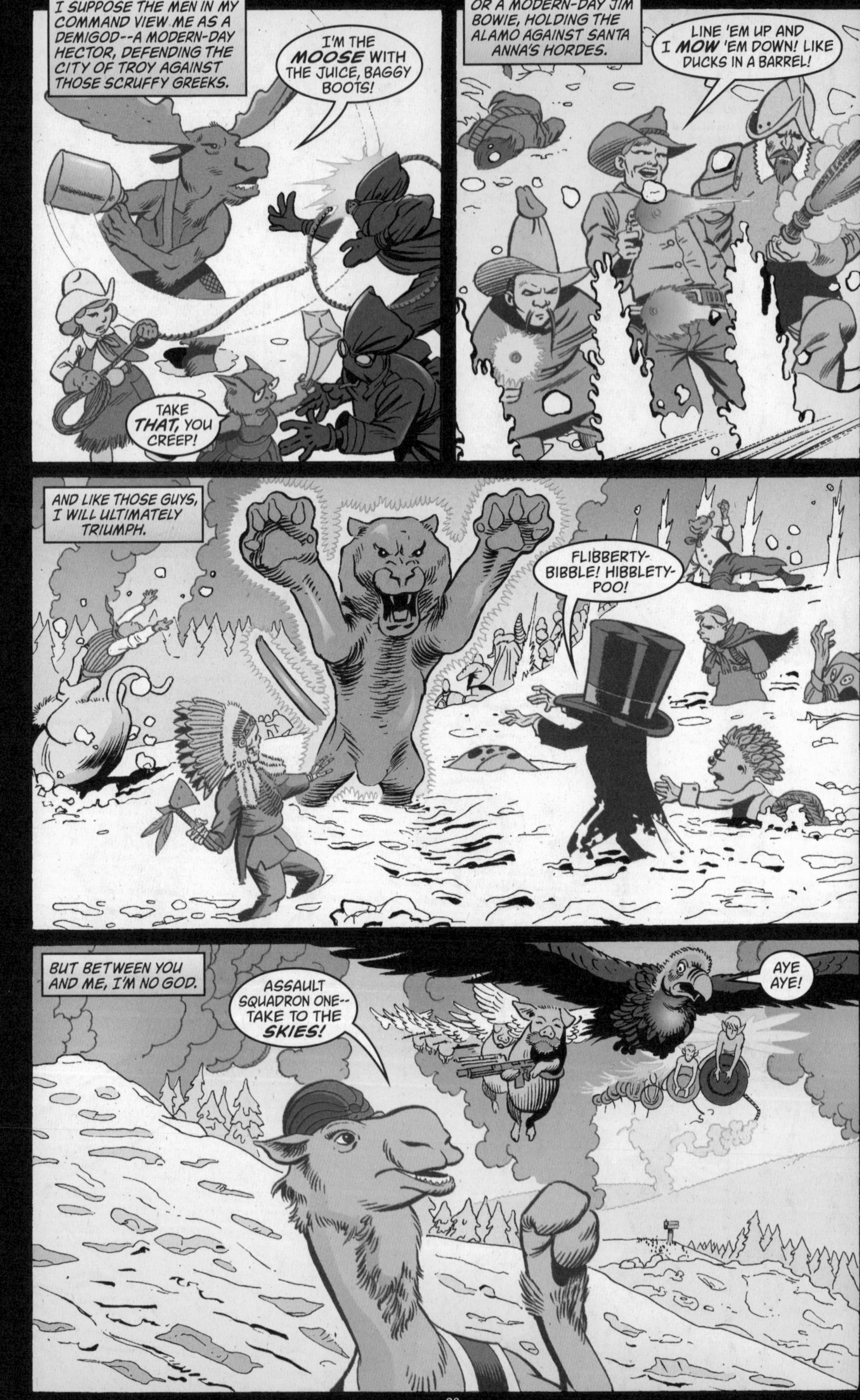
I SUPPOSE THE MEN IN MY COMMAND VIEW ME AS A DEMIGOD--A MODERN-DAY HECTOR, DEFENDING THE CITY OF TROY AGAINST THOSE SCRUFFY GREEKS.
I'M THE MOOSE WITH THE JUICE, BAGGY BOOTS!
TAKE THAT, YOU CREEP!
OR A MODERN-DAY JIM BOWIE, HOLDING THE ALAMO AGAINST SANTA ANNA'S HORDES.
LINE 'EM UP AND I MOW 'EM DOWN! LIKE DUCKS IN A BARREL!
AND LIKE THOSE GUYS, I WILL ULTIMATELY TRIUMPH.
FLIBBERTY-BIBBLE! HIBBLETY-POO!
BUT BETWEEN YOU AND ME, I'M NO GOD.
ASSAULT SQUADRON ONE--TAKE TO THE SKIES!
AYE AYE!

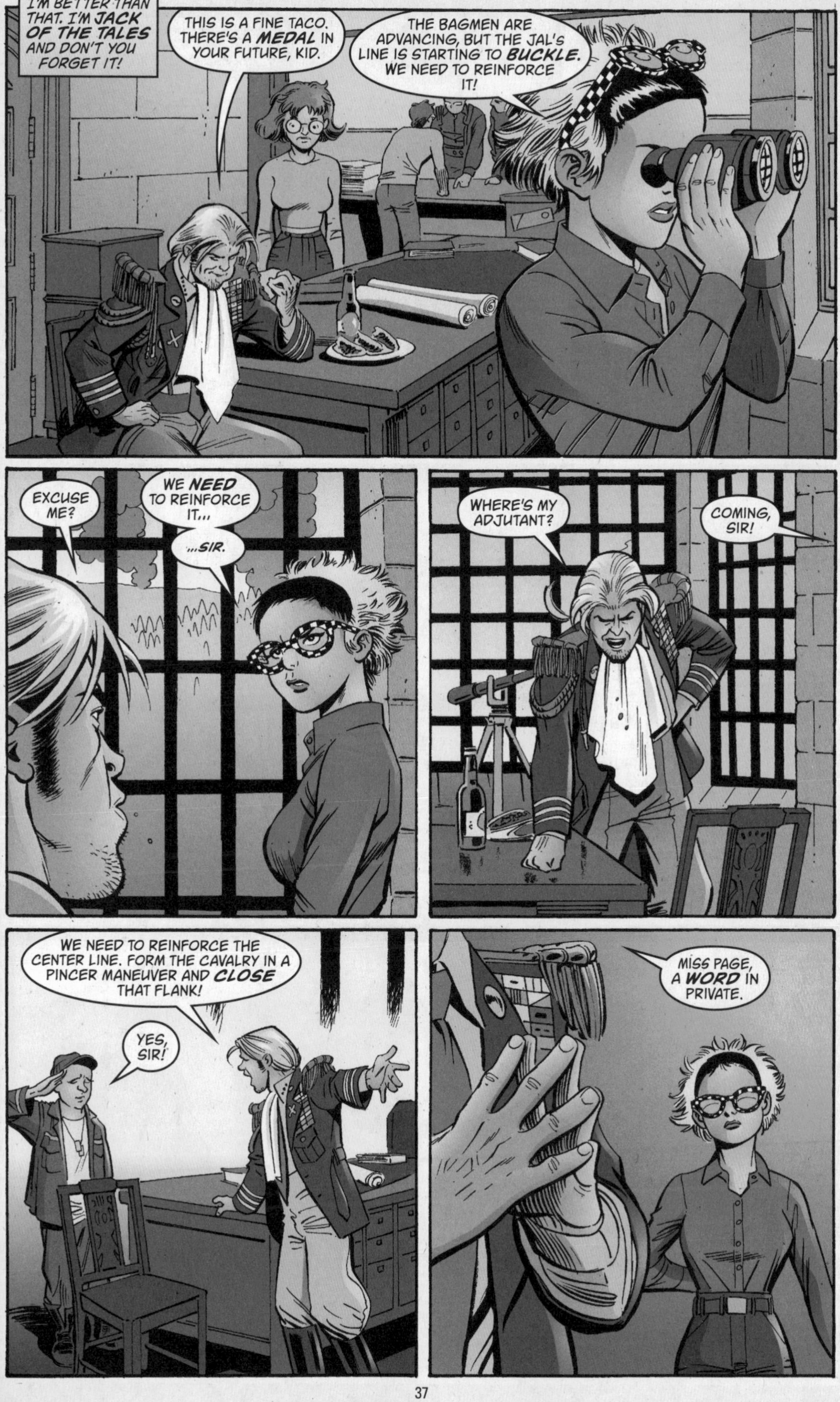
I'M BETTER THAN THAT. I'M JACK OF THE TALES AND DON'T YOU FORGET IT!
THIS IS A FINE TACO. THERE'S A MEDAL IN YOUR FUTURE, KID.
THE BAGMEN ARE ADVANCING, BUT THE JAL'S LINE IS STARTING TO BUCKLE. WE NEED TO REINFORCE IT!
EXCUSE ME?
WE NEED TO REINFORCE IT...
...SIR.
WHERE'S MY ADJUTANT?
COMING, SIR!
WE NEED TO REINFORCE THE CENTER LINE. FORM THE CAVALRY IN A PINCER MANEUVER AND CLOSE THAT FLANK!
YES, SIR!
MISS PAGE, A WORD IN PRIVATE.

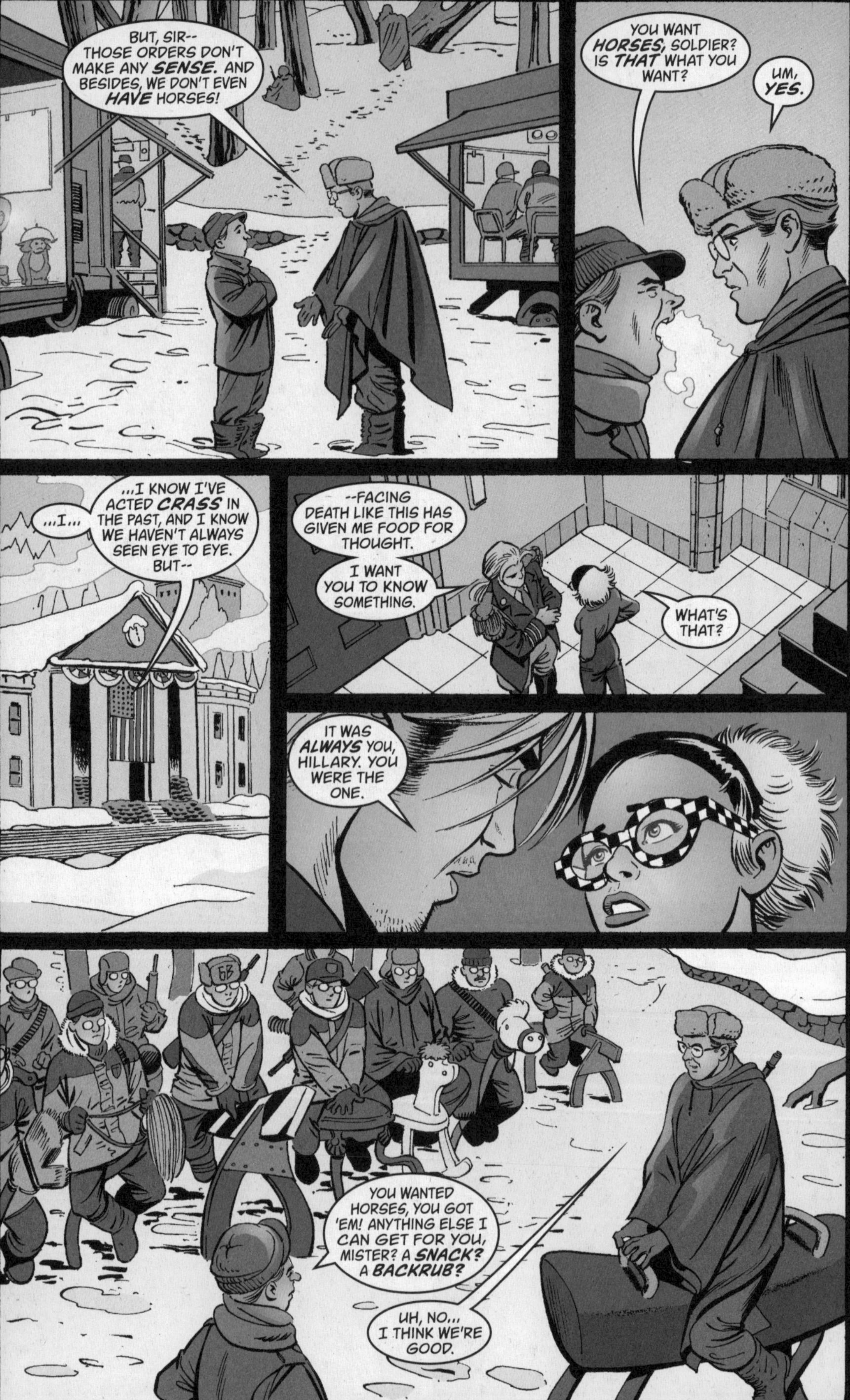
BUT, SIR-- THOSE ORDERS DON'T MAKE ANY SENSE. AND BESIDES, WE DON'T EVEN HAVE HORSES!
YOU WANT HORSES, SOLDIER? IS THAT WHAT YOU WANT?
UM, YES.
...I...
...I KNOW I'VE ACTED CRASS IN THE PAST, AND I KNOW WE HAVEN'T ALWAYS SEEN EYE TO EYE. BUT--
--FACING DEATH LIKE THIS HAS GIVEN ME FOOD FOR THOUGHT.
I WANT YOU TO KNOW SOMETHING.
WHAT'S THAT?
IT WAS ALWAYS YOU, HILLARY. YOU WERE THE ONE.
YOU WANTED HORSES, YOU GOT 'EM! ANYTHING ELSE I CAN GET FOR YOU, MISTER? A SNACK? A BACKRUB?
UH, NO... I THINK WE'RE GOOD.

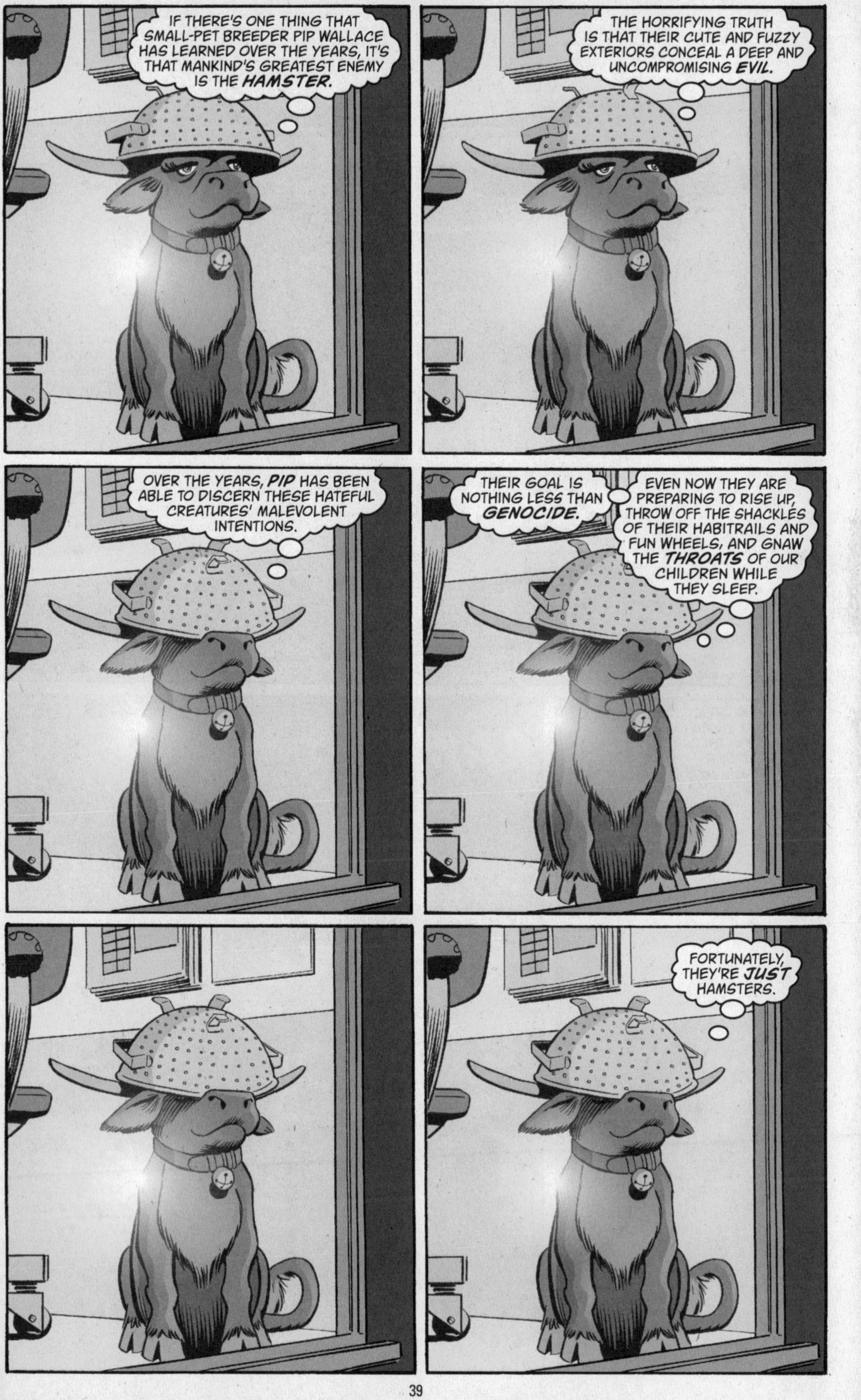
IF THERE'S ONE THING THAT SMALL-PET BREEDER PIP WALLACE HAS LEARNED OVER THE YEARS, IT'S THAT MANKIND'S GREATEST ENEMY IS THE HAMSTER.
THE HORRIFYING TRUTH IS THAT THEIR CUTE AND FUZZY EXTERIORS CONCEAL A DEEP AND UNCOMPROMISING EVIL.
OVER THE YEARS, PIP HAS BEEN ABLE TO DISCERN THESE HATEFUL CREATURES' MALEVOLENT INTENTIONS.
THEIR GOAL IS NOTHING LESS THAN GENOCIDE.
EVEN NOW THEY ARE PREPARING TO RISE UP, THROW OFF THE SHACKLES OF THEIR HABITRAILS AND FUN WHEELS, AND GNAW THE THROATS OF OUR CHILDREN WHILE THEY SLEEP.
FORTUNATELY, THEY'RE JUST HAMSTERS.

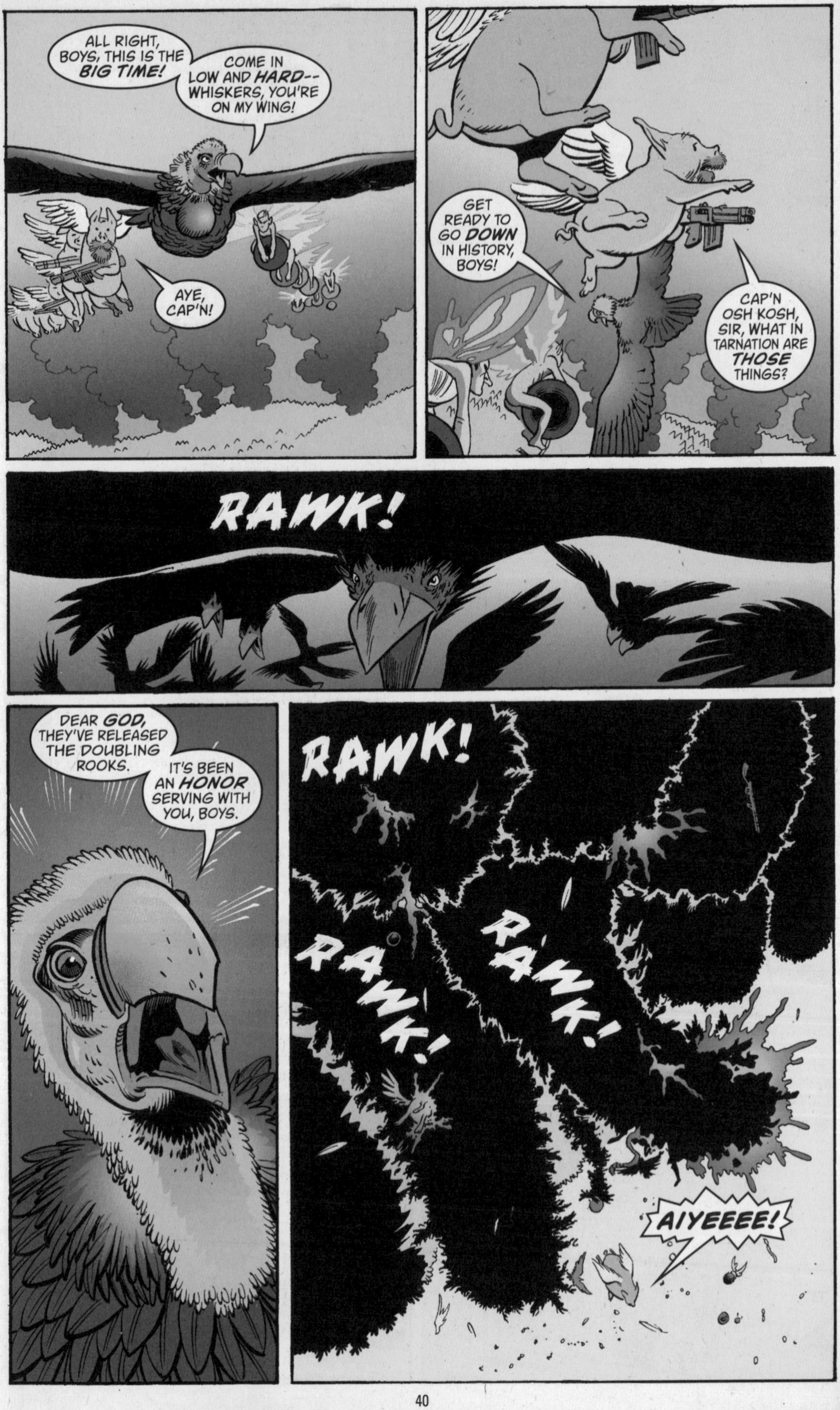
ALL RIGHT, BOYS, THIS IS THE BIG TIME!
COME IN LOW AND HARD-- WHISKERS, YOU'RE ON MY WING!
AYE, CAP'N!
GET READY TO GO DOWN IN HISTORY, BOYS!
CAP'N OSH KOSH, SIR, WHAT IN TARNATION ARE THOSE THINGS?
RAWK!
DEAR GOD, THEY'VE RELEASED THE DOUBLING ROOKS.
IT'S BEEN AN HONOR SERVING WITH YOU, BOYS.
RAWK!
RAWK!
RAWK!
AIYEEEE!

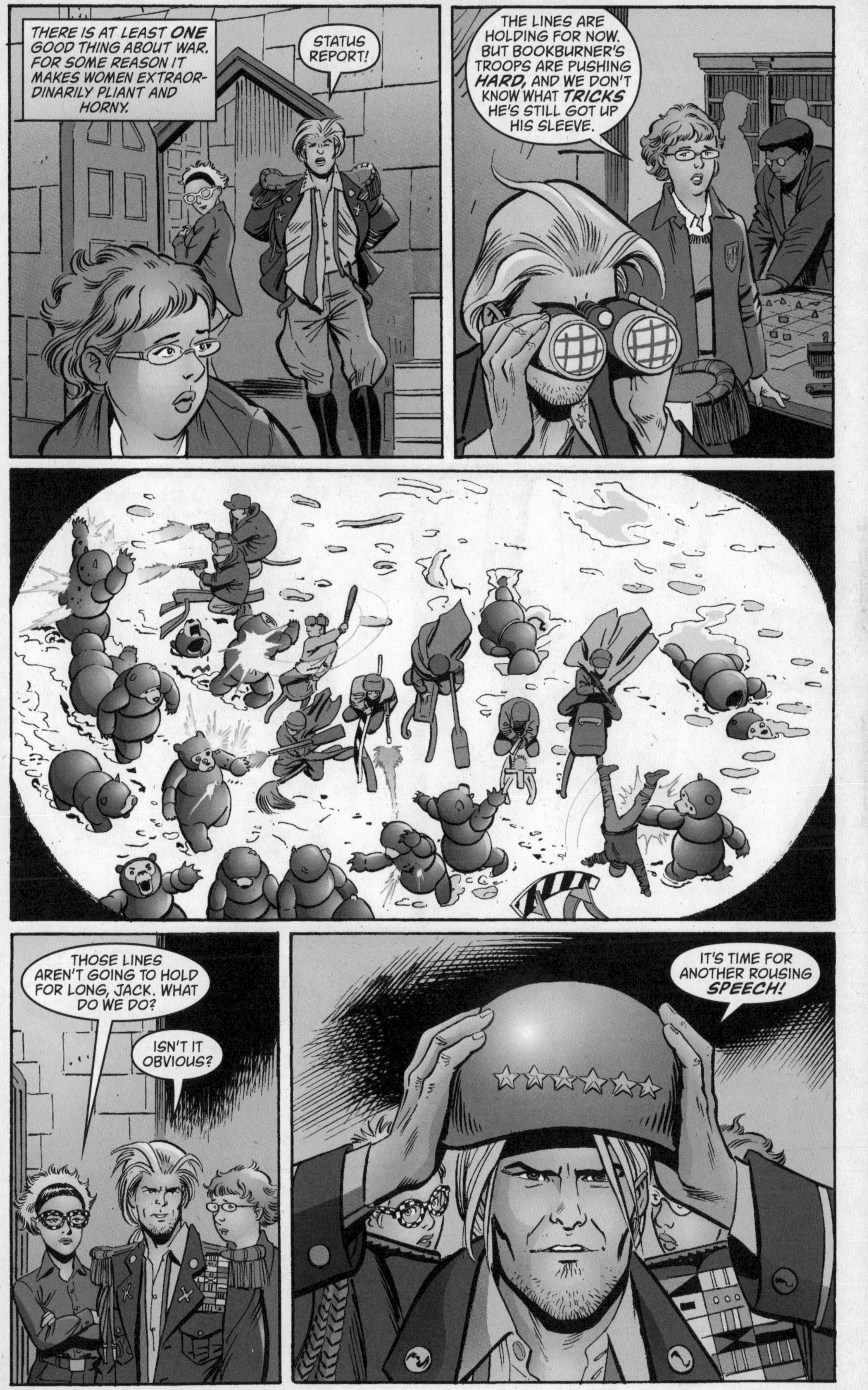
THERE IS AT LEAST ONE GOOD THING ABOUT WAR. FOR SOME REASON IT MAKES WOMEN EXTRAORDINARILY PLIANT AND HORNY.
STATUS REPORT!
THE LINES ARE HOLDING FOR NOW. BUT BOOKBURNER'S TROOPS ARE PUSHING HARD, AND WE DON'T KNOW WHAT TRICKS HE'S STILL GOT UP HIS SLEEVE.
THOSE LINES AREN'T GOING TO HOLD FOR LONG, JACK. WHAT DO WE DO?
ISN'T IT OBVIOUS?
IT'S TIME FOR ANOTHER ROUSING SPEECH!

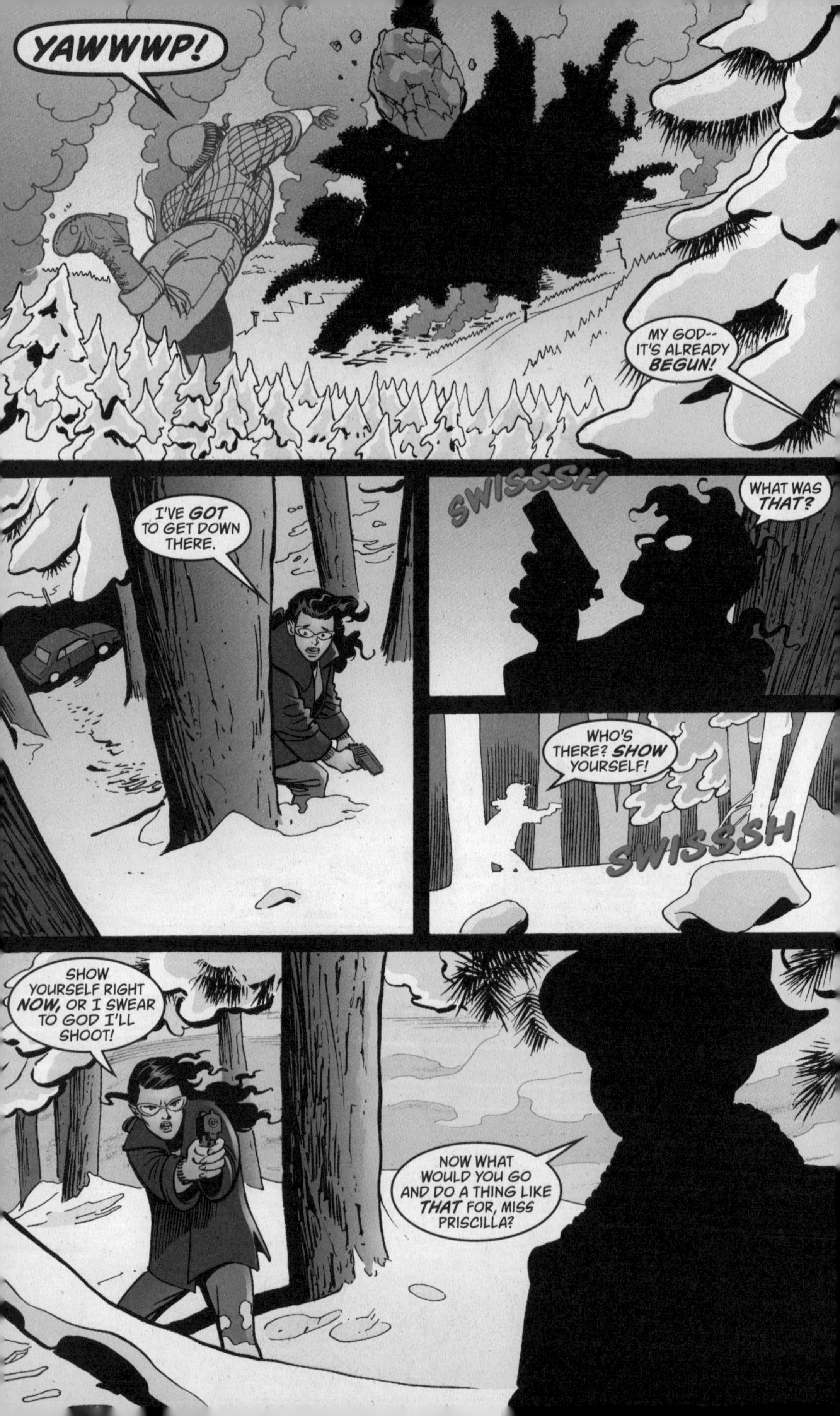
YAWWWP!
MY GOD-- IT'S ALREADY BEGUN!
I'VE GOT TO GET DOWN THERE.
SWISSSH
WHAT WAS THAT?
WHO'S THERE? SHOW YOURSELF!
SWISSSH
SHOW YOURSELF RIGHT NOW, OR I SWEAR TO GOD I'LL SHOOT!
NOW WHAT WOULD YOU GO AND DO A THING LIKE THAT FOR, MISS PRISCILLA?

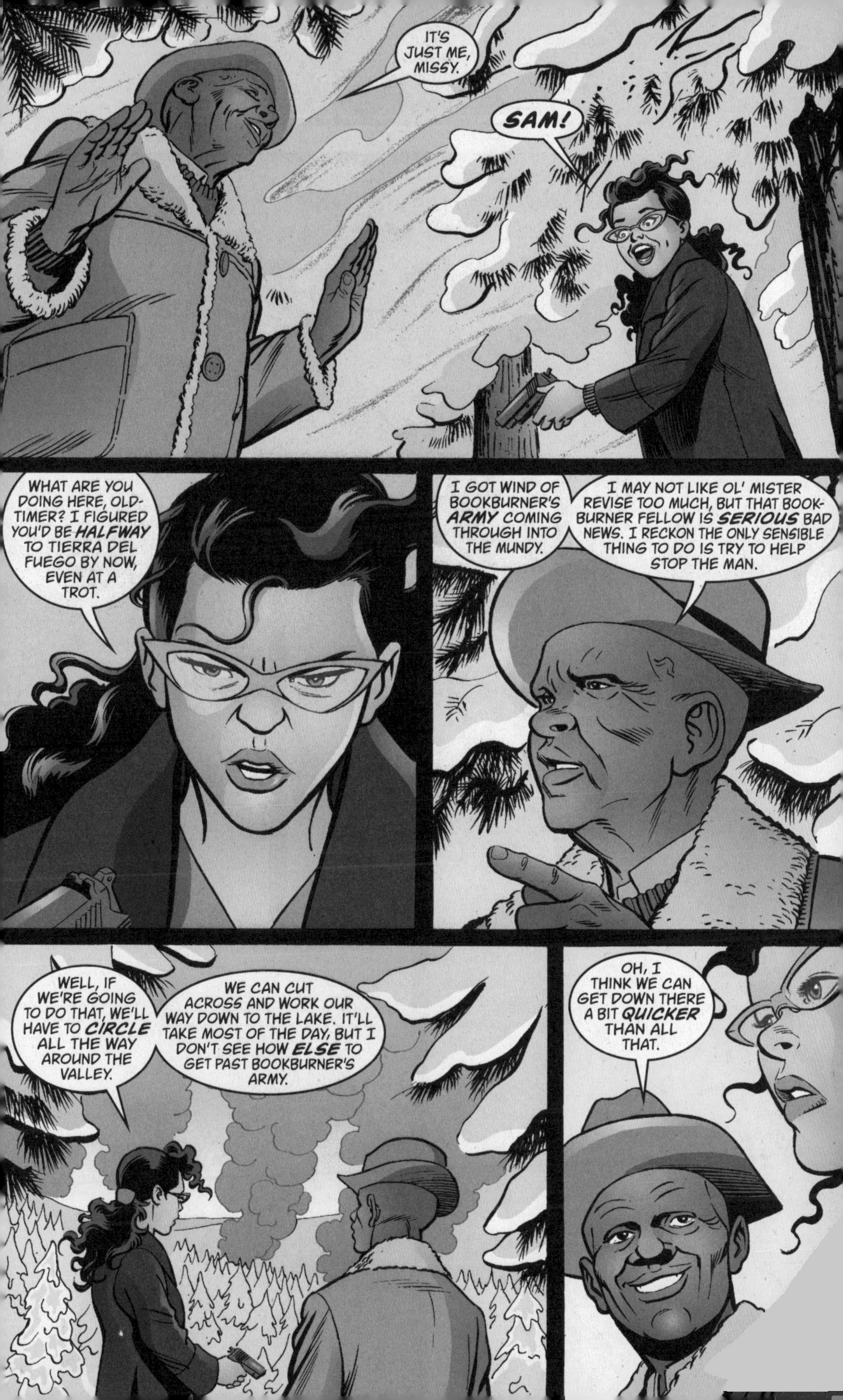
IT'S JUST ME, MISSY.
SAM!
WHAT ARE YOU DOING HERE, OLD-TIMER? I FIGURED YOU'D BE HALFWAY TO TIERRA DEL FUEGO BY NOW, EVEN AT A TROT.
I GOT WIND OF BOOKBURNER'S ARMY COMING THROUGH INTO THE MUNDY.
I MAY NOT LIKE OL' MISTER REVISE TOO MUCH, BUT THAT BOOK-BURNER FELLOW IS SERIOUS BAD NEWS. I RECKON THE ONLY SENSIBLE THING TO DO IS TRY TO HELP STOP THE MAN.
WELL, IF WE'RE GOING TO DO THAT, WE'LL HAVE TO CIRCLE ALL THE WAY AROUND THE VALLEY.
WE CAN CUT ACROSS AND WORK OUR WAY DOWN TO THE LAKE. IT'LL TAKE MOST OF THE DAY, BUT I DON'T SEE HOW ELSE TO GET PAST BOOKBURNER'S ARMY.
OH, I THINK WE CAN GET DOWN THERE A BIT QUICKER THAN ALL THAT.

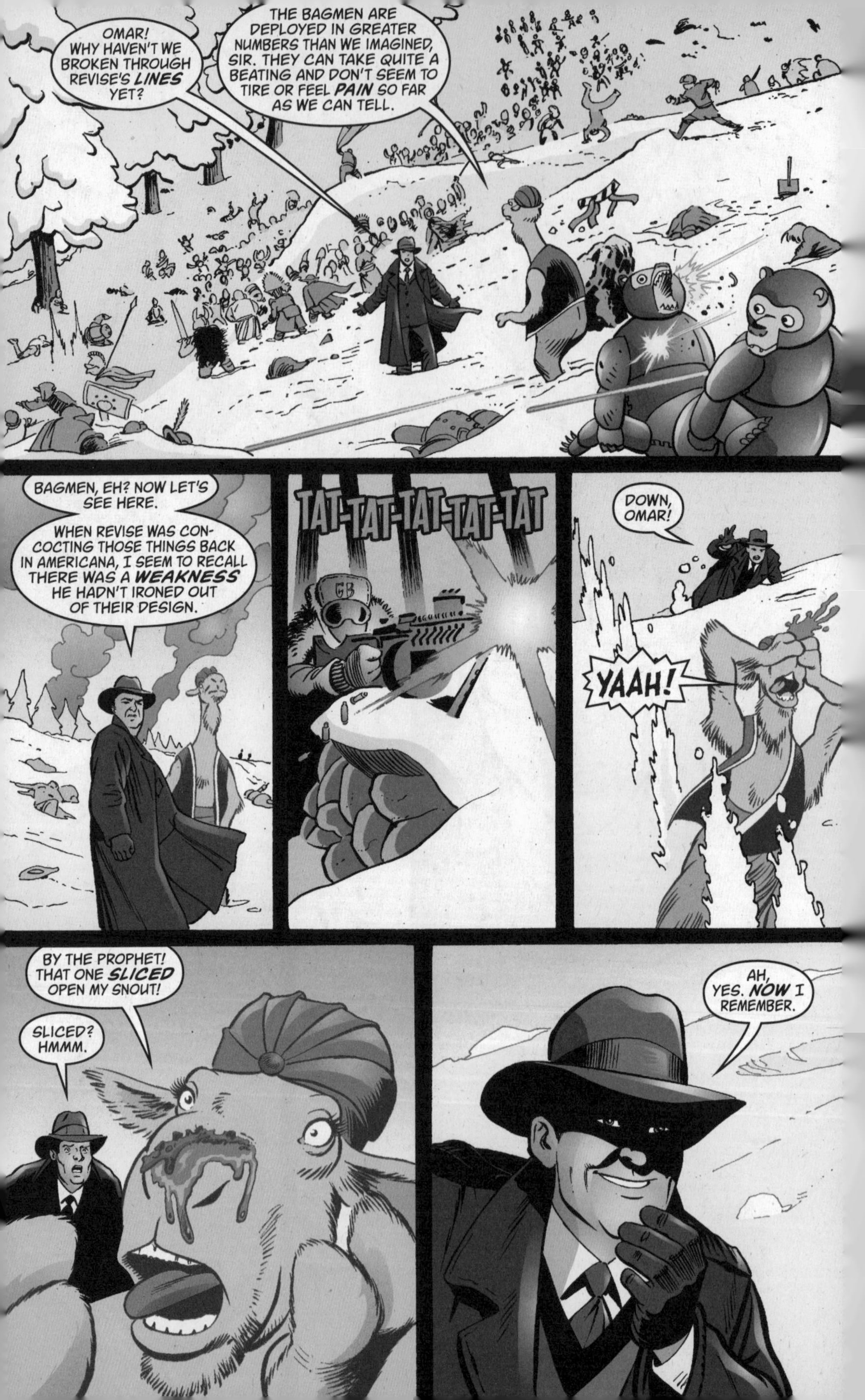

OMAR! WHY HAVEN'T WE BROKEN THROUGH REVISE'S LINES YET?
THE BAGMEN ARE DEPLOYED IN GREATER NUMBERS THAN WE IMAGINED, SIR. THEY CAN TAKE QUITE A BEATING AND DON'T SEEM TO TIRE OR FEEL PAIN SO FAR AS WE CAN TELL.
BAGMEN, EH? NOW LET'S SEE HERE.
WHEN REVISE WAS CONCOCTING THOSE THINGS BACK IN AMERICANA, I SEEM TO RECALL THERE WAS A WEAKNESS HE HADN'T IRONED OUT OF THEIR DESIGN.
TAT-TAT-TAT-TAT-TAT
GB
DOWN, OMAR!
YAAH!
BY THE PROPHET! THAT ONE SLICED OPEN MY SNOUT!
SLICED? HMMM.
AH, YES. NOW I REMEMBER.

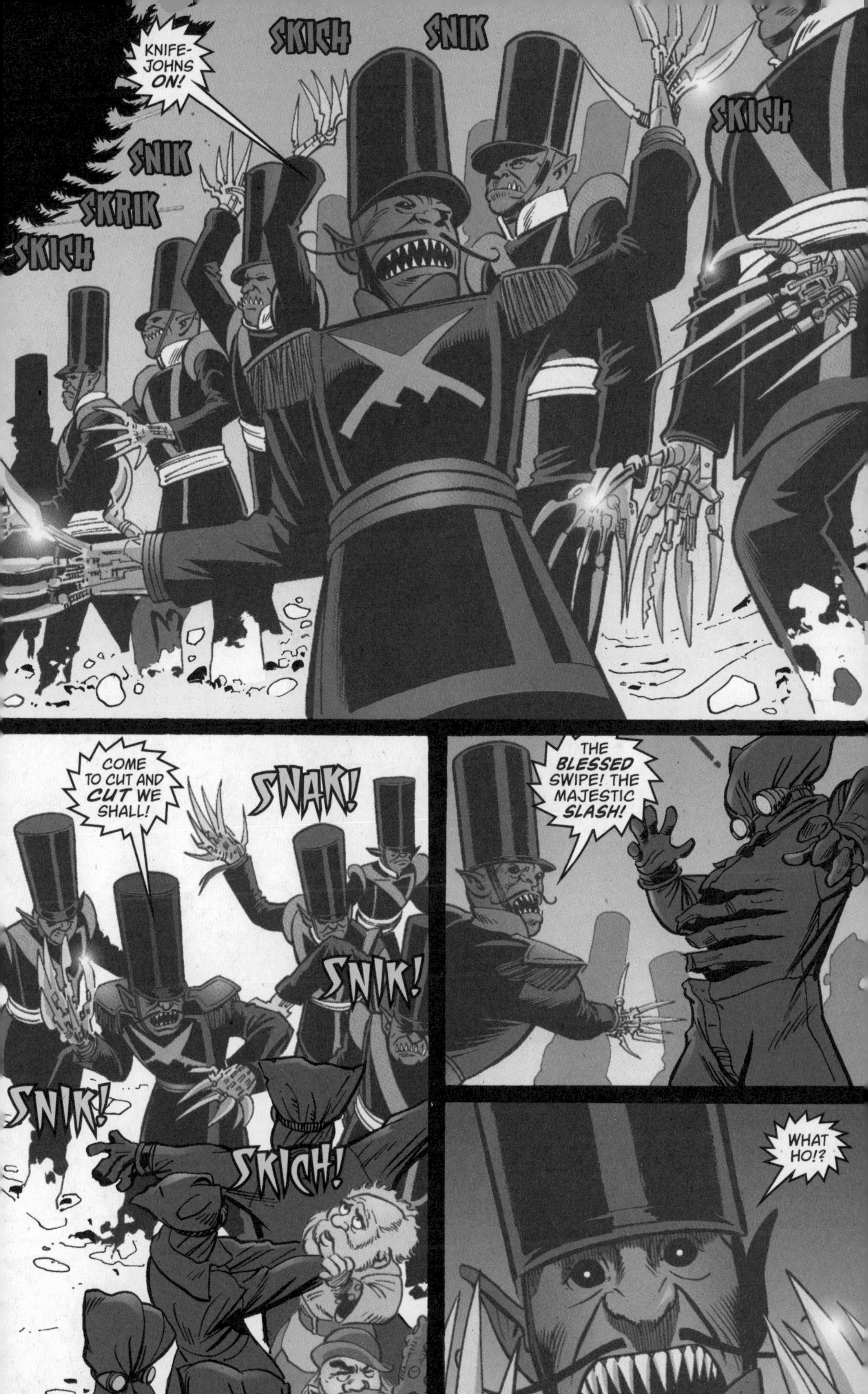
KNIFE-JOHNS ON!
SKICH
SNIK
SNIK
SKRIK
SKICH
SKICH
COME TO CUT AND CUT WE SHALL!
SNAK!
SNIK!
SNIK!
SKICH!
THE BLESSED SWIPE! THE MAJESTIC SLASH!
WHAT HO!?

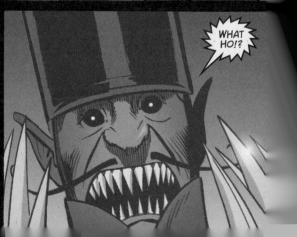

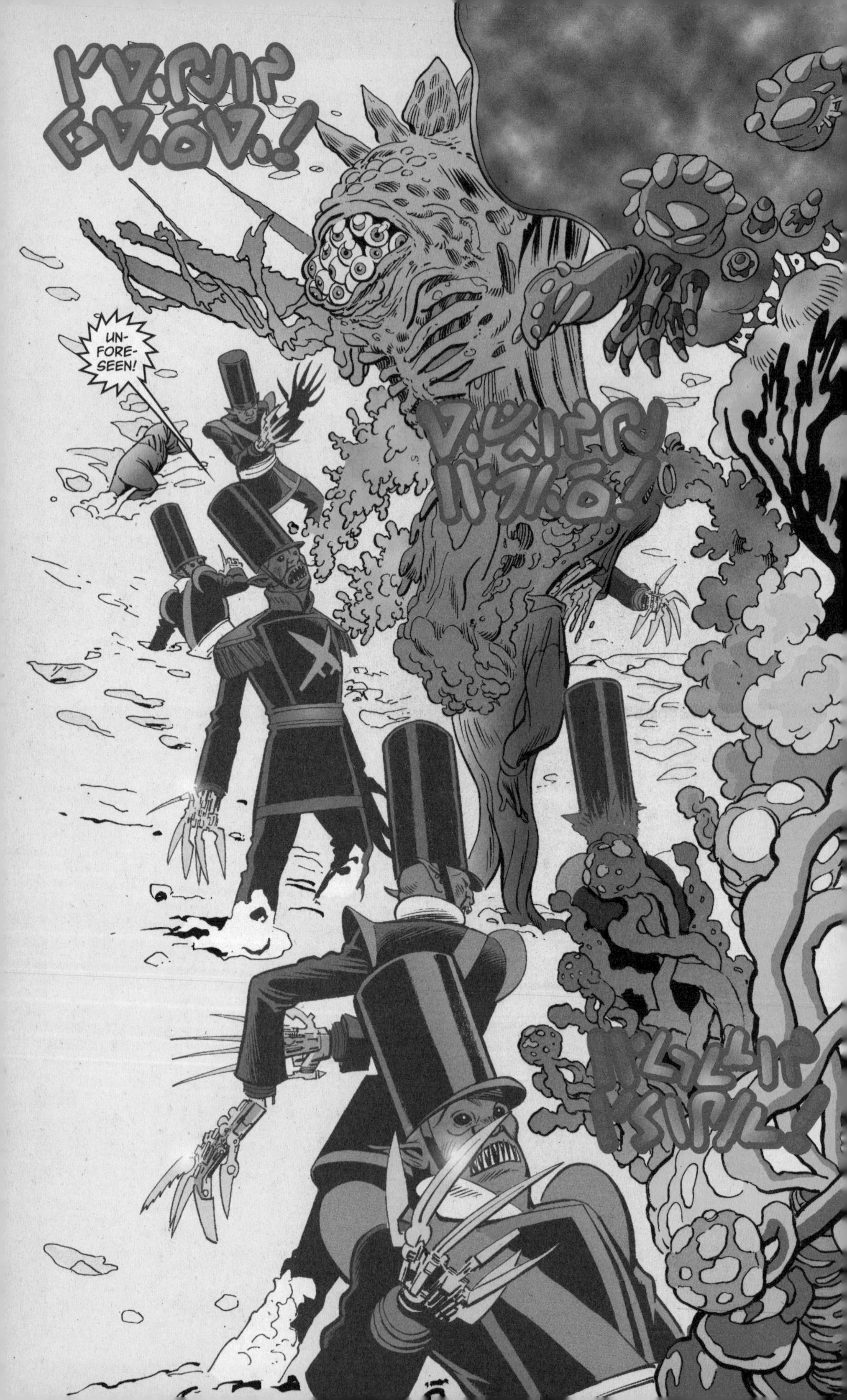
UN-FORE-SEEN!

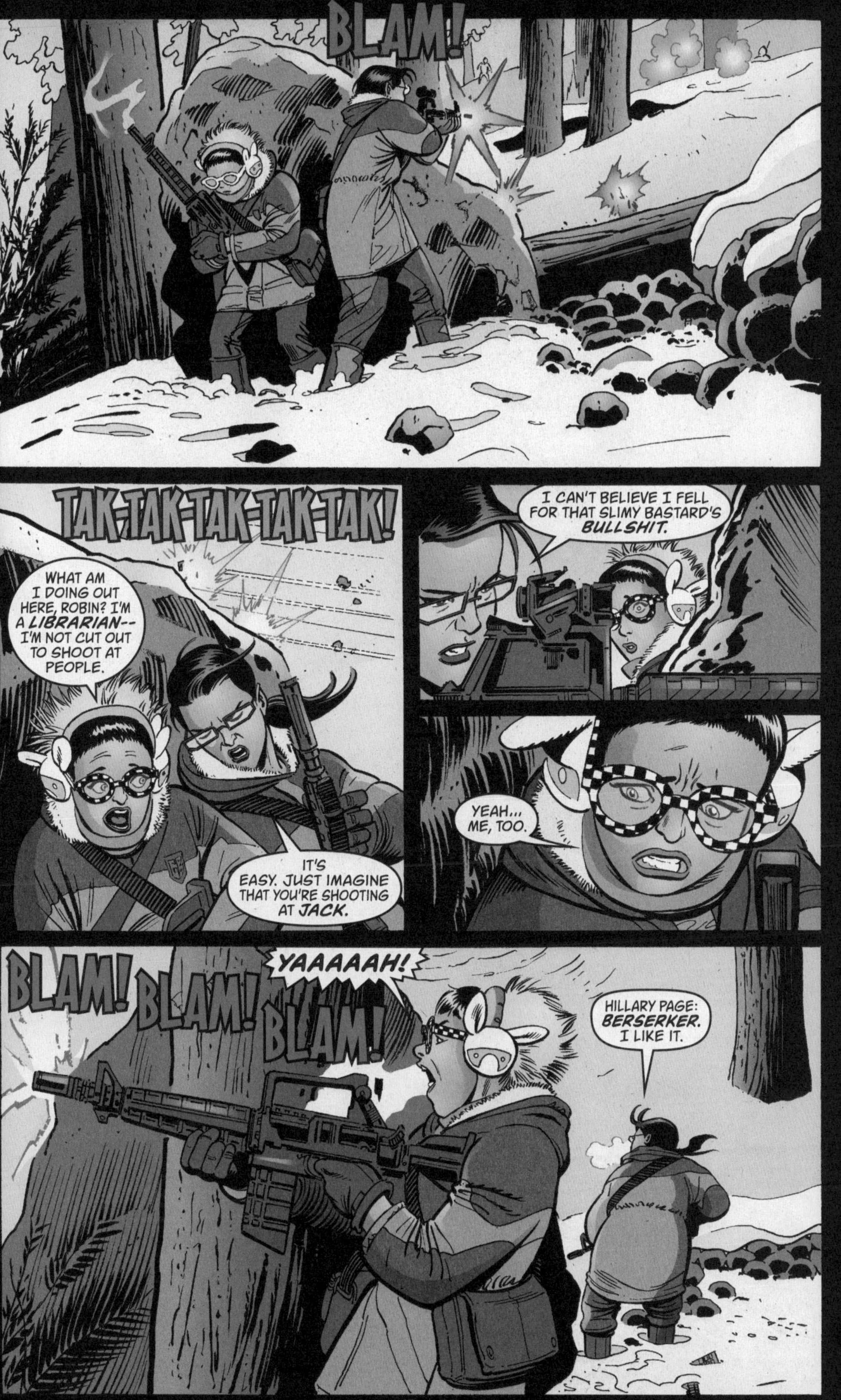
BLAM!
TAK-TAK-TAK-TAK-TAK!
WHAT AM I DOING OUT HERE, ROBIN? I'M A *LIBRARIAN*-- I'M NOT CUT OUT TO SHOOT AT PEOPLE.
IT'S EASY. JUST IMAGINE THAT YOU'RE SHOOTING AT **JACK**.
I CAN'T BELIEVE I FELL FOR THAT SLIMY BASTARD'S ***BULLSHIT***.
YEAH... ME, TOO.
BLAM! BLAM! BLAM!
YAAAAAH!
HILLARY PAGE: ***BERSERKER***. I LIKE IT.

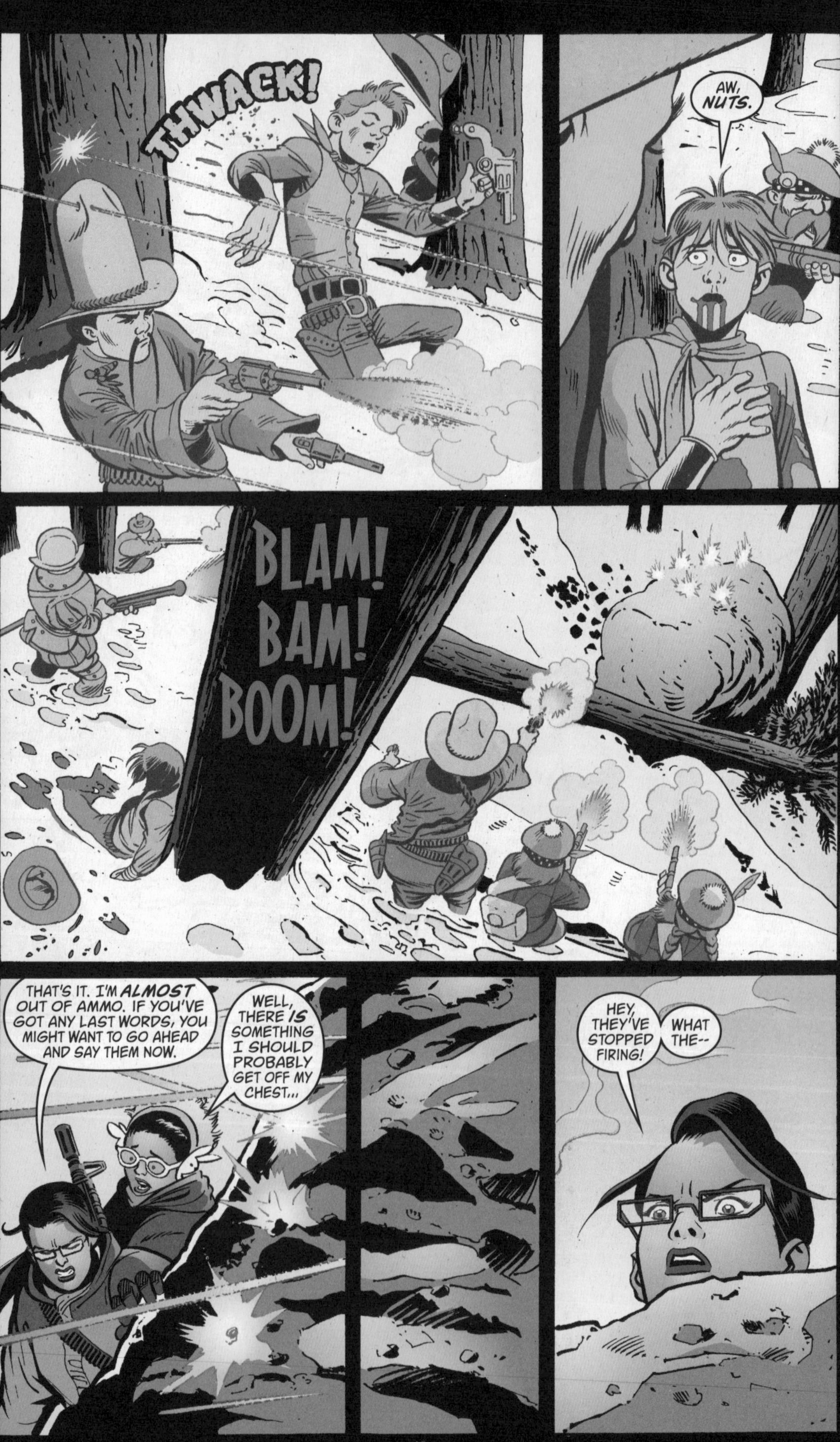
THWACK!
AW, NUTS.
BLAM! BAM! BOOM!
THAT'S IT. I'M ALMOST OUT OF AMMO. IF YOU'VE GOT ANY LAST WORDS, YOU MIGHT WANT TO GO AHEAD AND SAY THEM NOW.
WELL, THERE IS SOMETHING I SHOULD PROBABLY GET OFF MY CHEST...
HEY, THEY'VE STOPPED FIRING!
WHAT THE--

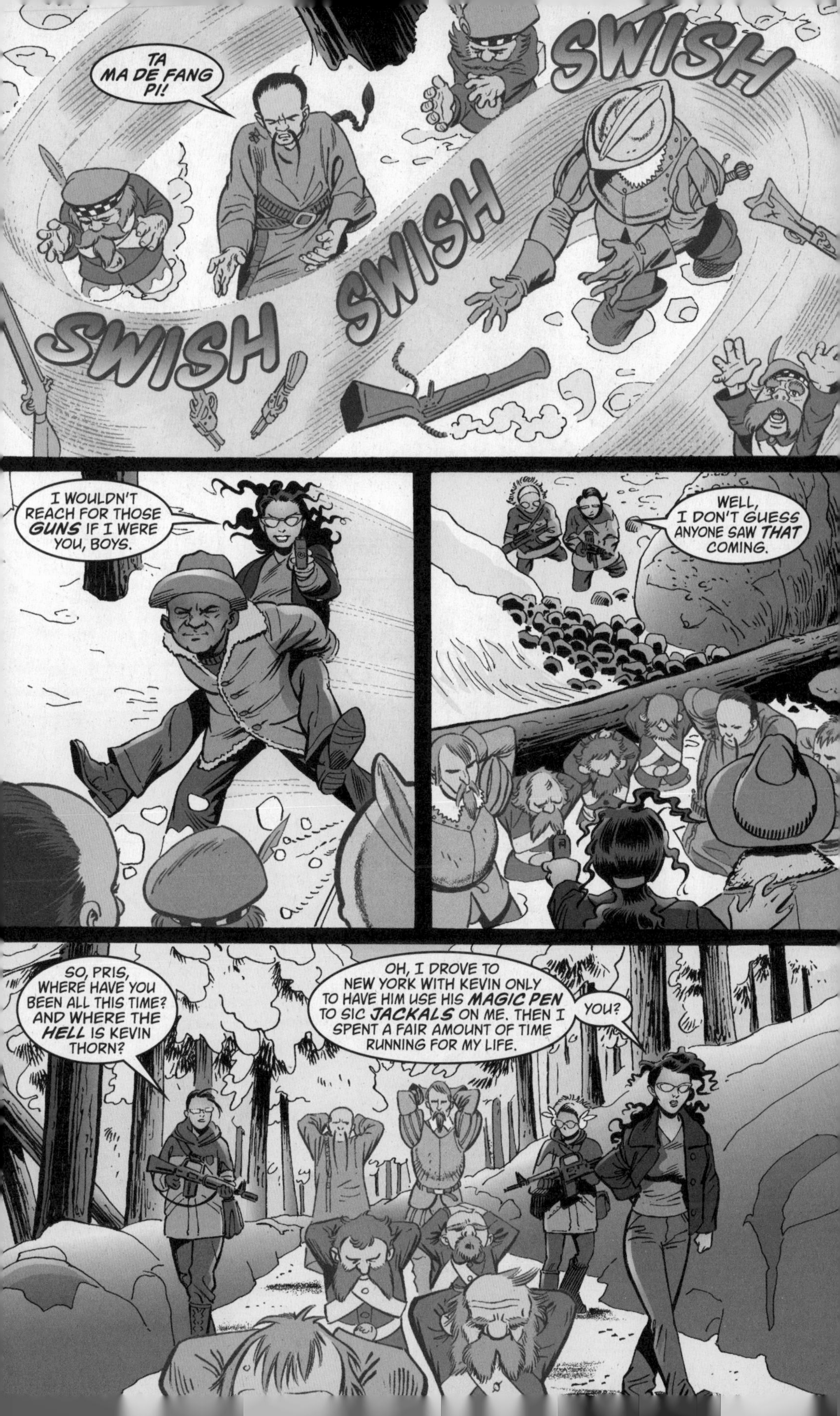
TA MA DE FANG PI!
SWISH
SWISH
SWISH
I WOULDN'T REACH FOR THOSE GUNS IF I WERE YOU, BOYS.
WELL, I DON'T GUESS ANYONE SAW THAT COMING.
SO, PRIS, WHERE HAVE YOU BEEN ALL THIS TIME? AND WHERE THE HELL IS KEVIN THORN?
OH, I DROVE TO NEW YORK WITH KEVIN ONLY TO HAVE HIM USE HIS MAGIC PEN TO SIC JACKALS ON ME. THEN I SPENT A FAIR AMOUNT OF TIME RUNNING FOR MY LIFE.
YOU?

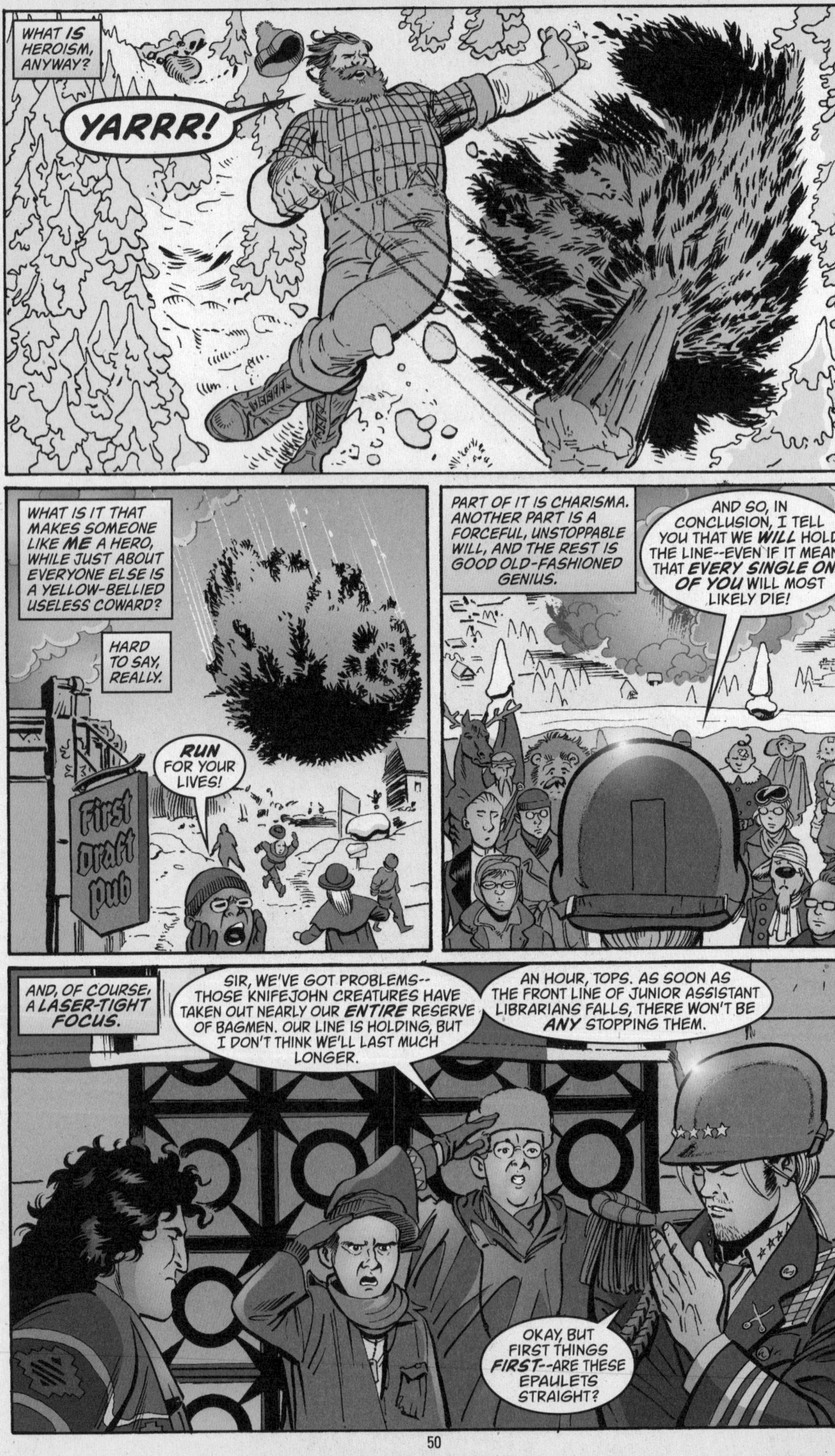

WHAT IS HEROISM, ANYWAY?
YARRR!
WHAT IS IT THAT MAKES SOMEONE LIKE ME A HERO, WHILE JUST ABOUT EVERYONE ELSE IS A YELLOW-BELLIED USELESS COWARD?
HARD TO SAY, REALLY.
RUN FOR YOUR LIVES!
First Draft Pub
PART OF IT IS CHARISMA. ANOTHER PART IS A FORCEFUL, UNSTOPPABLE WILL, AND THE REST IS GOOD OLD-FASHIONED GENIUS.
AND SO, IN CONCLUSION, I TELL YOU THAT WE WILL HOLD THE LINE--EVEN IF IT MEANS THAT EVERY SINGLE ONE OF YOU WILL MOST LIKELY DIE!
AND, OF COURSE, A LASER-TIGHT FOCUS.
SIR, WE'VE GOT PROBLEMS-- THOSE KNIFEJOHN CREATURES HAVE TAKEN OUT NEARLY OUR ENTIRE RESERVE OF BAGMEN. OUR LINE IS HOLDING, BUT I DON'T THINK WE'LL LAST MUCH LONGER.
AN HOUR, TOPS. AS SOON AS THE FRONT LINE OF JUNIOR ASSISTANT LIBRARIANS FALLS, THERE WON'T BE ANY STOPPING THEM.
OKAY, BUT FIRST THINGS FIRST--ARE THESE EPAULETS STRAIGHT?

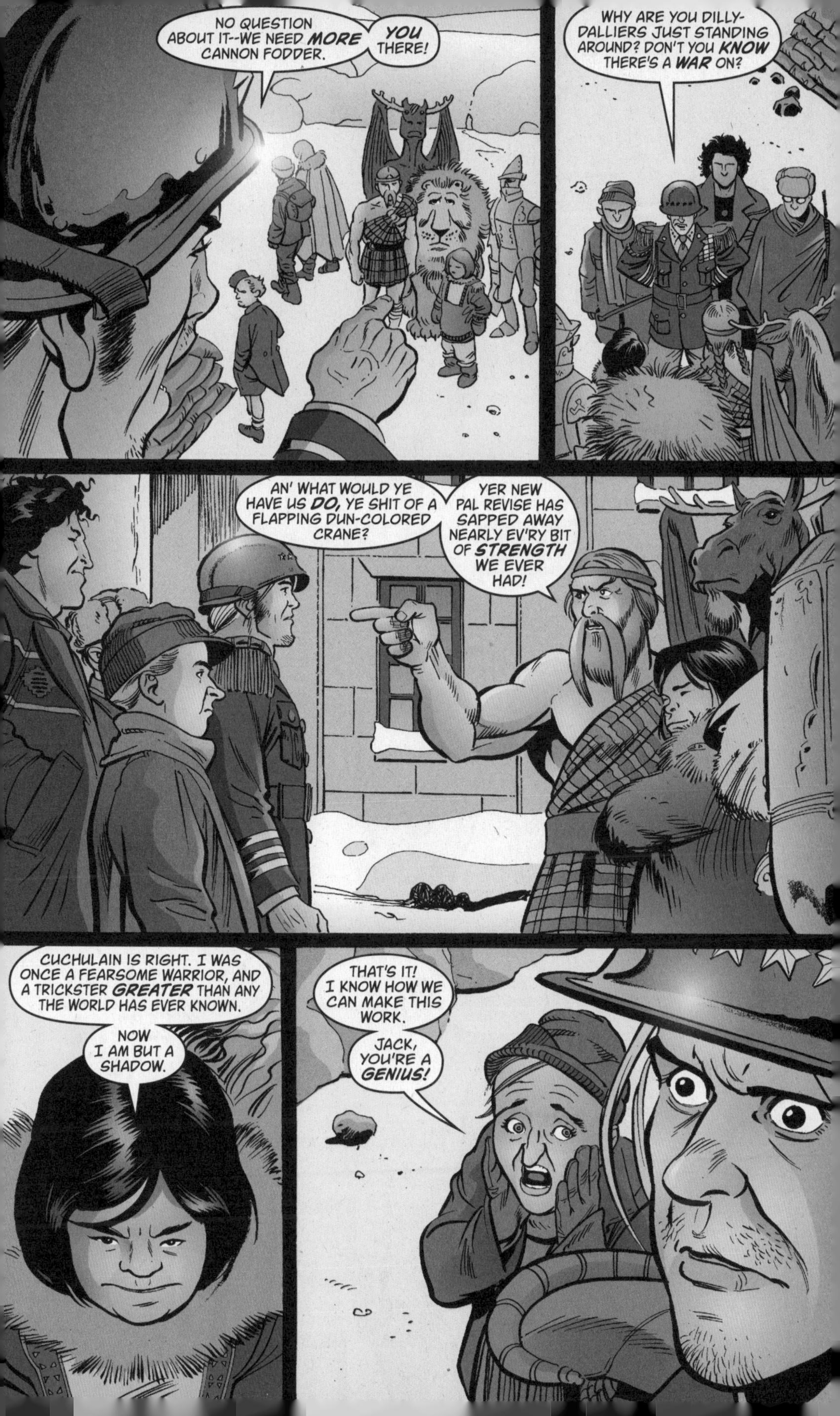
NO QUESTION ABOUT IT--WE NEED MORE CANNON FODDER.
YOU THERE!
WHY ARE YOU DILLY-DALLIERS JUST STANDING AROUND? DON'T YOU KNOW THERE'S A WAR ON?
AN' WHAT WOULD YE HAVE US DO, YE SHIT OF A FLAPPING DUN-COLORED CRANE?
YER NEW PAL REVISE HAS SAPPED AWAY NEARLY EV'RY BIT OF STRENGTH WE EVER HAD!
CUCHULAIN IS RIGHT. I WAS ONCE A FEARSOME WARRIOR, AND A TRICKSTER GREATER THAN ANY THE WORLD HAS EVER KNOWN.
NOW I AM BUT A SHADOW.
THAT'S IT! I KNOW HOW WE CAN MAKE THIS WORK.
JACK, YOU'RE A GENIUS!

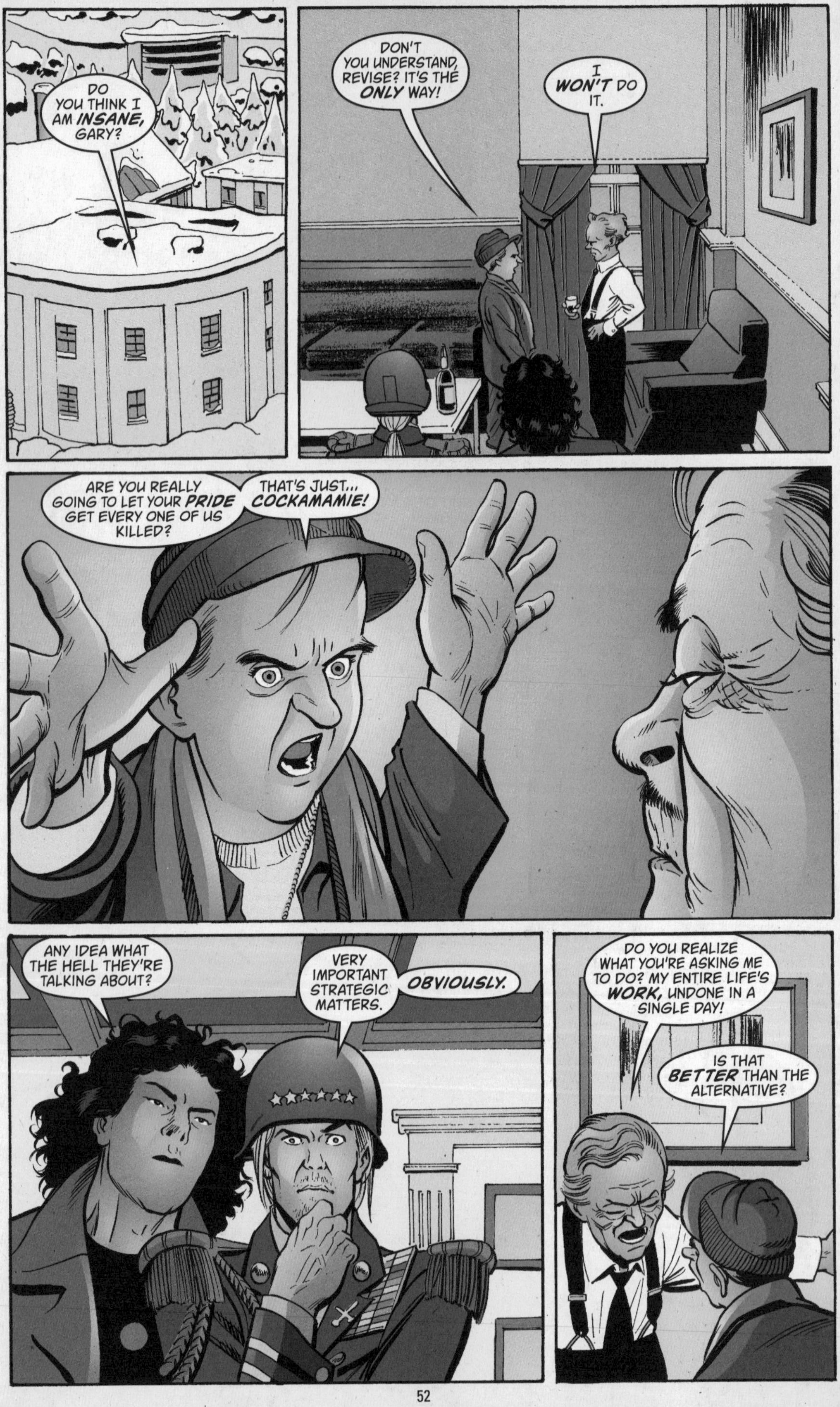
DO YOU THINK I AM INSANE, GARY?
DON'T YOU UNDERSTAND, REVISE? IT'S THE ONLY WAY!
I WON'T DO IT.
ARE YOU REALLY GOING TO LET YOUR PRIDE GET EVERY ONE OF US KILLED?
THAT'S JUST... COCKAMAMIE!
ANY IDEA WHAT THE HELL THEY'RE TALKING ABOUT?
VERY IMPORTANT STRATEGIC MATTERS.
OBVIOUSLY.
DO YOU REALIZE WHAT YOU'RE ASKING ME TO DO? MY ENTIRE LIFE'S WORK, UNDONE IN A SINGLE DAY!
IS THAT BETTER THAN THE ALTERNATIVE?

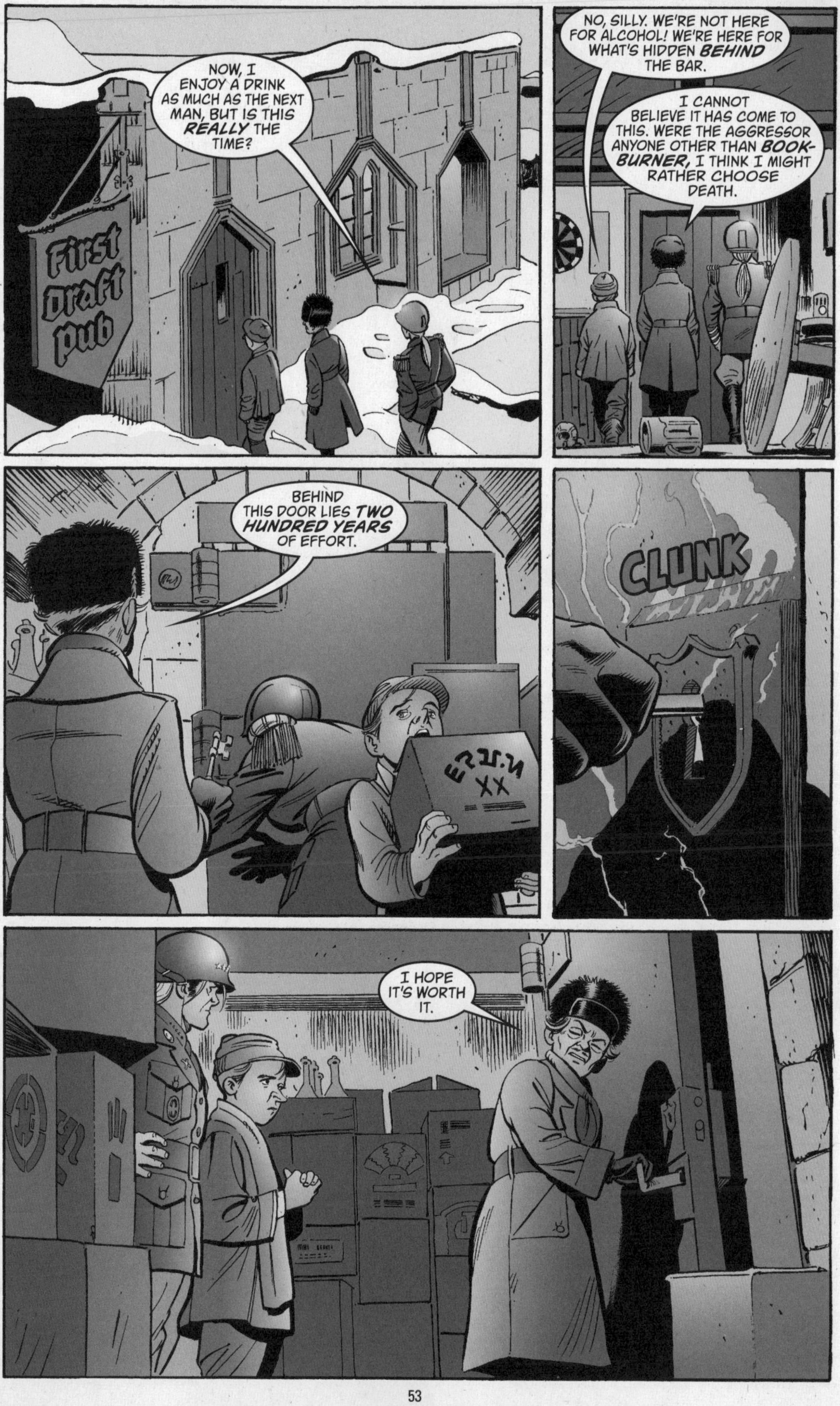
First Draft pub
NOW, I ENJOY A DRINK AS MUCH AS THE NEXT MAN, BUT IS THIS REALLY THE TIME?
NO, SILLY. WE'RE NOT HERE FOR ALCOHOL! WE'RE HERE FOR WHAT'S HIDDEN BEHIND THE BAR.
I CANNOT BELIEVE IT HAS COME TO THIS. WERE THE AGGRESSOR ANYONE OTHER THAN BOOK-BURNER, I THINK I MIGHT RATHER CHOOSE DEATH.
BEHIND THIS DOOR LIES TWO HUNDRED YEARS OF EFFORT.
CLUNK
I HOPE IT'S WORTH IT.

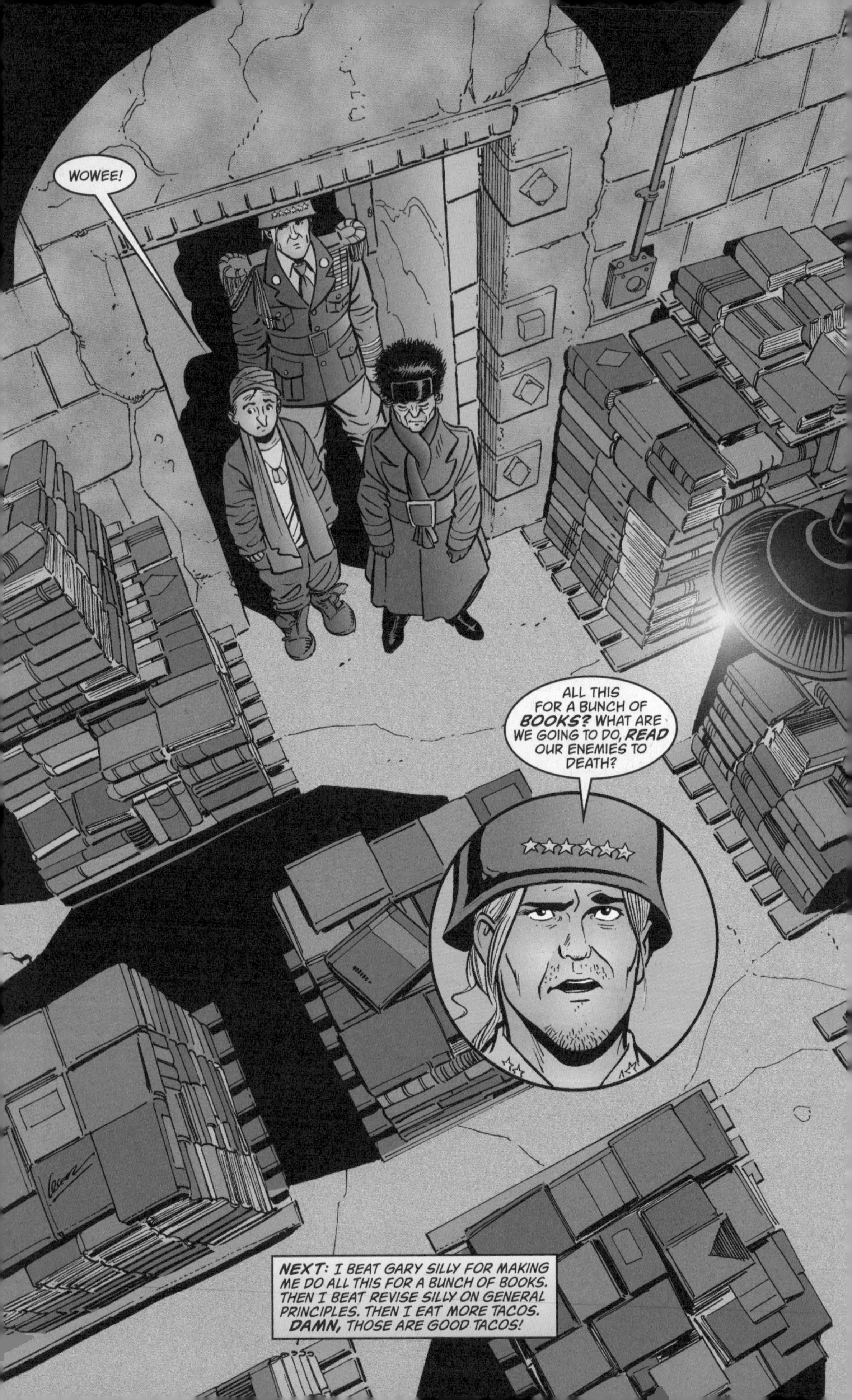
WOWEE!
ALL THIS FOR A BUNCH OF **BOOKS?** WHAT ARE WE GOING TO DO, **READ** OUR ENEMIES TO DEATH?
NEXT: I BEAT GARY SILLY FOR MAKING ME DO ALL THIS FOR A BUNCH OF BOOKS. THEN I BEAT REVISE SILLY ON GENERAL PRINCIPLES. THEN I EAT MORE TACOS. **DAMN,** THOSE ARE GOOD TACOS!

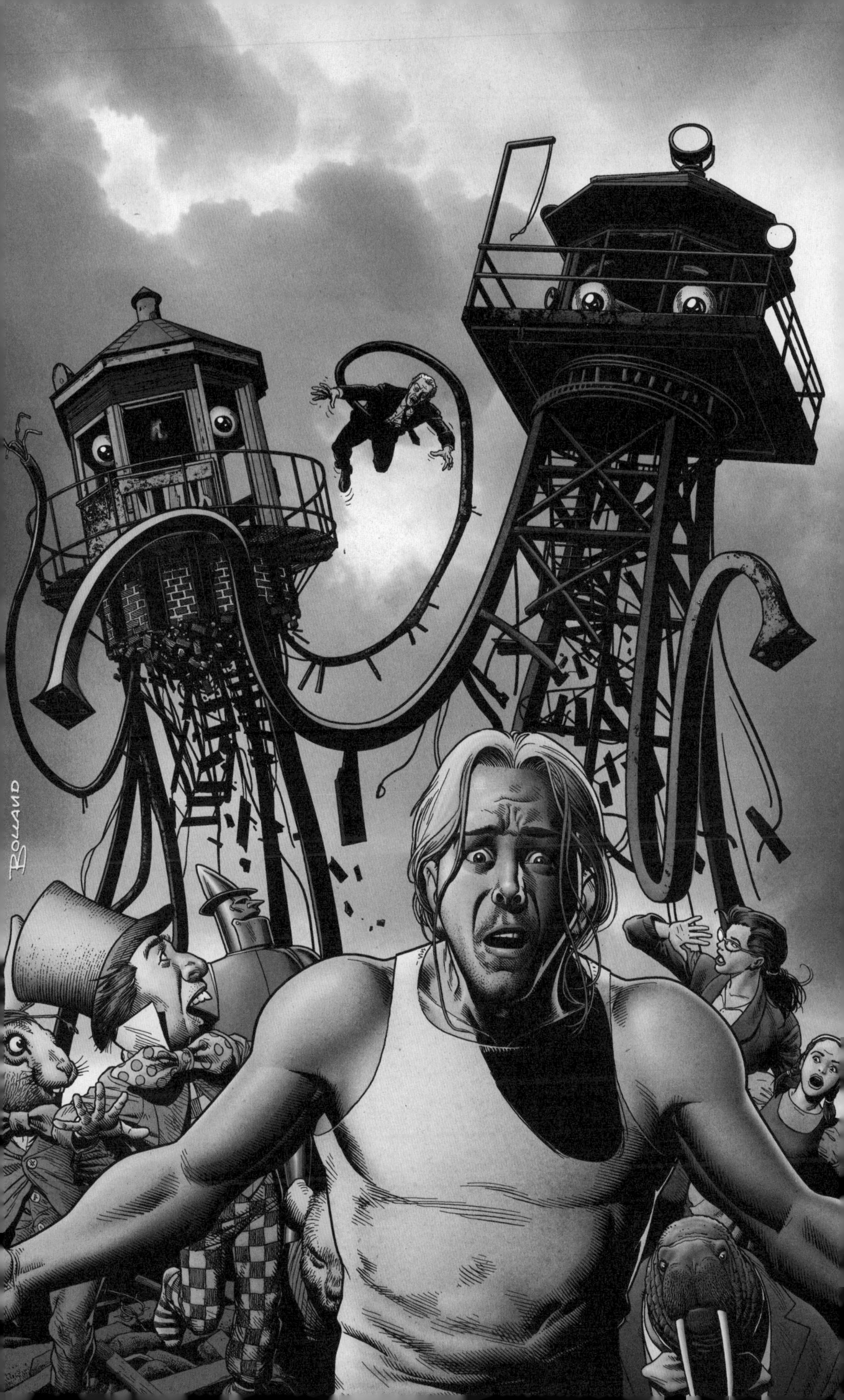
BOLLAND

*"Let the **revolution** begin!"*

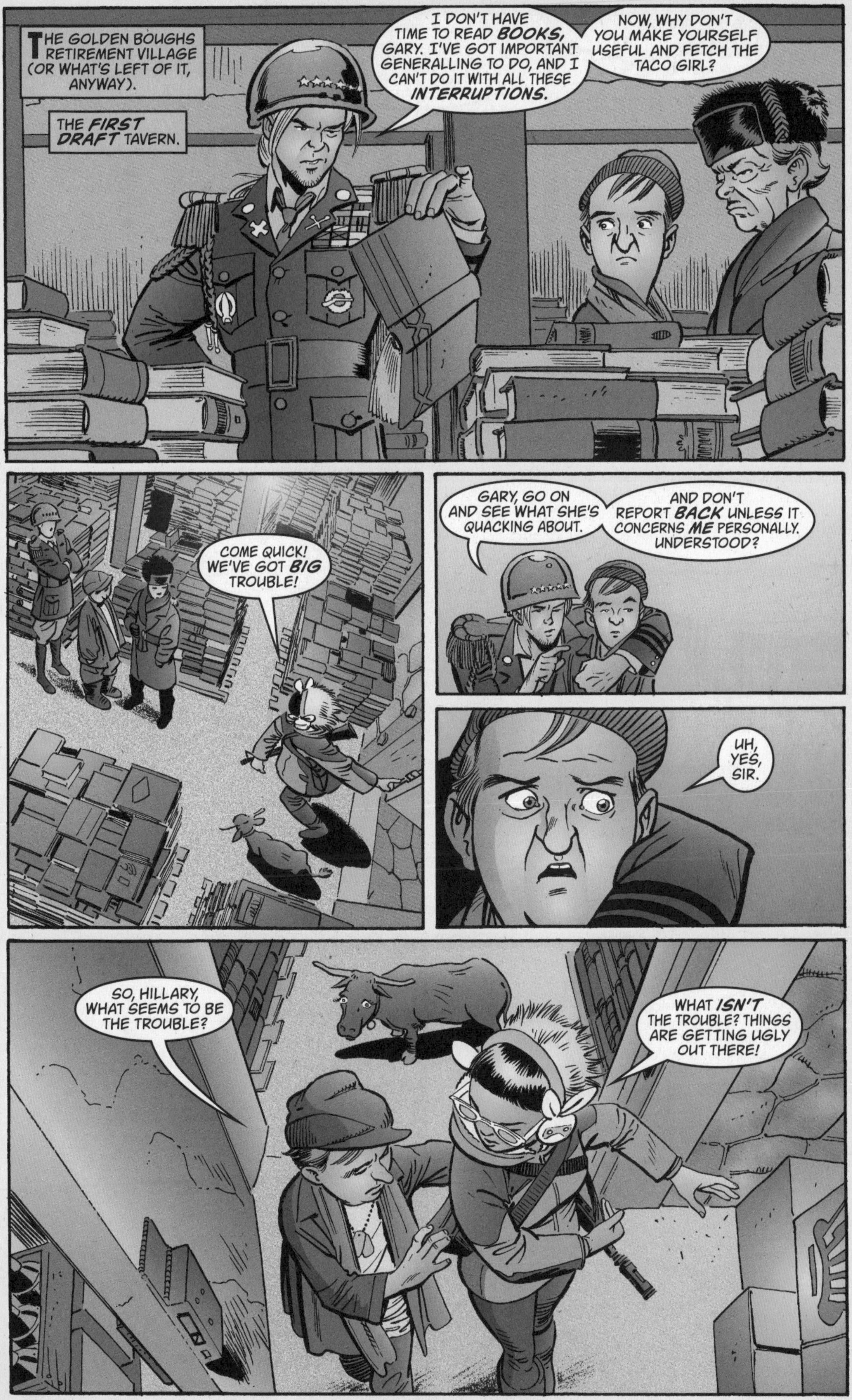
THE GOLDEN BOUGHS RETIREMENT VILLAGE (OR WHAT'S LEFT OF IT, ANYWAY).
THE FIRST DRAFT TAVERN.
I DON'T HAVE TIME TO READ BOOKS, GARY. I'VE GOT IMPORTANT GENERALLING TO DO, AND I CAN'T DO IT WITH ALL THESE INTERRUPTIONS.
NOW, WHY DON'T YOU MAKE YOURSELF USEFUL AND FETCH THE TACO GIRL?
COME QUICK! WE'VE GOT BIG TROUBLE!
GARY, GO ON AND SEE WHAT SHE'S QUACKING ABOUT.
AND DON'T REPORT BACK UNLESS IT CONCERNS ME PERSONALLY. UNDERSTOOD?
UH, YES, SIR.
SO, HILLARY, WHAT SEEMS TO BE THE TROUBLE?
WHAT ISN'T THE TROUBLE? THINGS ARE GETTING UGLY OUT THERE!

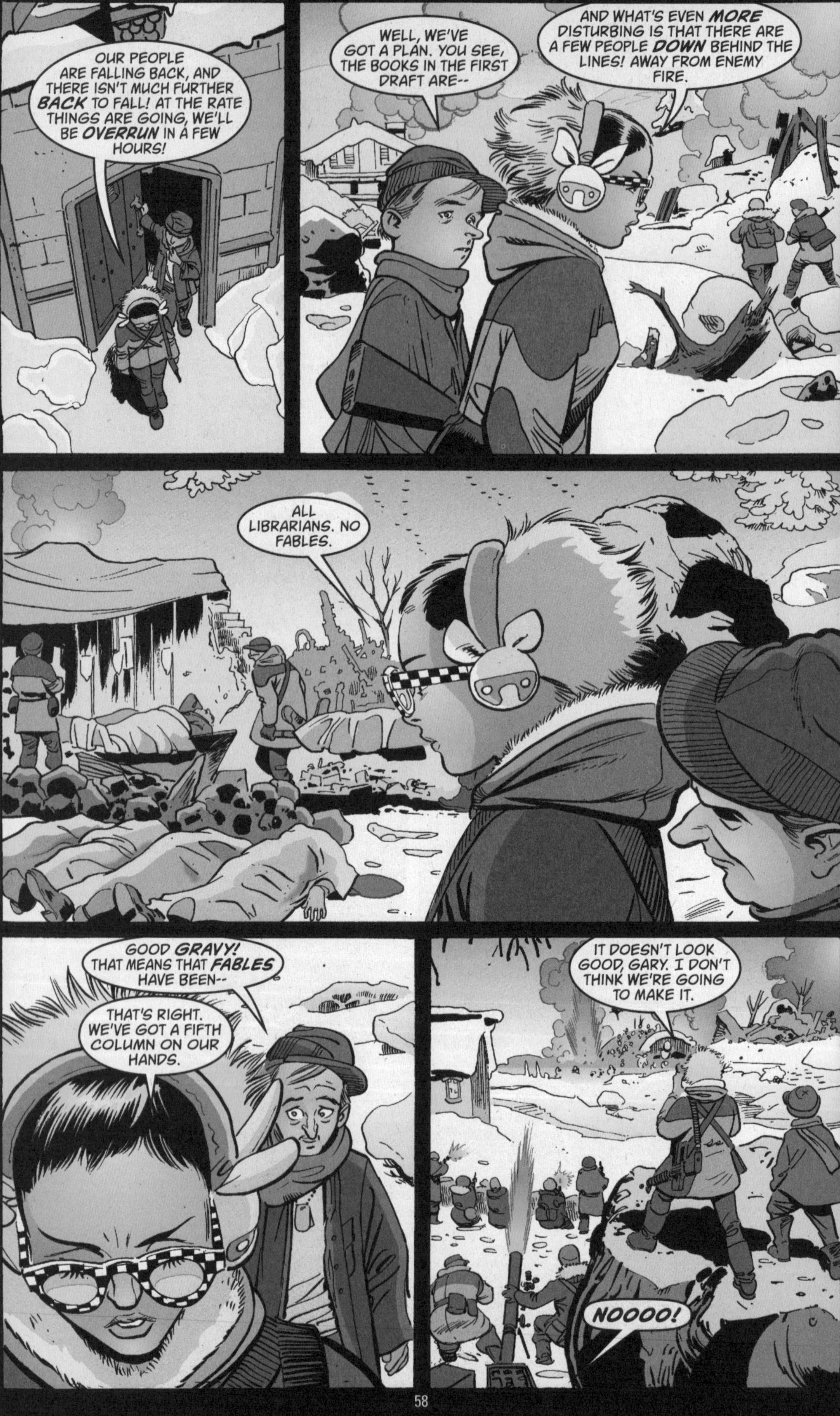
OUR PEOPLE ARE FALLING BACK, AND THERE ISN'T MUCH FURTHER BACK TO FALL! AT THE RATE THINGS ARE GOING, WE'LL BE OVERRUN IN A FEW HOURS!
WELL, WE'VE GOT A PLAN. YOU SEE, THE BOOKS IN THE FIRST DRAFT ARE--
AND WHAT'S EVEN MORE DISTURBING IS THAT THERE ARE A FEW PEOPLE DOWN BEHIND THE LINES! AWAY FROM ENEMY FIRE.
ALL LIBRARIANS. NO FABLES.
GOOD GRAVY! THAT MEANS THAT FABLES HAVE BEEN--
THAT'S RIGHT. WE'VE GOT A FIFTH COLUMN ON OUR HANDS.
IT DOESN'T LOOK GOOD, GARY. I DON'T THINK WE'RE GOING TO MAKE IT.
NOOOO!

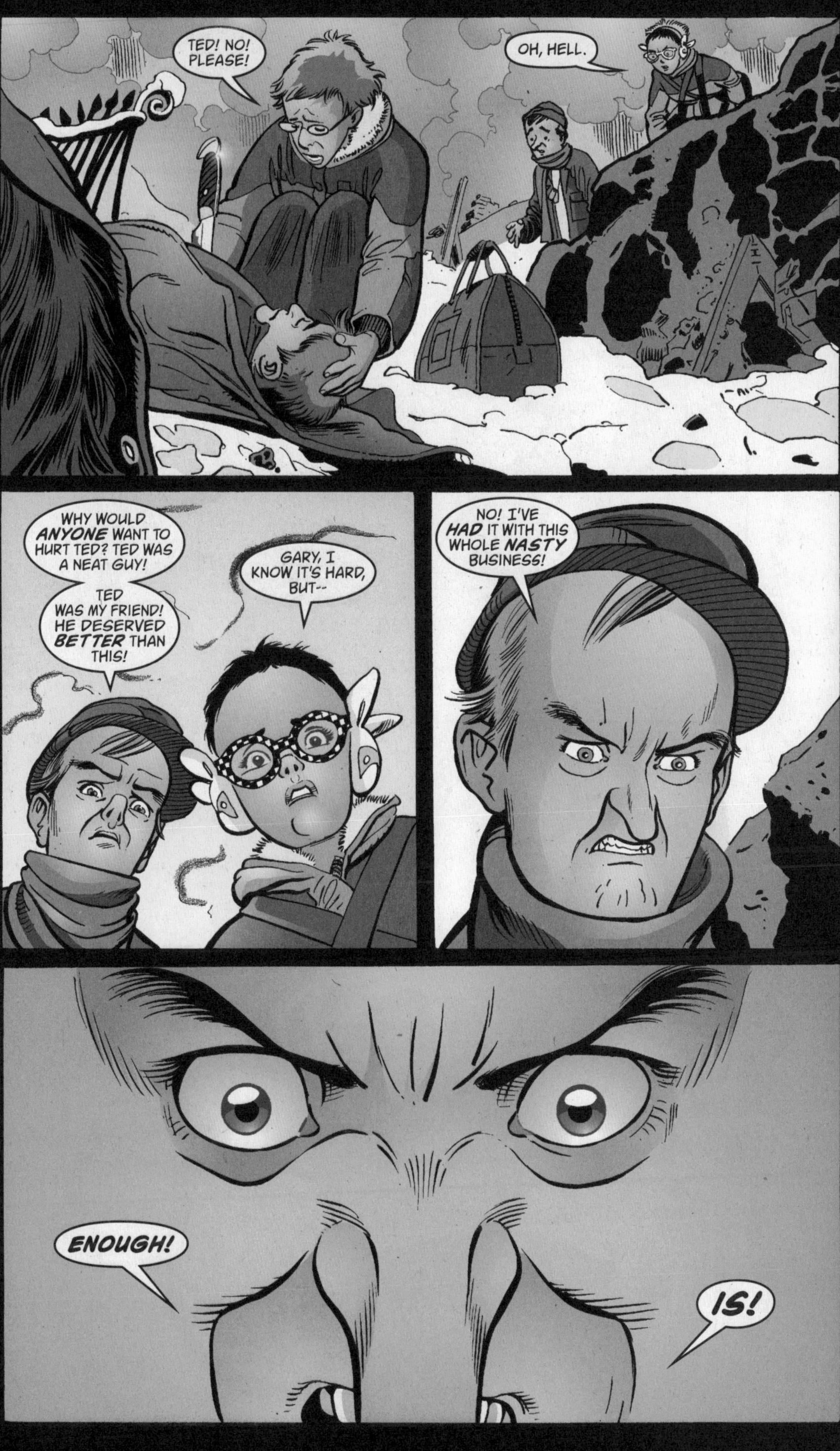
TED! NO! PLEASE!
OH, HELL.
WHY WOULD ANYONE WANT TO HURT TED? TED WAS A NEAT GUY!
TED WAS MY FRIEND! HE DESERVED BETTER THAN THIS!
GARY, I KNOW IT'S HARD, BUT--
NO! I'VE HAD IT WITH THIS WHOLE NASTY BUSINESS!
ENOUGH!
IS!

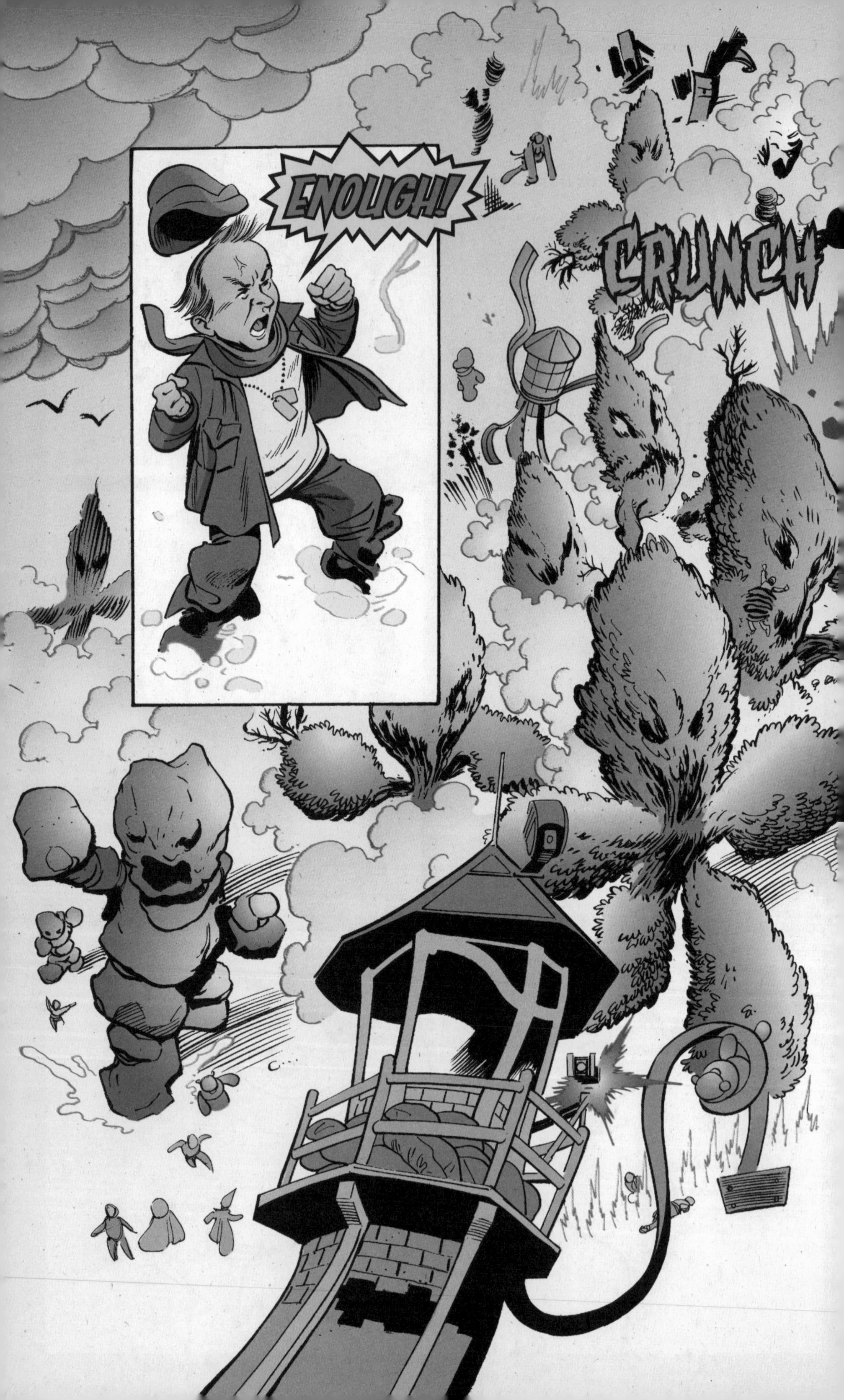

ENOUGH!
CRUNCH

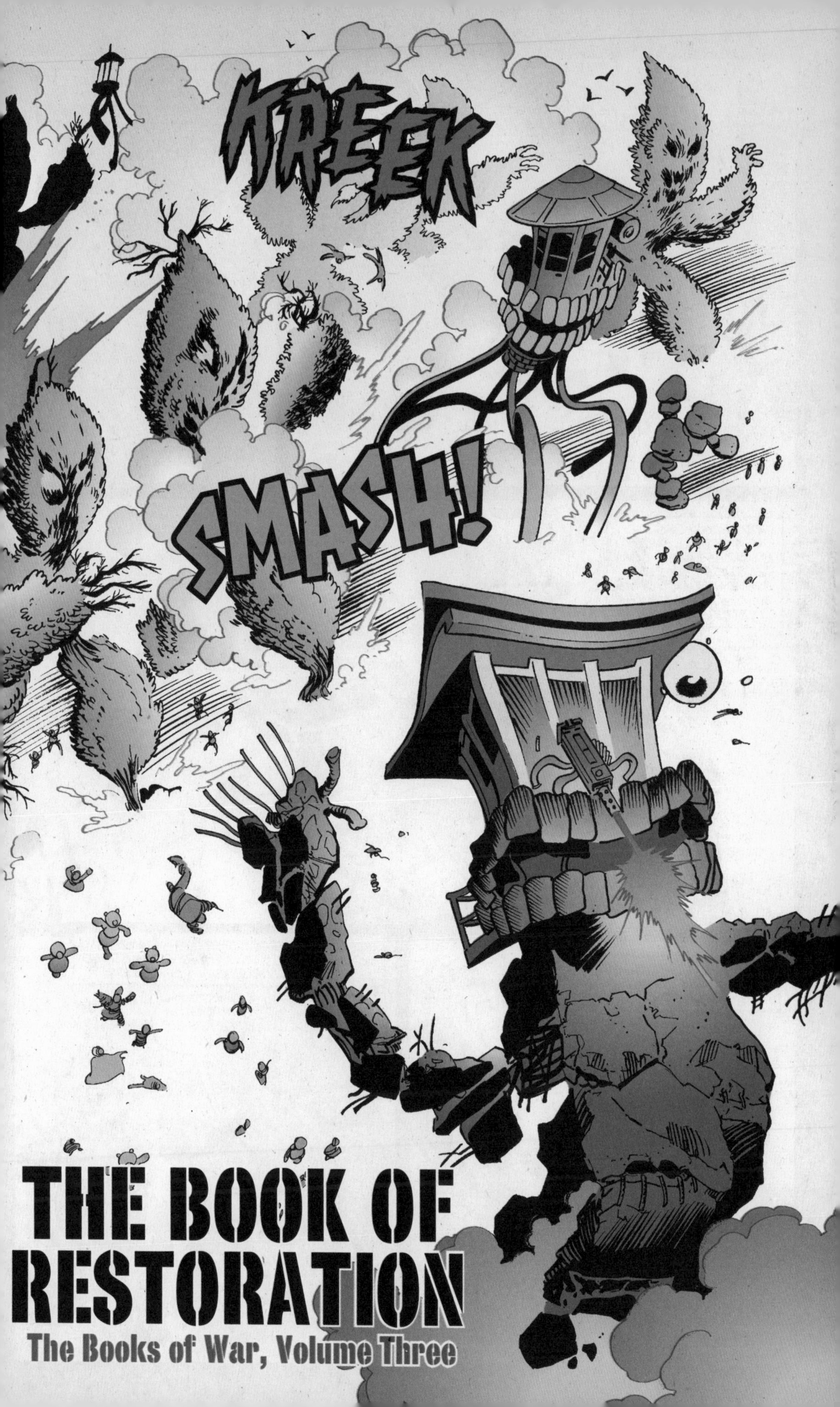
KREEK
SMASH!

THE BOOK OF RESTORATION
The Books of War, Volume Three

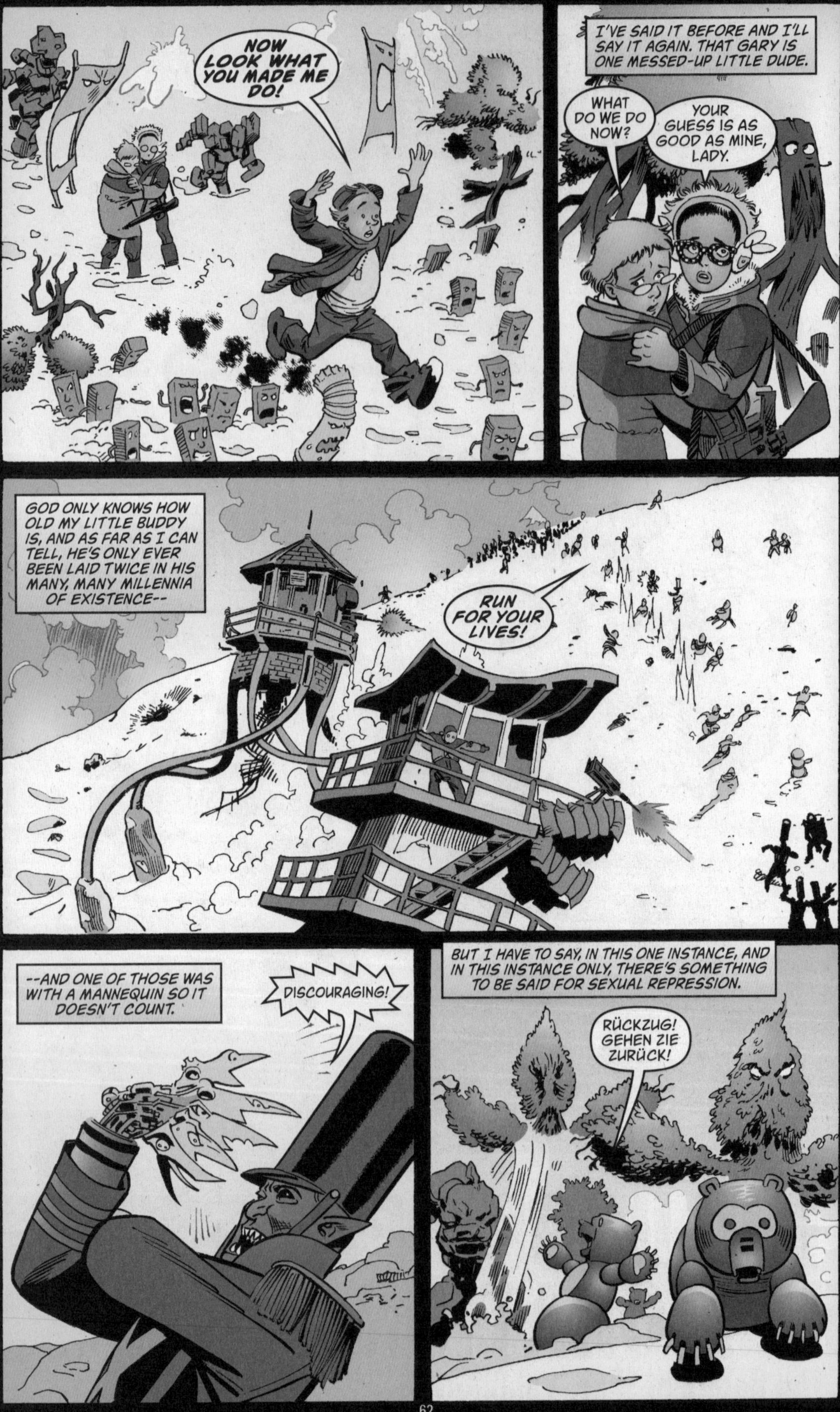
NOW LOOK WHAT YOU MADE ME DO!
I'VE SAID IT BEFORE AND I'LL SAY IT AGAIN. THAT GARY IS ONE MESSED-UP LITTLE DUDE.
WHAT DO WE DO NOW?
YOUR GUESS IS AS GOOD AS MINE, LADY.
GOD ONLY KNOWS HOW OLD MY LITTLE BUDDY IS, AND AS FAR AS I CAN TELL, HE'S ONLY EVER BEEN LAID TWICE IN HIS MANY, MANY MILLENNIA OF EXISTENCE--
RUN FOR YOUR LIVES!
--AND ONE OF THOSE WAS WITH A MANNEQUIN SO IT DOESN'T COUNT.
DISCOURAGING!
BUT I HAVE TO SAY, IN THIS ONE INSTANCE, AND IN THIS INSTANCE ONLY, THERE'S SOMETHING TO BE SAID FOR SEXUAL REPRESSION.
RÜCKZUG! GEHEN ZIE ZURÜCK!

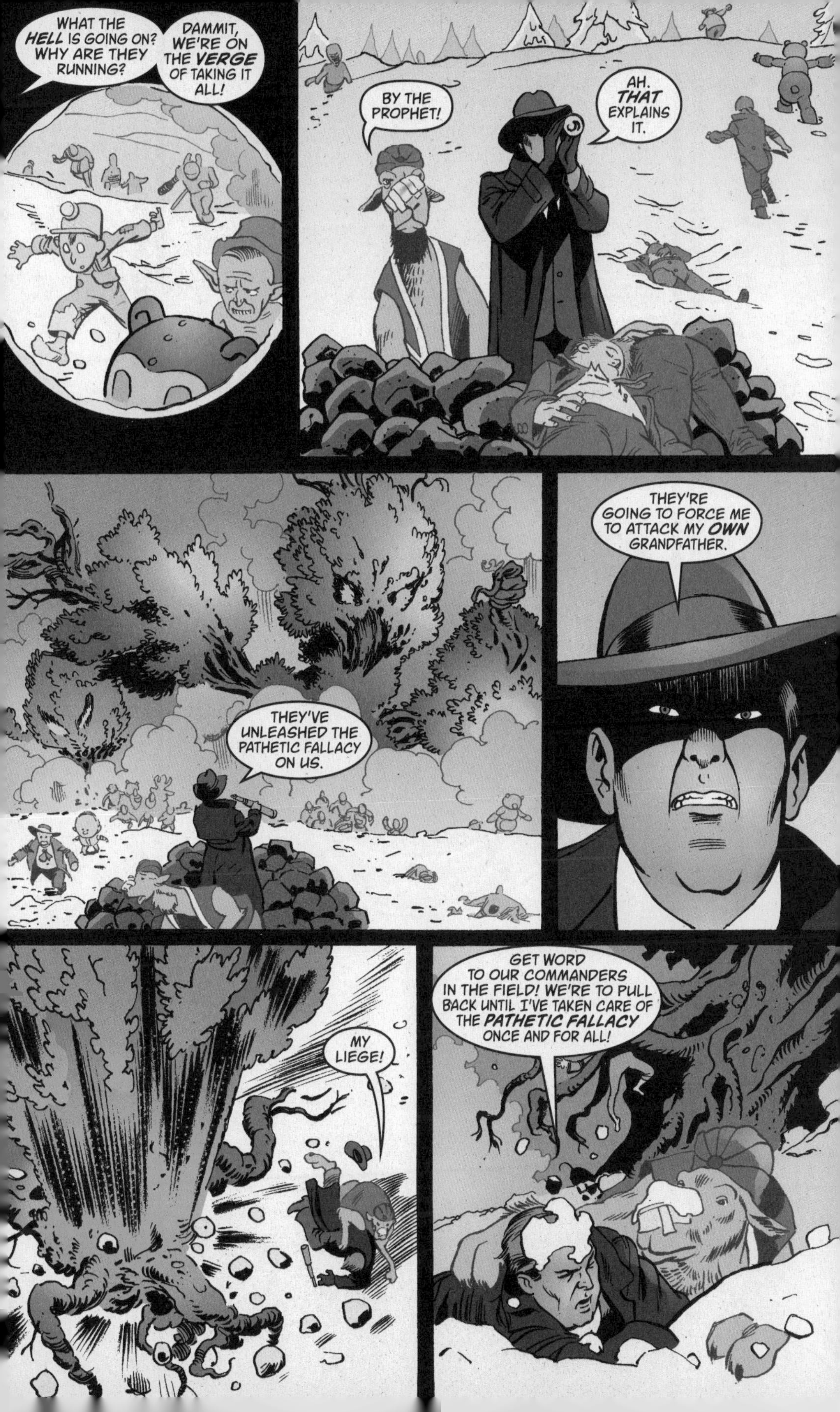
WHAT THE HELL IS GOING ON? WHY ARE THEY RUNNING?
DAMMIT, WE'RE ON THE VERGE OF TAKING IT ALL!
BY THE PROPHET!
AH. THAT EXPLAINS IT.
THEY'VE UNLEASHED THE PATHETIC FALLACY ON US.
THEY'RE GOING TO FORCE ME TO ATTACK MY OWN GRANDFATHER.
MY LIEGE!
GET WORD TO OUR COMMANDERS IN THE FIELD! WE'RE TO PULL BACK UNTIL I'VE TAKEN CARE OF THE PATHETIC FALLACY ONCE AND FOR ALL!

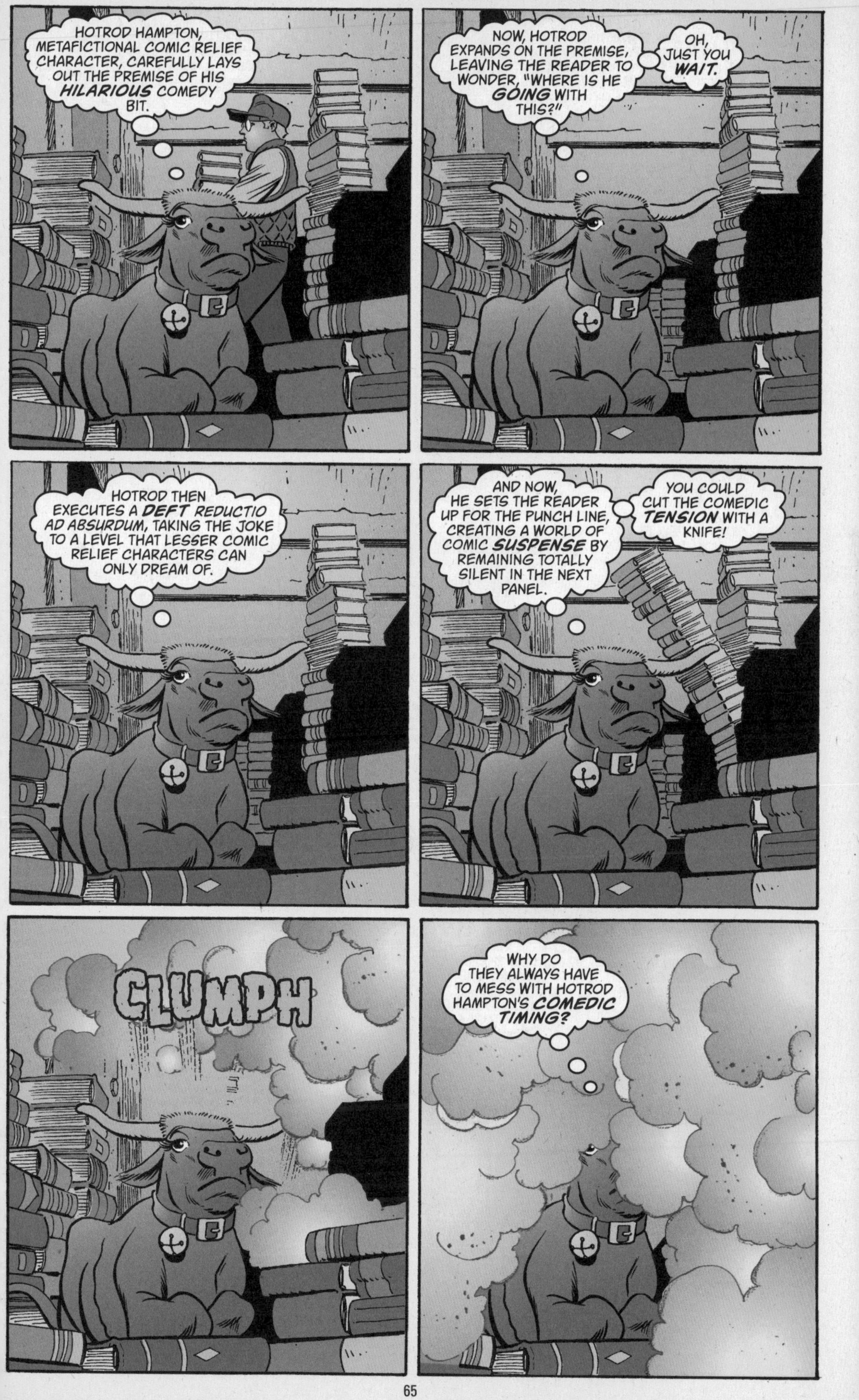
HOTROD HAMPTON, METAFICTIONAL COMIC RELIEF CHARACTER, CAREFULLY LAYS OUT THE PREMISE OF HIS *HILARIOUS* COMEDY BIT.
NOW, HOTROD EXPANDS ON THE PREMISE, LEAVING THE READER TO WONDER, "WHERE IS HE *GOING* WITH THIS?"
OH, JUST YOU *WAIT.*
HOTROD THEN EXECUTES A *DEFT* REDUCTIO AD ABSURDUM, TAKING THE JOKE TO A LEVEL THAT LESSER COMIC RELIEF CHARACTERS CAN ONLY DREAM OF.
AND NOW, HE SETS THE READER UP FOR THE PUNCH LINE, CREATING A WORLD OF COMIC *SUSPENSE* BY REMAINING TOTALLY SILENT IN THE NEXT PANEL.
YOU COULD CUT THE COMEDIC *TENSION* WITH A KNIFE!
CLUMPH
WHY DO THEY ALWAYS HAVE TO MESS WITH HOTROD HAMPTON'S *COMEDIC TIMING?*

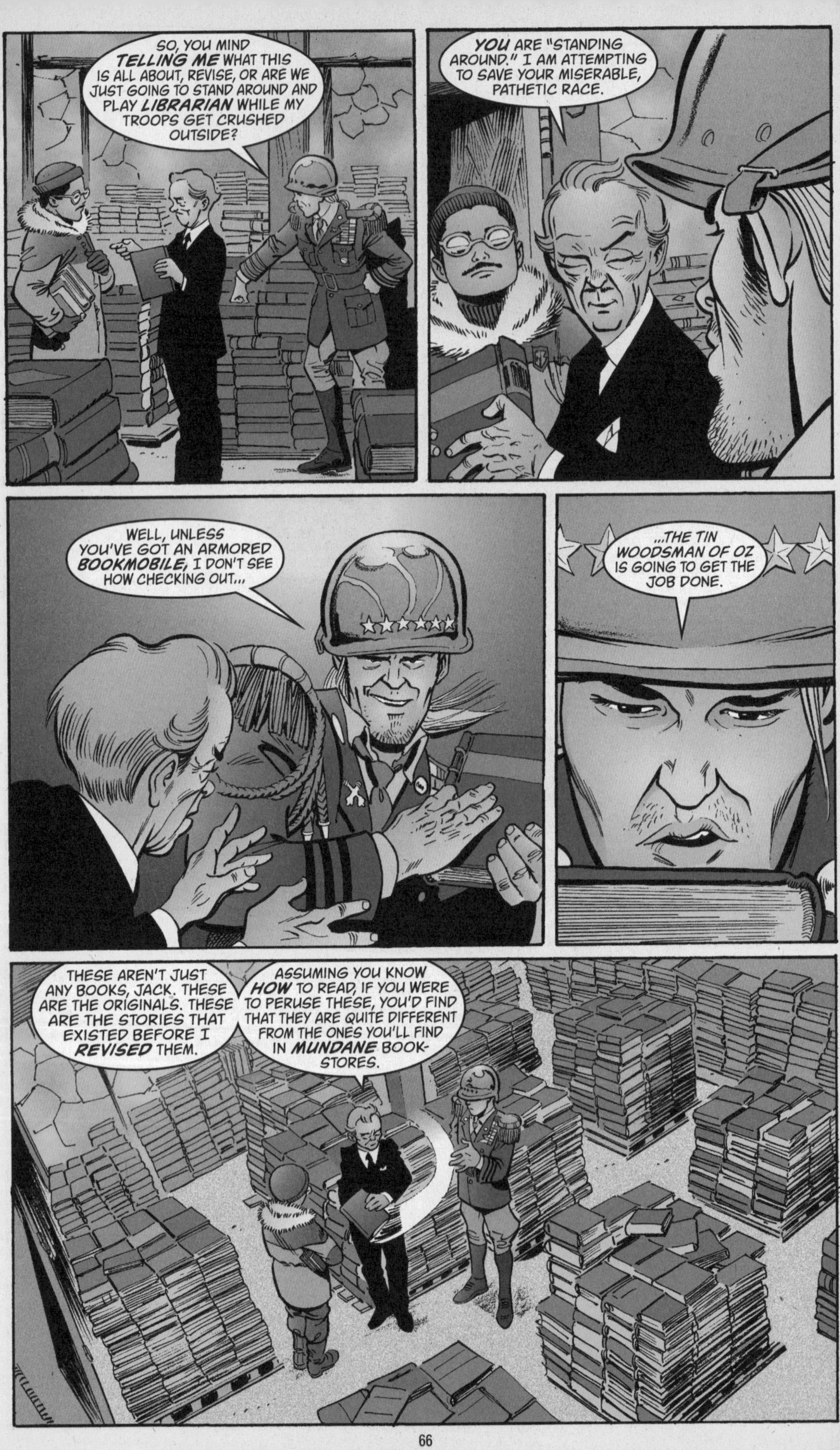
SO, YOU MIND TELLING ME WHAT THIS IS ALL ABOUT, REVISE, OR ARE WE JUST GOING TO STAND AROUND AND PLAY LIBRARIAN WHILE MY TROOPS GET CRUSHED OUTSIDE?
YOU ARE "STANDING AROUND." I AM ATTEMPTING TO SAVE YOUR MISERABLE, PATHETIC RACE.
WELL, UNLESS YOU'VE GOT AN ARMORED BOOKMOBILE, I DON'T SEE HOW CHECKING OUT...
...THE TIN WOODSMAN OF OZ IS GOING TO GET THE JOB DONE.
THESE AREN'T JUST ANY BOOKS, JACK. THESE ARE THE ORIGINALS. THESE ARE THE STORIES THAT EXISTED BEFORE I REVISED THEM.
ASSUMING YOU KNOW HOW TO READ, IF YOU WERE TO PERUSE THESE, YOU'D FIND THAT THEY ARE QUITE DIFFERENT FROM THE ONES YOU'LL FIND IN MUNDANE BOOK-STORES.

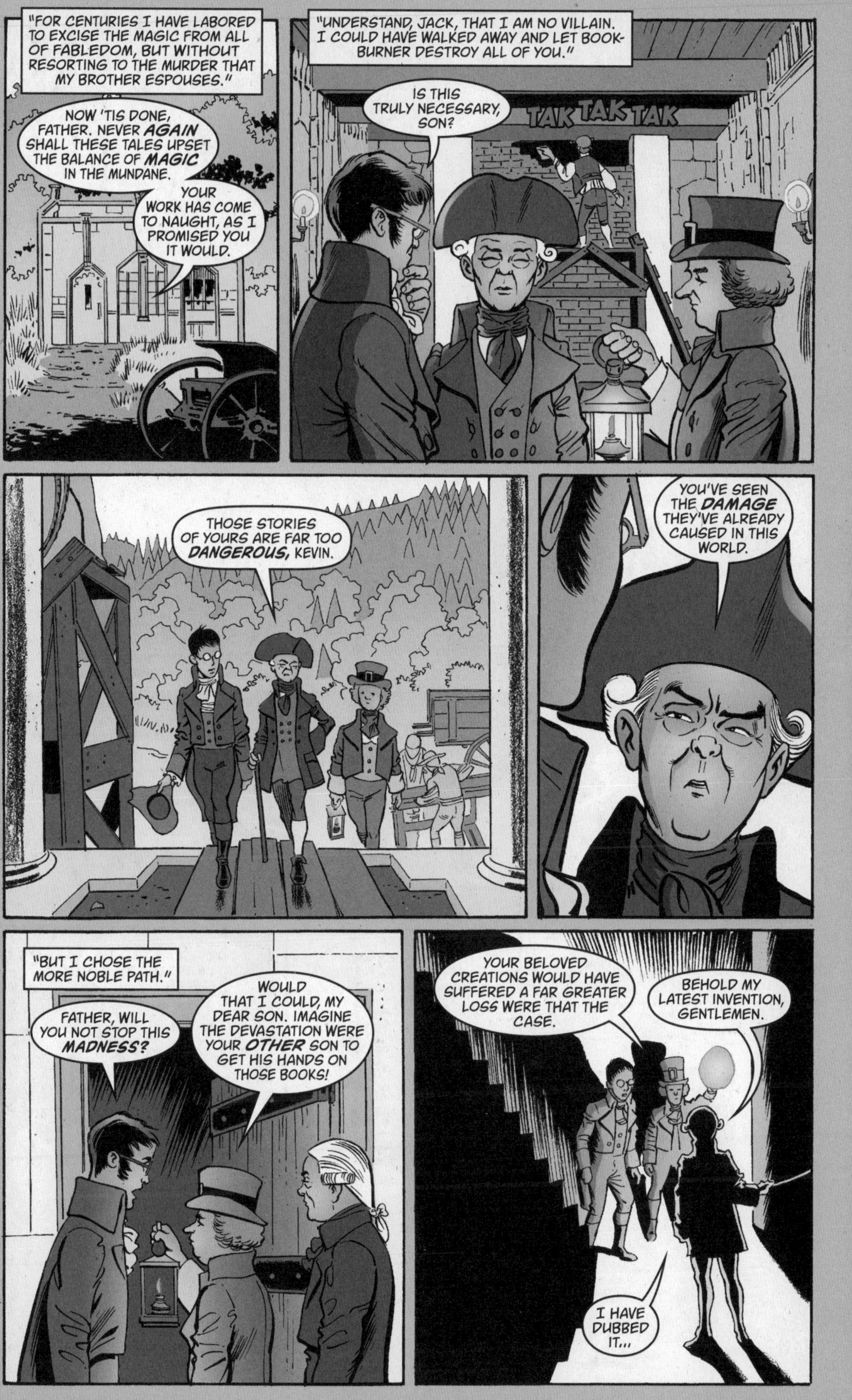
"FOR CENTURIES I HAVE LABORED TO EXCISE THE MAGIC FROM ALL OF FABLEDOM, BUT WITHOUT RESORTING TO THE MURDER THAT MY BROTHER ESPOUSES."
NOW 'TIS DONE, FATHER. NEVER AGAIN SHALL THESE TALES UPSET THE BALANCE OF MAGIC IN THE MUNDANE.
YOUR WORK HAS COME TO NAUGHT, AS I PROMISED YOU IT WOULD.
"UNDERSTAND, JACK, THAT I AM NO VILLAIN. I COULD HAVE WALKED AWAY AND LET BOOK-BURNER DESTROY ALL OF YOU."
IS THIS TRULY NECESSARY, SON?
TAK TAK TAK
THOSE STORIES OF YOURS ARE FAR TOO DANGEROUS, KEVIN.
YOU'VE SEEN THE DAMAGE THEY'VE ALREADY CAUSED IN THIS WORLD.
"BUT I CHOSE THE MORE NOBLE PATH."
FATHER, WILL YOU NOT STOP THIS MADNESS?
WOULD THAT I COULD, MY DEAR SON. IMAGINE THE DEVASTATION WERE YOUR OTHER SON TO GET HIS HANDS ON THOSE BOOKS!
YOUR BELOVED CREATIONS WOULD HAVE SUFFERED A FAR GREATER LOSS WERE THAT THE CASE.
BEHOLD MY LATEST INVENTION, GENTLEMEN.
I HAVE DUBBED IT...

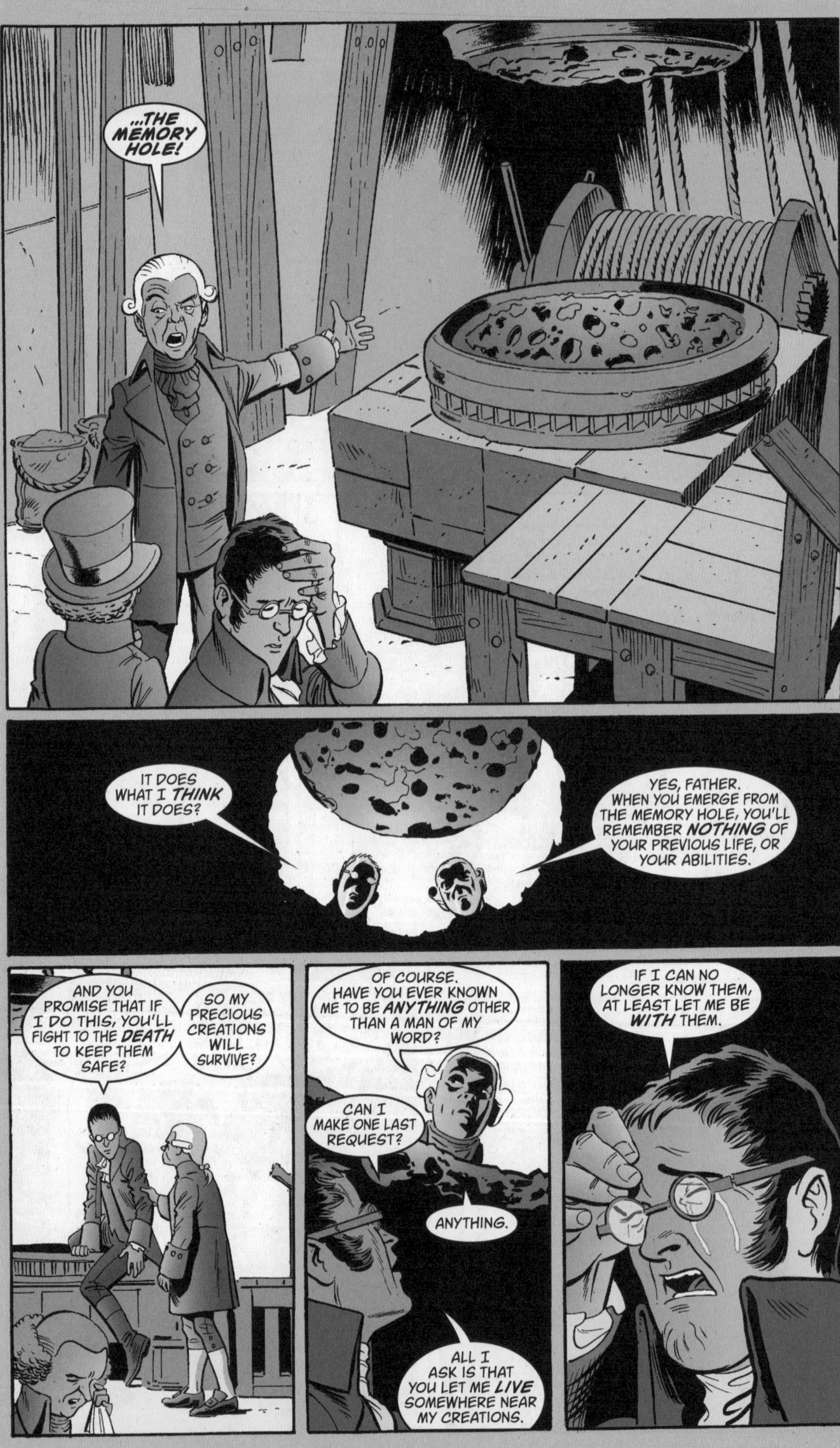
...THE MEMORY HOLE!
IT DOES WHAT I THINK IT DOES?
YES, FATHER. WHEN YOU EMERGE FROM THE MEMORY HOLE, YOU'LL REMEMBER NOTHING OF YOUR PREVIOUS LIFE, OR YOUR ABILITIES.
AND YOU PROMISE THAT IF I DO THIS, YOU'LL FIGHT TO THE DEATH TO KEEP THEM SAFE?
SO MY PRECIOUS CREATIONS WILL SURVIVE?
OF COURSE. HAVE YOU EVER KNOWN ME TO BE ANYTHING OTHER THAN A MAN OF MY WORD?
CAN I MAKE ONE LAST REQUEST?
ANYTHING.
ALL I ASK IS THAT YOU LET ME LIVE SOMEWHERE NEAR MY CREATIONS.
IF I CAN NO LONGER KNOW THEM, AT LEAST LET ME BE WITH THEM.

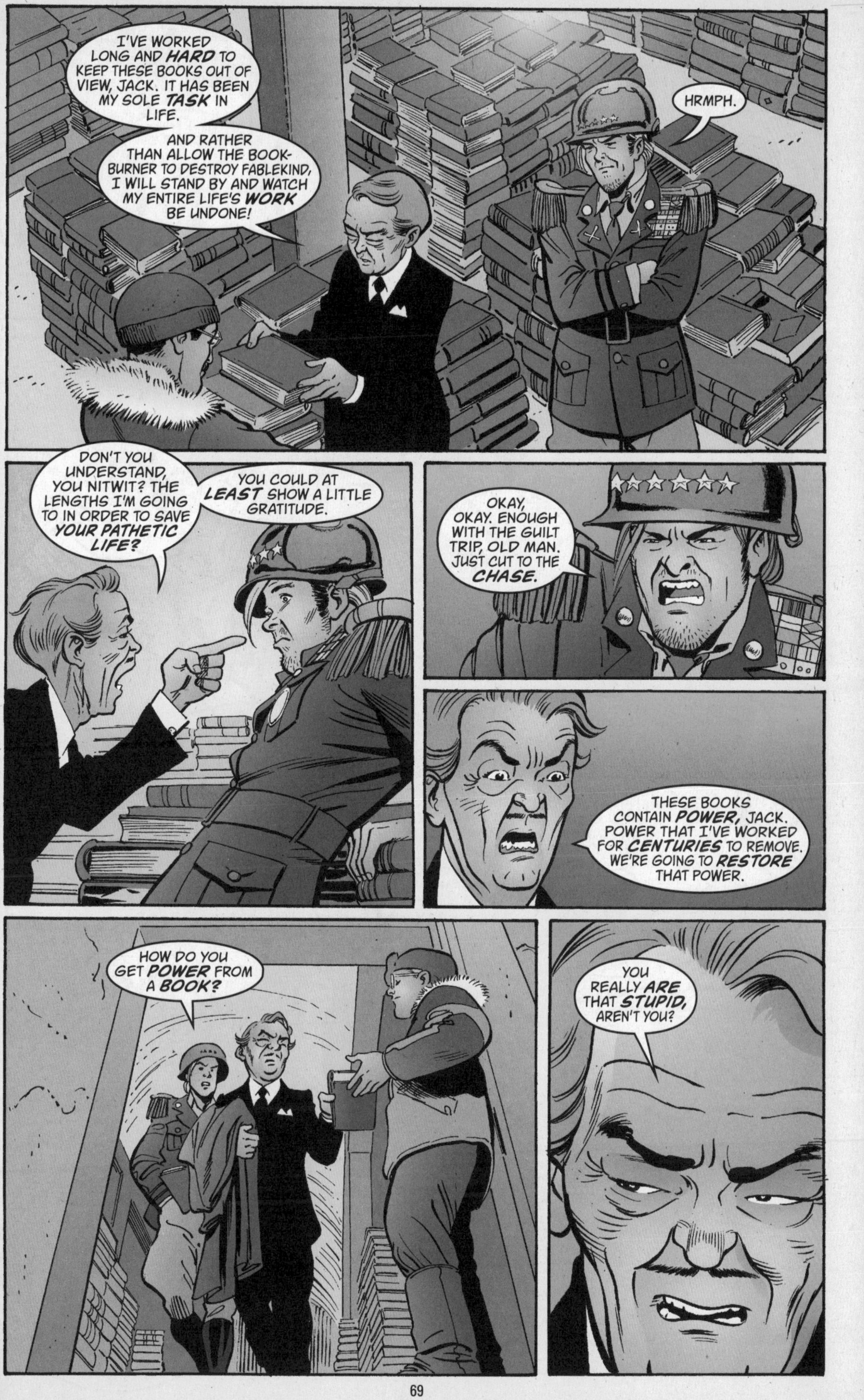
I'VE WORKED LONG AND HARD TO KEEP THESE BOOKS OUT OF VIEW, JACK. IT HAS BEEN MY SOLE TASK IN LIFE.
AND RATHER THAN ALLOW THE BOOK-BURNER TO DESTROY FABLEKIND, I WILL STAND BY AND WATCH MY ENTIRE LIFE'S WORK BE UNDONE!
HRMPH.
DON'T YOU UNDERSTAND, YOU NITWIT? THE LENGTHS I'M GOING TO IN ORDER TO SAVE YOUR PATHETIC LIFE?
YOU COULD AT LEAST SHOW A LITTLE GRATITUDE.
OKAY, OKAY. ENOUGH WITH THE GUILT TRIP, OLD MAN. JUST CUT TO THE CHASE.
THESE BOOKS CONTAIN POWER, JACK. POWER THAT I'VE WORKED FOR CENTURIES TO REMOVE. WE'RE GOING TO RESTORE THAT POWER.
HOW DO YOU GET POWER FROM A BOOK?
YOU REALLY ARE THAT STUPID, AREN'T YOU?

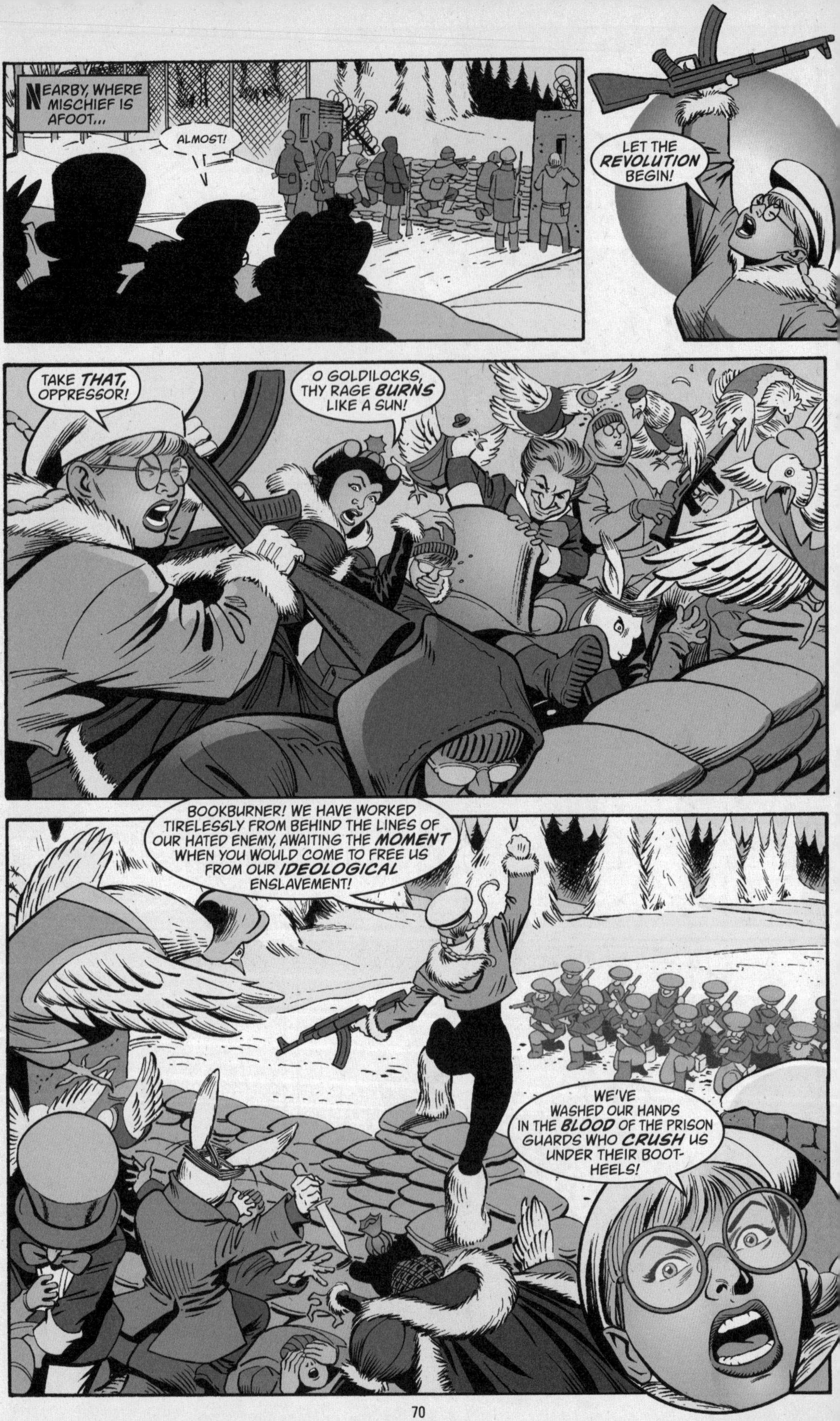
NEARBY, WHERE MISCHIEF IS AFOOT...
ALMOST!
LET THE REVOLUTION BEGIN!
TAKE THAT, OPPRESSOR!
O GOLDILOCKS, THY RAGE BURNS LIKE A SUN!
BOOKBURNER! WE HAVE WORKED TIRELESSLY FROM BEHIND THE LINES OF OUR HATED ENEMY, AWAITING THE MOMENT WHEN YOU WOULD COME TO FREE US FROM OUR IDEOLOGICAL ENSLAVEMENT!
WE'VE WASHED OUR HANDS IN THE BLOOD OF THE PRISON GUARDS WHO CRUSH US UNDER THEIR BOOT-HEELS!

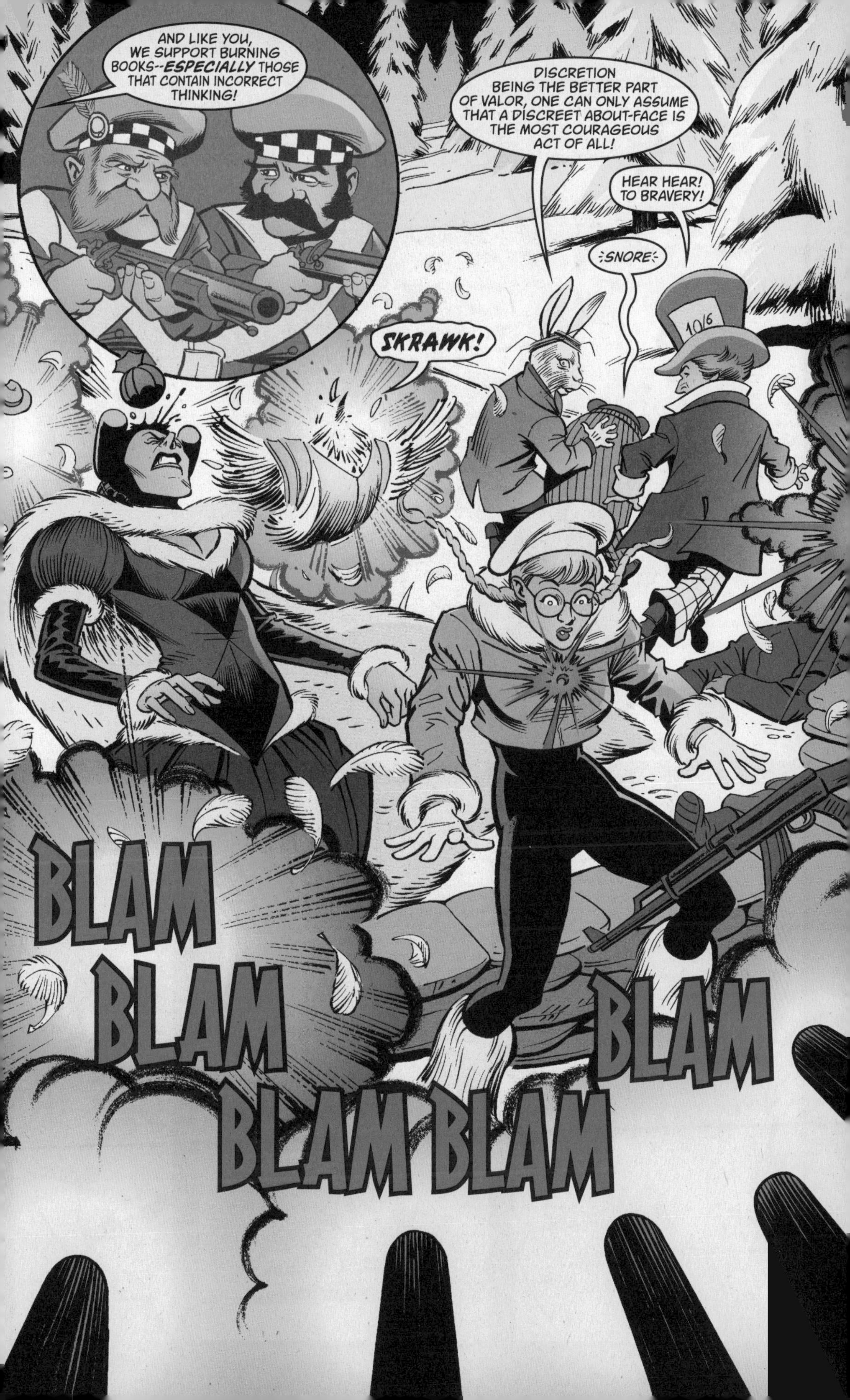
AND LIKE YOU, WE SUPPORT BURNING BOOKS--ESPECIALLY THOSE THAT CONTAIN INCORRECT THINKING!
DISCRETION BEING THE BETTER PART OF VALOR, ONE CAN ONLY ASSUME THAT A DISCREET ABOUT-FACE IS THE MOST COURAGEOUS ACT OF ALL!
HEAR HEAR! TO BRAVERY!
SNORE
10/6
SKRAWK!
BLAM
BLAM
BLAM
BLAM BLAM BLAM

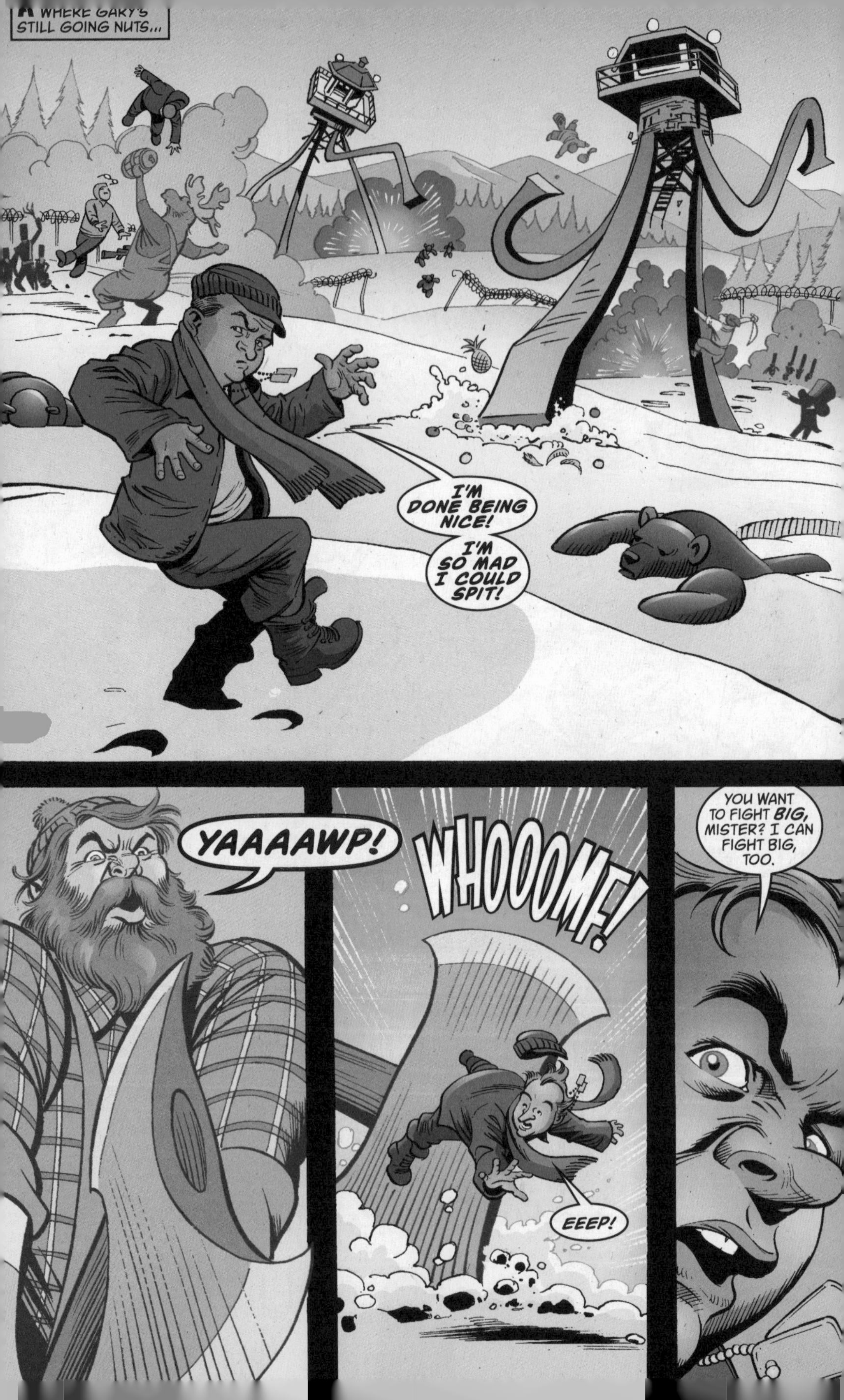
WHERE GARY'S STILL GOING NUTS...
I'M DONE BEING NICE!
I'M SO MAD I COULD SPIT!
YAAAAWP!
WHOOOMF!
EEEP!
YOU WANT TO FIGHT BIG, MISTER? I CAN FIGHT BIG, TOO.

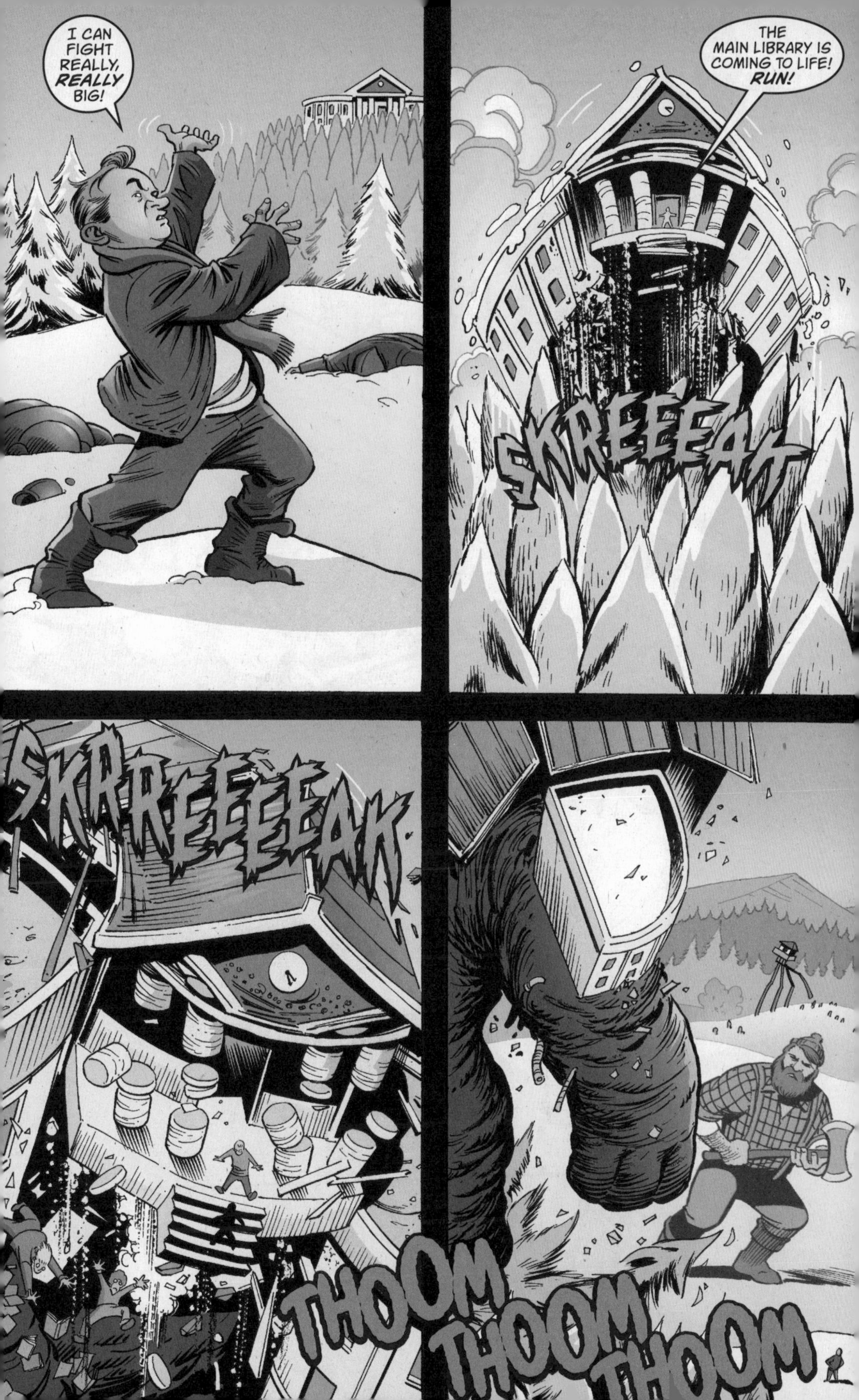
I CAN FIGHT REALLY, REALLY BIG!
THE MAIN LIBRARY IS COMING TO LIFE! RUN!
SKREEEAK
SKRREEEEAK
THOOM
THOOM
THOOM

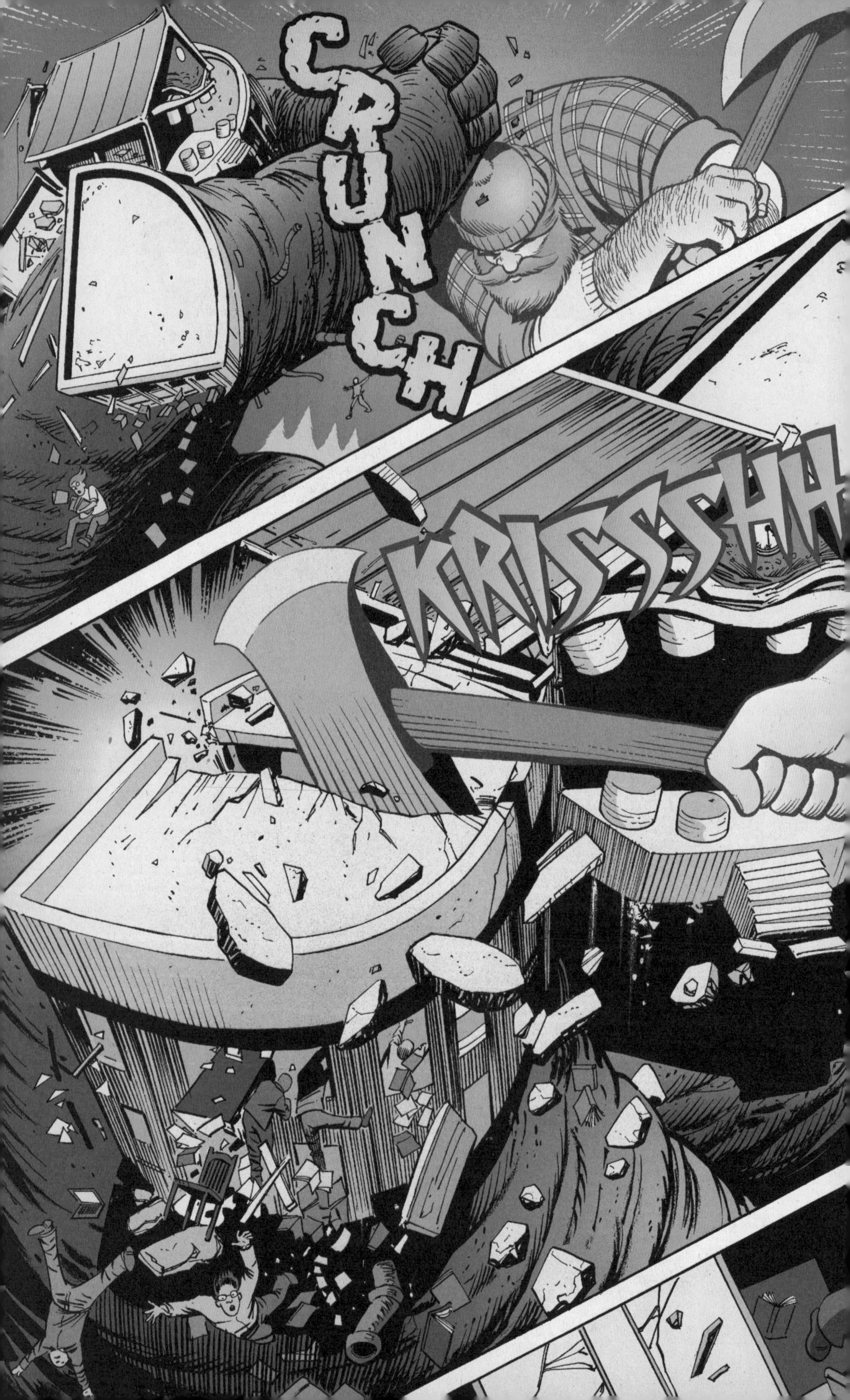
CRUNCH
KRISSSHH

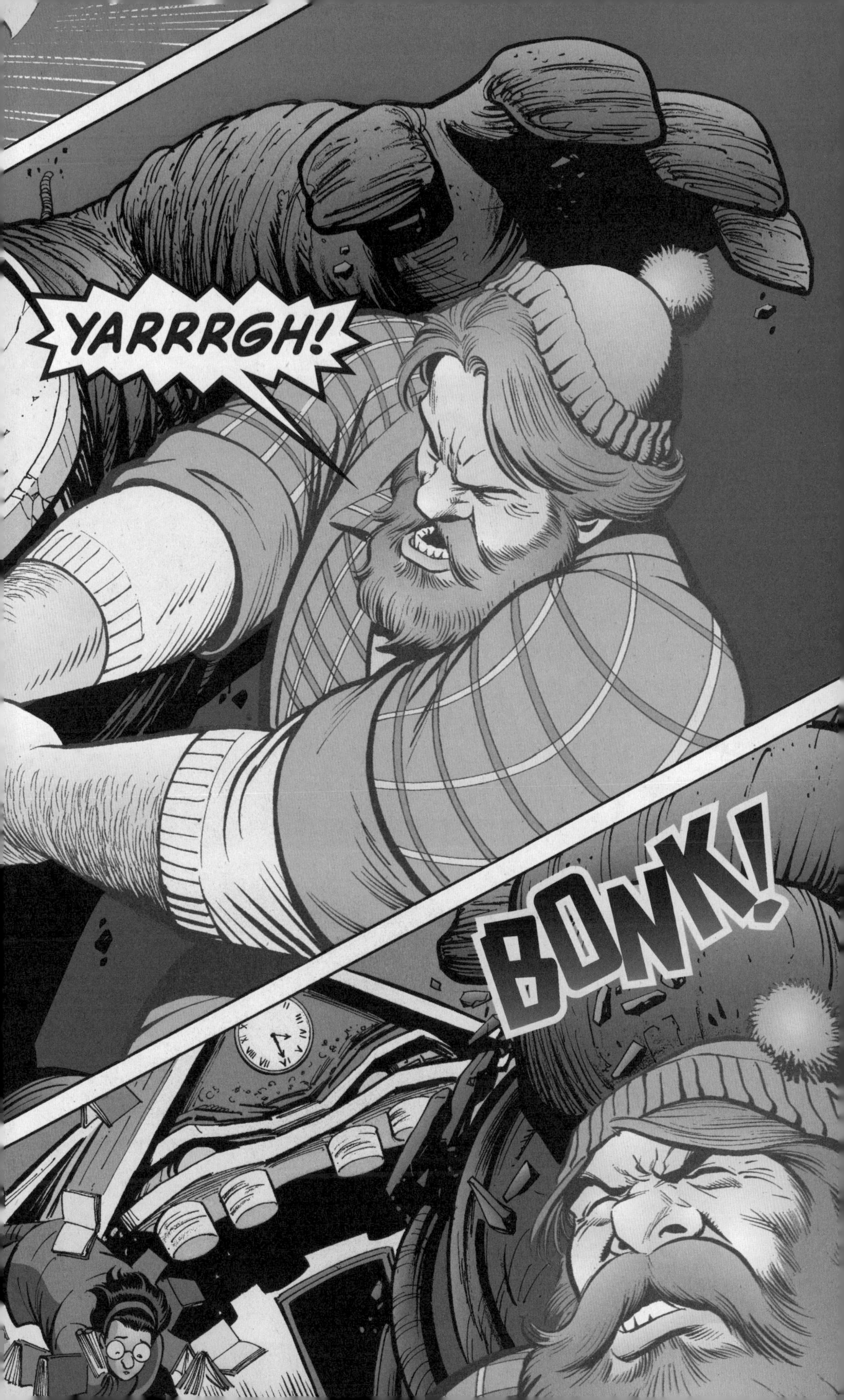
YARRRGH!
BONK!

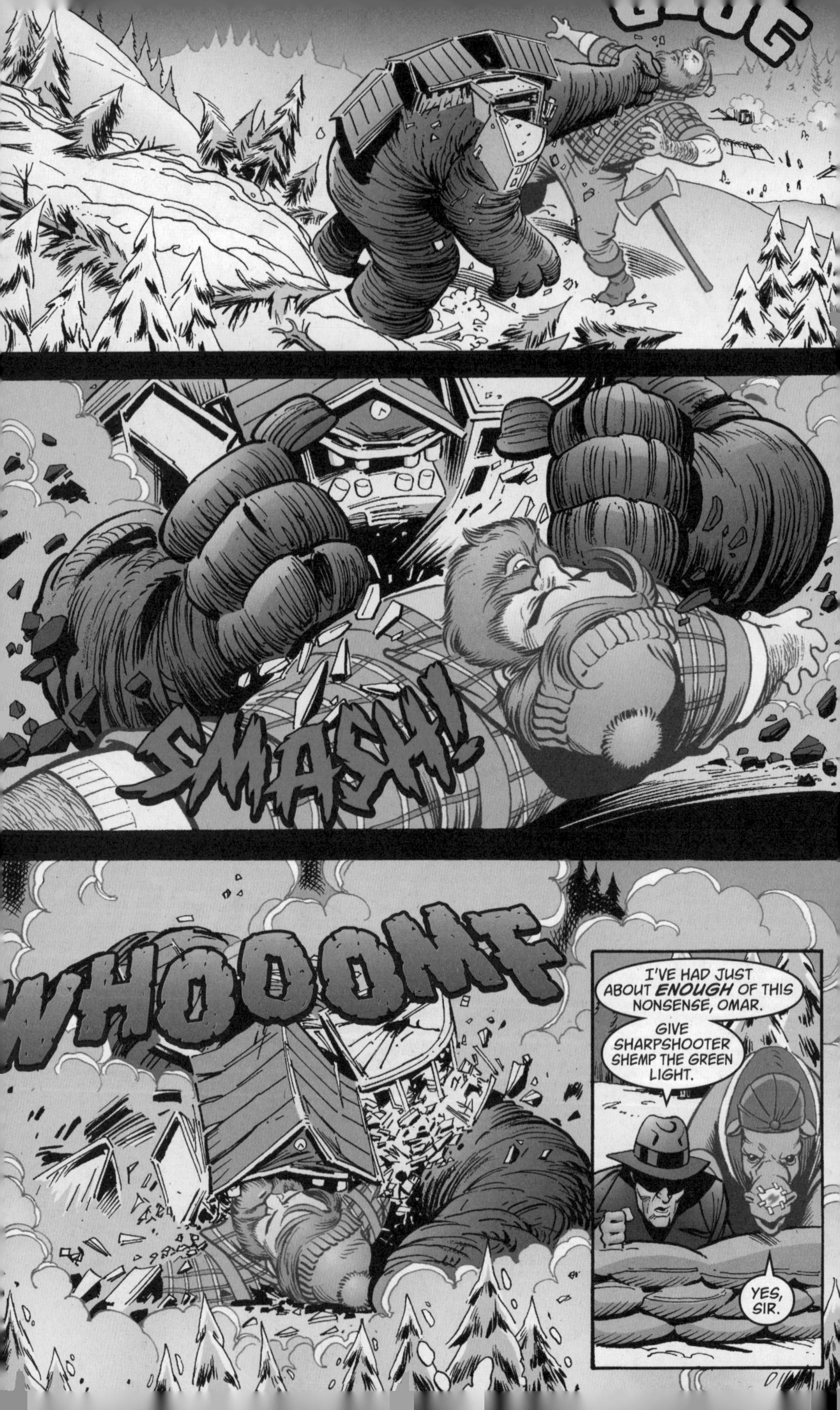
SMASH!
WHOOOMF
I'VE HAD JUST ABOUT ENOUGH OF THIS NONSENSE, OMAR.
GIVE SHARPSHOOTER SHEMP THE GREEN LIGHT.
YES, SIR.

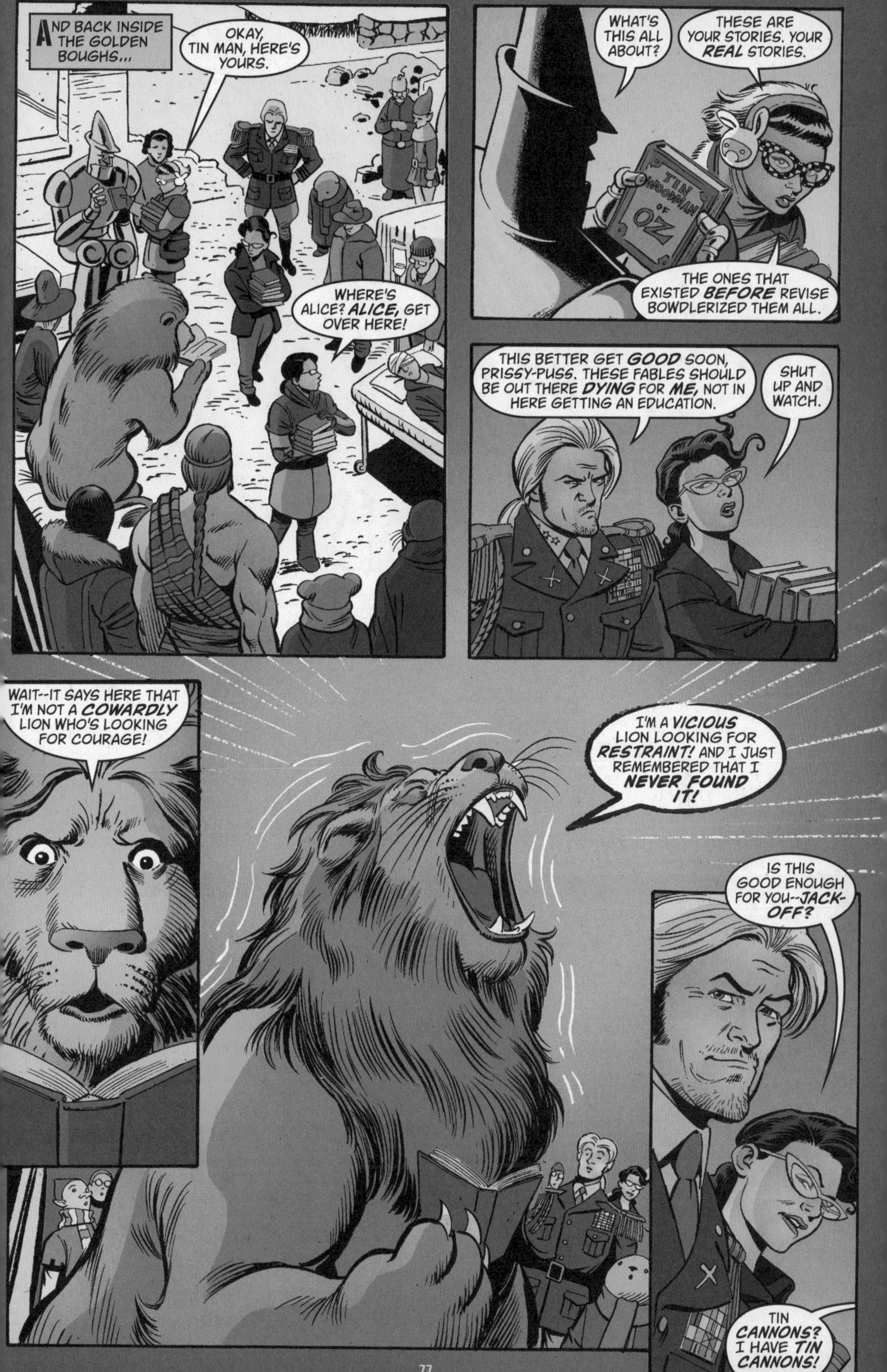
AND BACK INSIDE THE GOLDEN BOUGHS...
OKAY, TIN MAN, HERE'S YOURS.
WHERE'S ALICE? ALICE, GET OVER HERE!
WHAT'S THIS ALL ABOUT?
THESE ARE YOUR STORIES. YOUR REAL STORIES.
TIN WOODMAN OF OZ
THE ONES THAT EXISTED BEFORE REVISE BOWDLERIZED THEM ALL.
THIS BETTER GET GOOD SOON, PRISSY-PUSS. THESE FABLES SHOULD BE OUT THERE DYING FOR ME, NOT IN HERE GETTING AN EDUCATION.
SHUT UP AND WATCH.
WAIT--IT SAYS HERE THAT I'M NOT A COWARDLY LION WHO'S LOOKING FOR COURAGE!
I'M A VICIOUS LION LOOKING FOR RESTRAINT! AND I JUST REMEMBERED THAT I NEVER FOUND IT!
IS THIS GOOD ENOUGH FOR YOU--JACK-OFF?
TIN CANNONS? I HAVE TIN CANNONS!

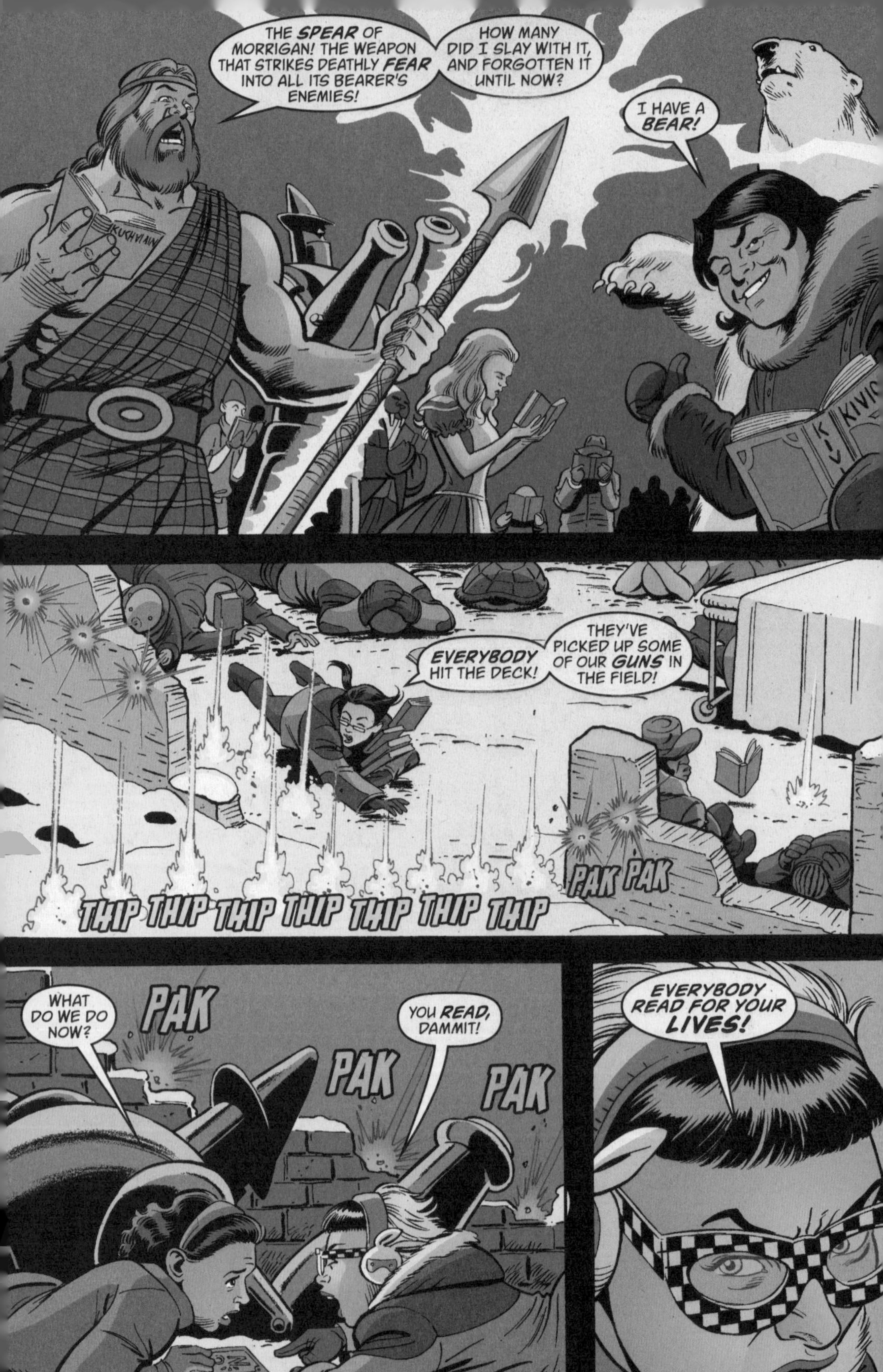
THE SPEAR OF MORRIGAN! THE WEAPON THAT STRIKES DEATHLY FEAR INTO ALL ITS BEARER'S ENEMIES!
HOW MANY DID I SLAY WITH IT, AND FORGOTTEN IT UNTIL NOW?
I HAVE A BEAR!
EVERYBODY HIT THE DECK!
THEY'VE PICKED UP SOME OF OUR GUNS IN THE FIELD!
PAK PAK
THIP THIP THIP THIP THIP THIP THIP
WHAT DO WE DO NOW?
PAK
PAK
YOU READ, DAMMIT!
PAK
EVERYBODY READ FOR YOUR LIVES!

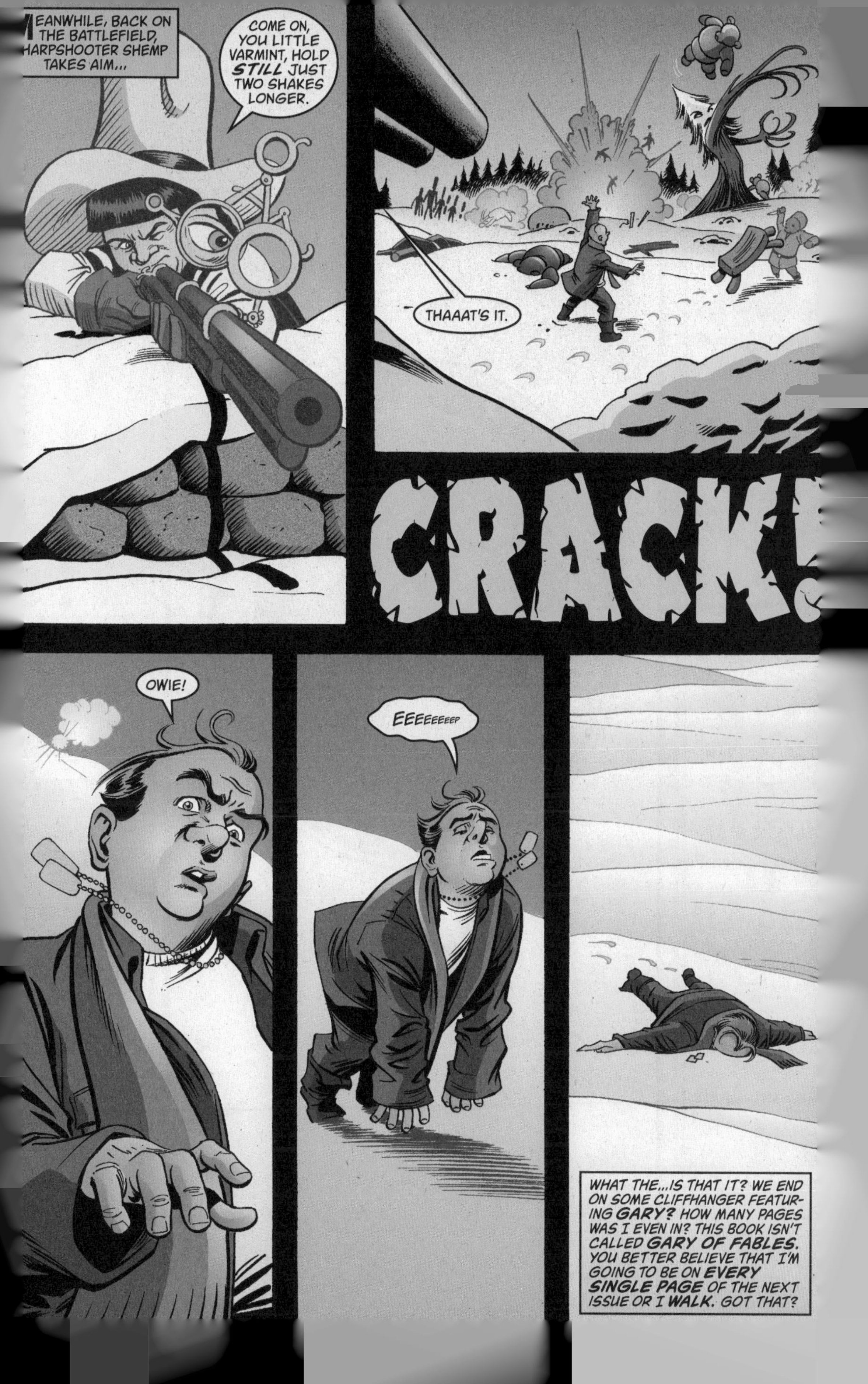
MEANWHILE, BACK ON THE BATTLEFIELD, SHARPSHOOTER SHEMP TAKES AIM...
COME ON, YOU LITTLE VARMINT, HOLD STILL JUST TWO SHAKES LONGER.
THAAAT'S IT.
CRACK!
OWIE!
EEEEeeeep
WHAT THE...IS THAT IT? WE END ON SOME CLIFFHANGER FEATURING GARY? HOW MANY PAGES WAS I EVEN IN? THIS BOOK ISN'T CALLED GARY OF FABLES. YOU BETTER BELIEVE THAT I'M GOING TO BE ON EVERY SINGLE PAGE OF THE NEXT ISSUE OR I WALK. GOT THAT?

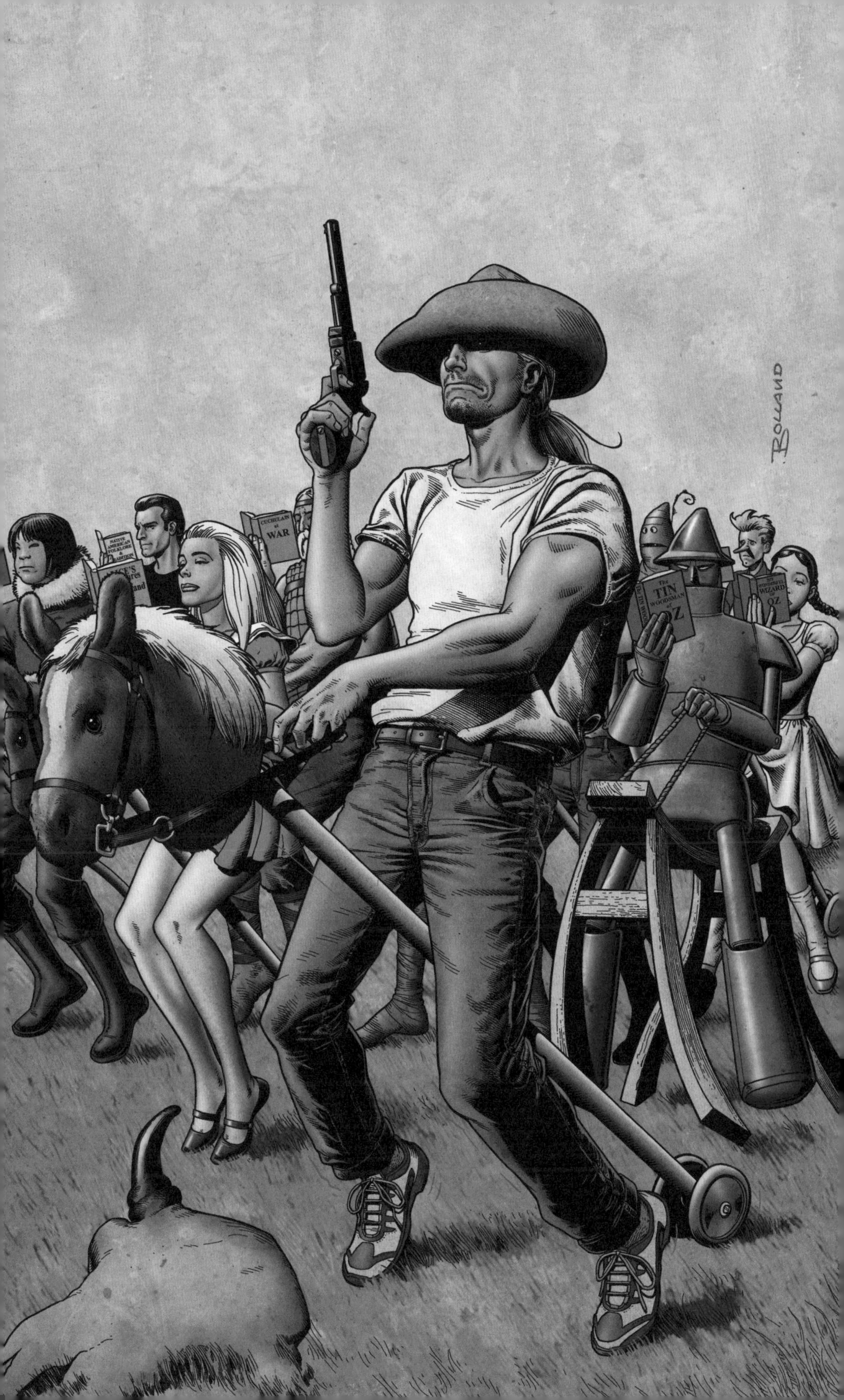
BOLLAND
NATIVE AMERICAN FOLKLORE & TRADITION
CUCHULAIN at WAR
The TIN WOODSMAN of OZ
WIZARD of OZ

*"So, brother. It comes to **this**, after all these years."*

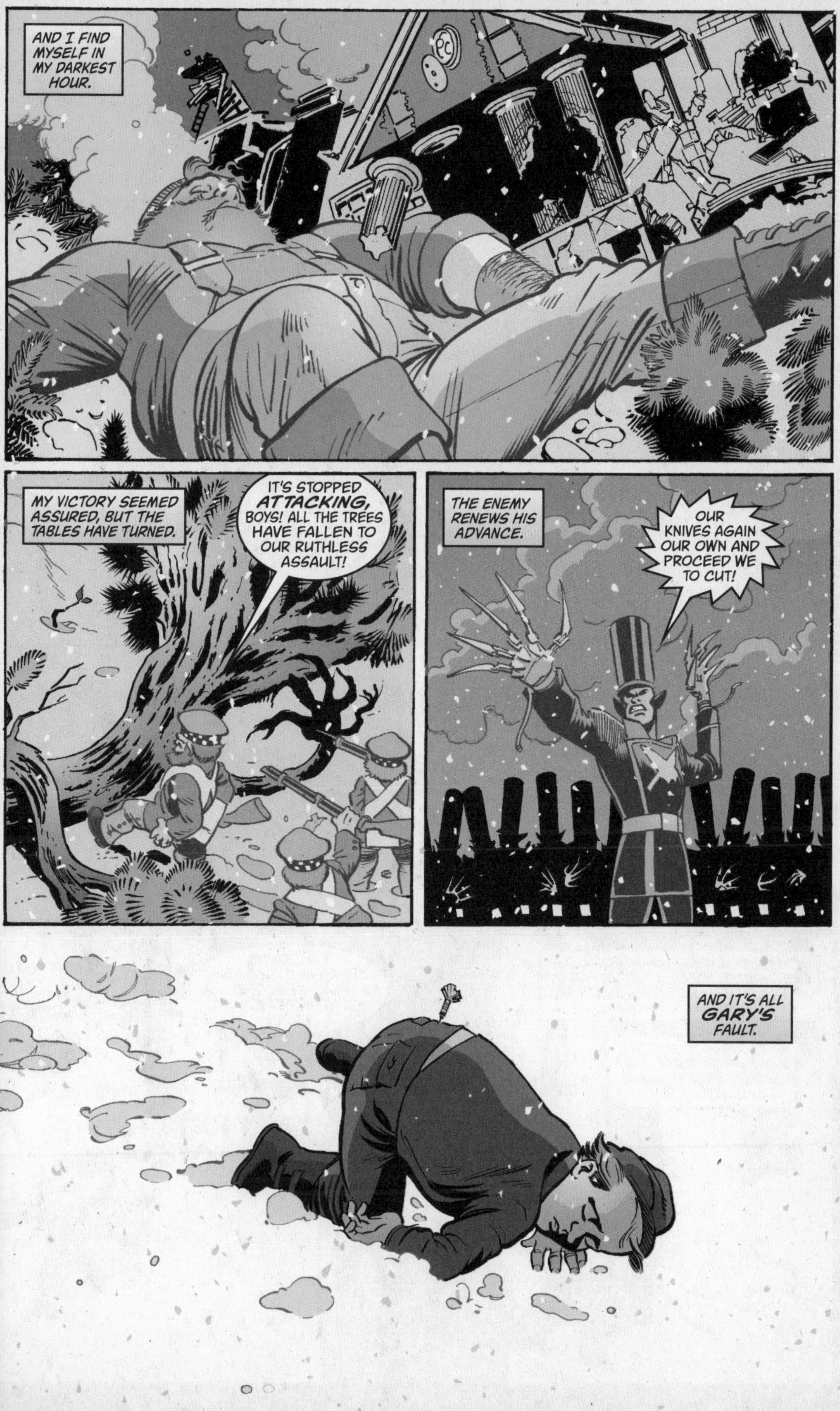
AND I FIND MYSELF IN MY DARKEST HOUR.
MY VICTORY SEEMED ASSURED, BUT THE TABLES HAVE TURNED.
IT'S STOPPED ATTACKING, BOYS! ALL THE TREES HAVE FALLEN TO OUR RUTHLESS ASSAULT!
THE ENEMY RENEWS HIS ADVANCE.
OUR KNIVES AGAIN OUR OWN AND PROCEED WE TO CUT!
AND IT'S ALL GARY'S FAULT.

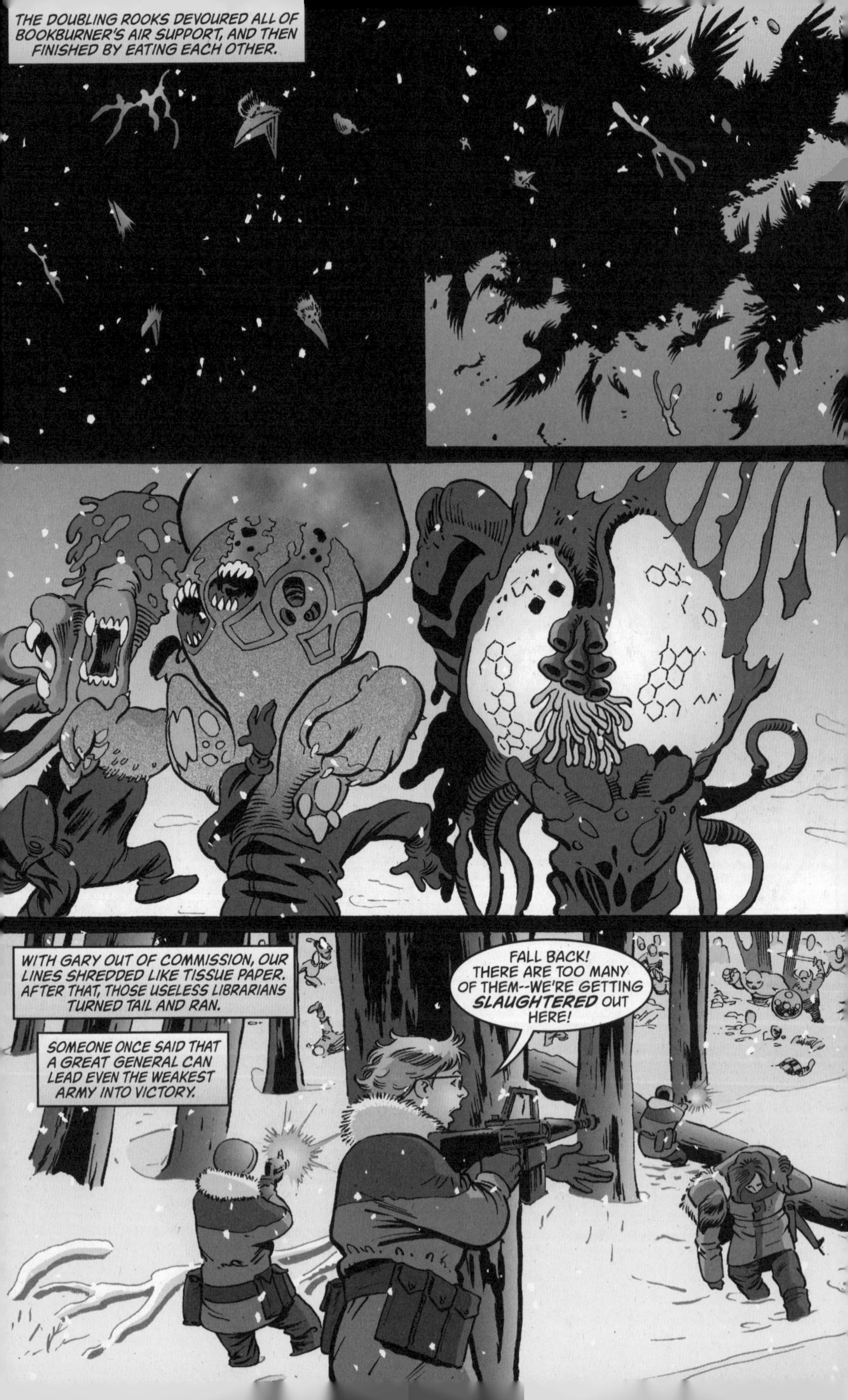
THE DOUBLING ROOKS DEVOURED ALL OF BOOKBURNER'S AIR SUPPORT, AND THEN FINISHED BY EATING EACH OTHER.
WITH GARY OUT OF COMMISSION, OUR LINES SHREDDED LIKE TISSUE PAPER. AFTER THAT, THOSE USELESS LIBRARIANS TURNED TAIL AND RAN.
SOMEONE ONCE SAID THAT A GREAT GENERAL CAN LEAD EVEN THE WEAKEST ARMY INTO VICTORY.
FALL BACK! THERE ARE TOO MANY OF THEM--WE'RE GETTING SLAUGHTERED OUT HERE!

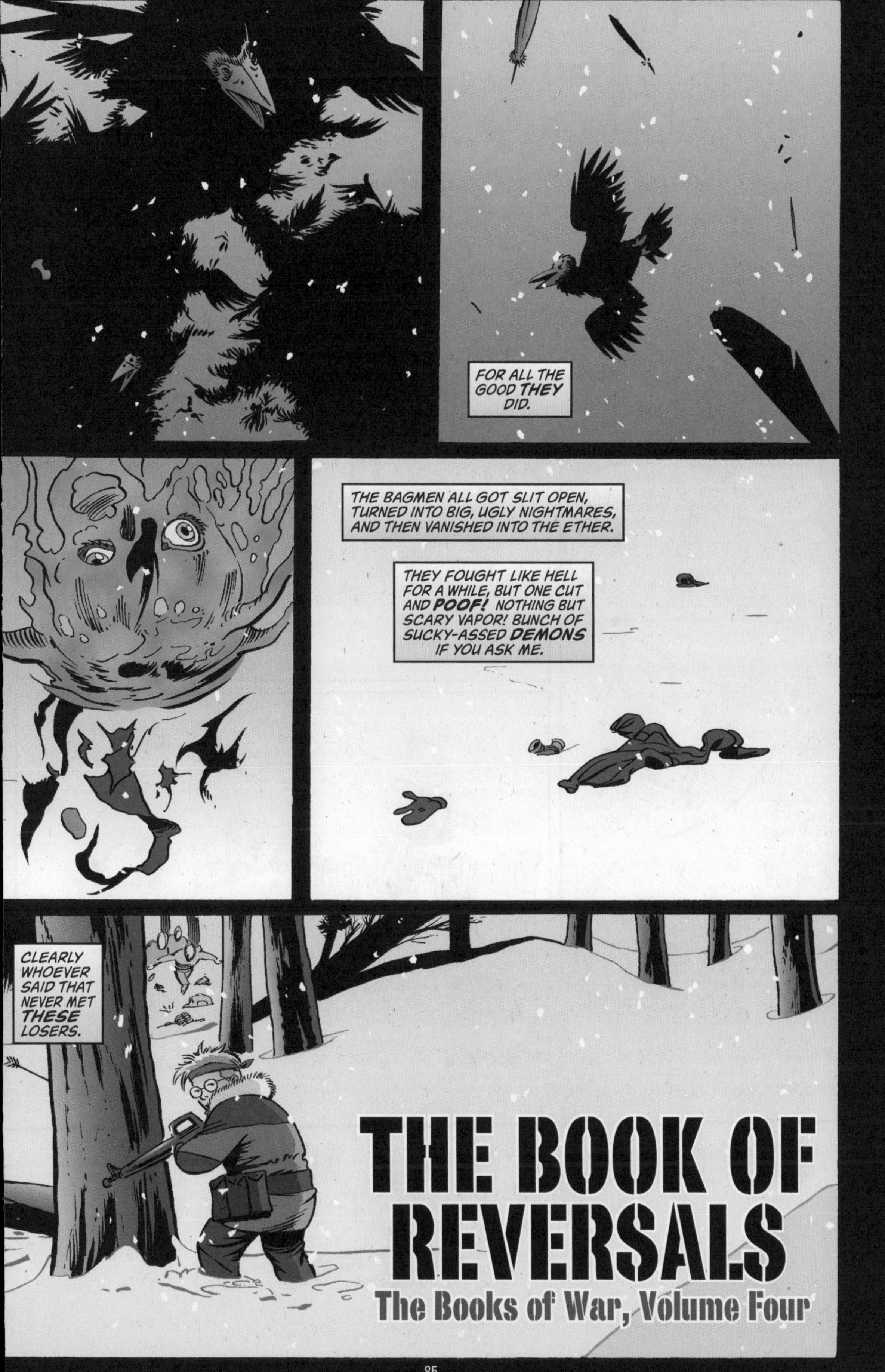
FOR ALL THE GOOD THEY DID.
THE BAGMEN ALL GOT SLIT OPEN, TURNED INTO BIG, UGLY NIGHTMARES, AND THEN VANISHED INTO THE ETHER.
THEY FOUGHT LIKE HELL FOR A WHILE, BUT ONE CUT AND POOF! NOTHING BUT SCARY VAPOR! BUNCH OF SUCKY-ASSED DEMONS IF YOU ASK ME.
CLEARLY WHOEVER SAID THAT NEVER MET THESE LOSERS.
THE BOOK OF REVERSALS
The Books of War, Volume Four

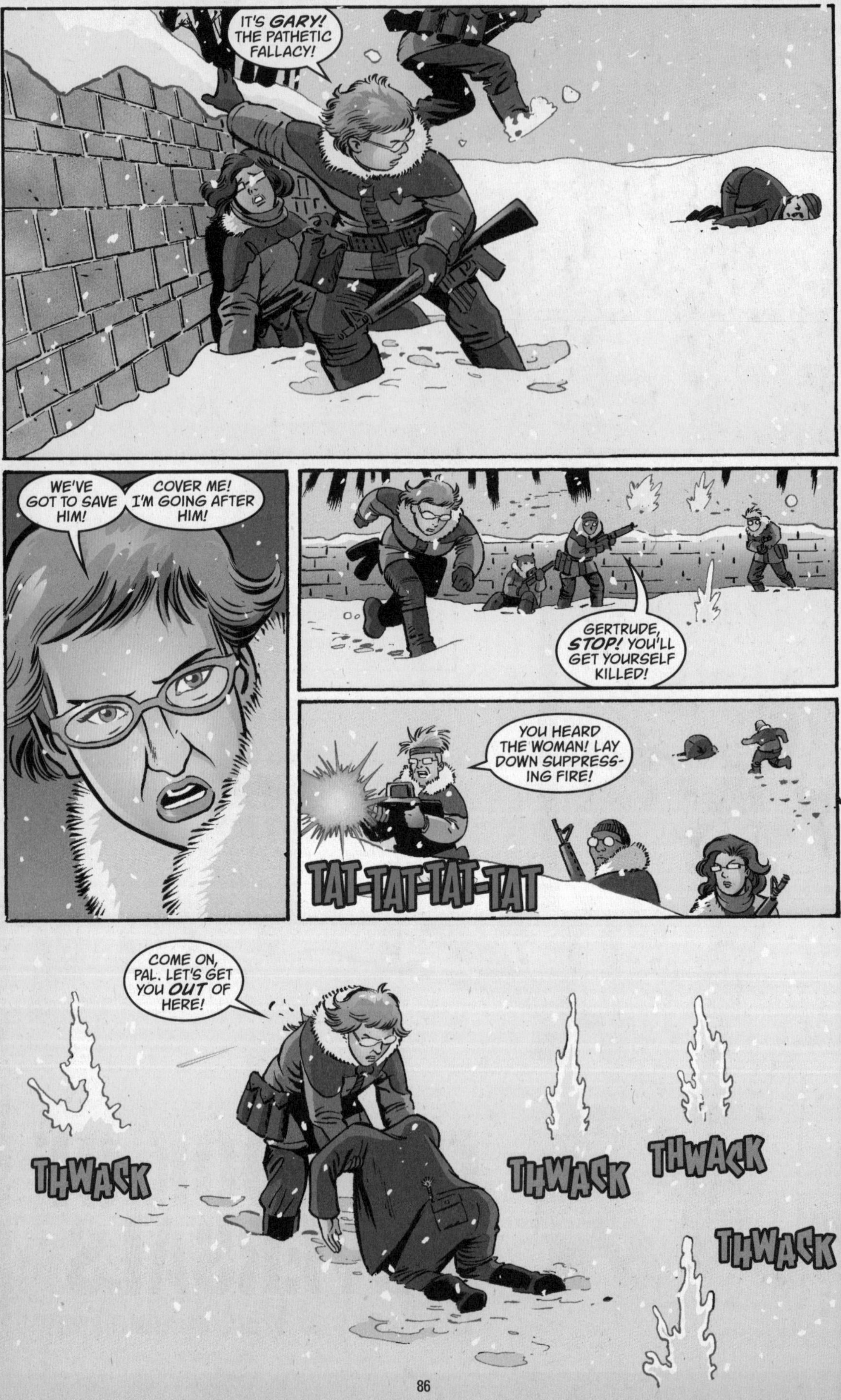
IT'S GARY! THE PATHETIC FALLACY!
WE'VE GOT TO SAVE HIM!
COVER ME! I'M GOING AFTER HIM!
GERTRUDE, STOP! YOU'LL GET YOURSELF KILLED!
YOU HEARD THE WOMAN! LAY DOWN SUPPRESS-ING FIRE!
TAT-TAT-TAT-TAT
COME ON, PAL. LET'S GET YOU OUT OF HERE!
THWACK
THWACK
THWACK
THWACK

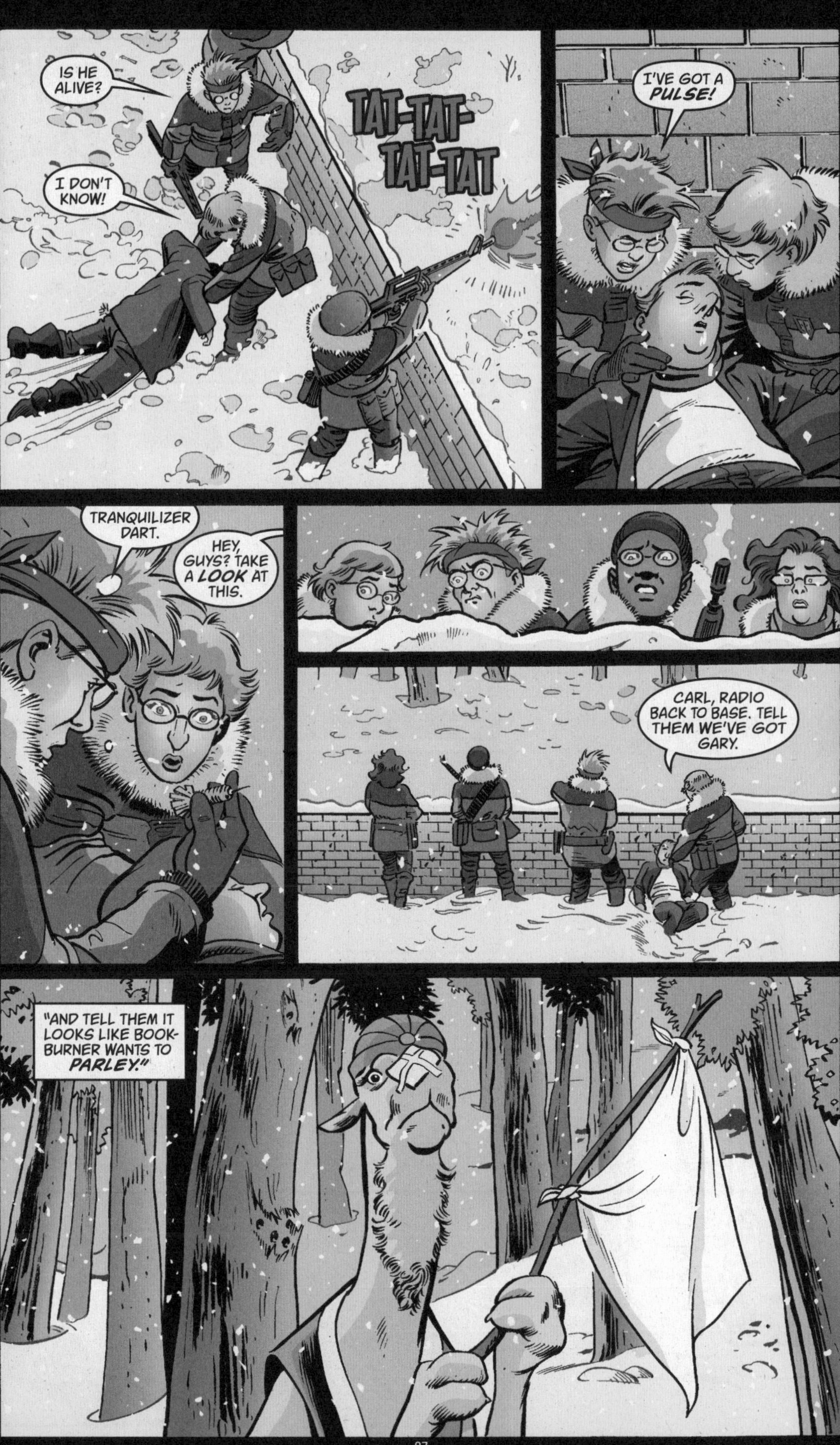

IS HE ALIVE?
I DON'T KNOW!
TAT-TAT-TAT-TAT
I'VE GOT A PULSE!
TRANQUILIZER DART.
HEY, GUYS? TAKE A LOOK AT THIS.
CARL, RADIO BACK TO BASE. TELL THEM WE'VE GOT GARY.
"AND TELL THEM IT LOOKS LIKE BOOK-BURNER WANTS TO PARLEY."

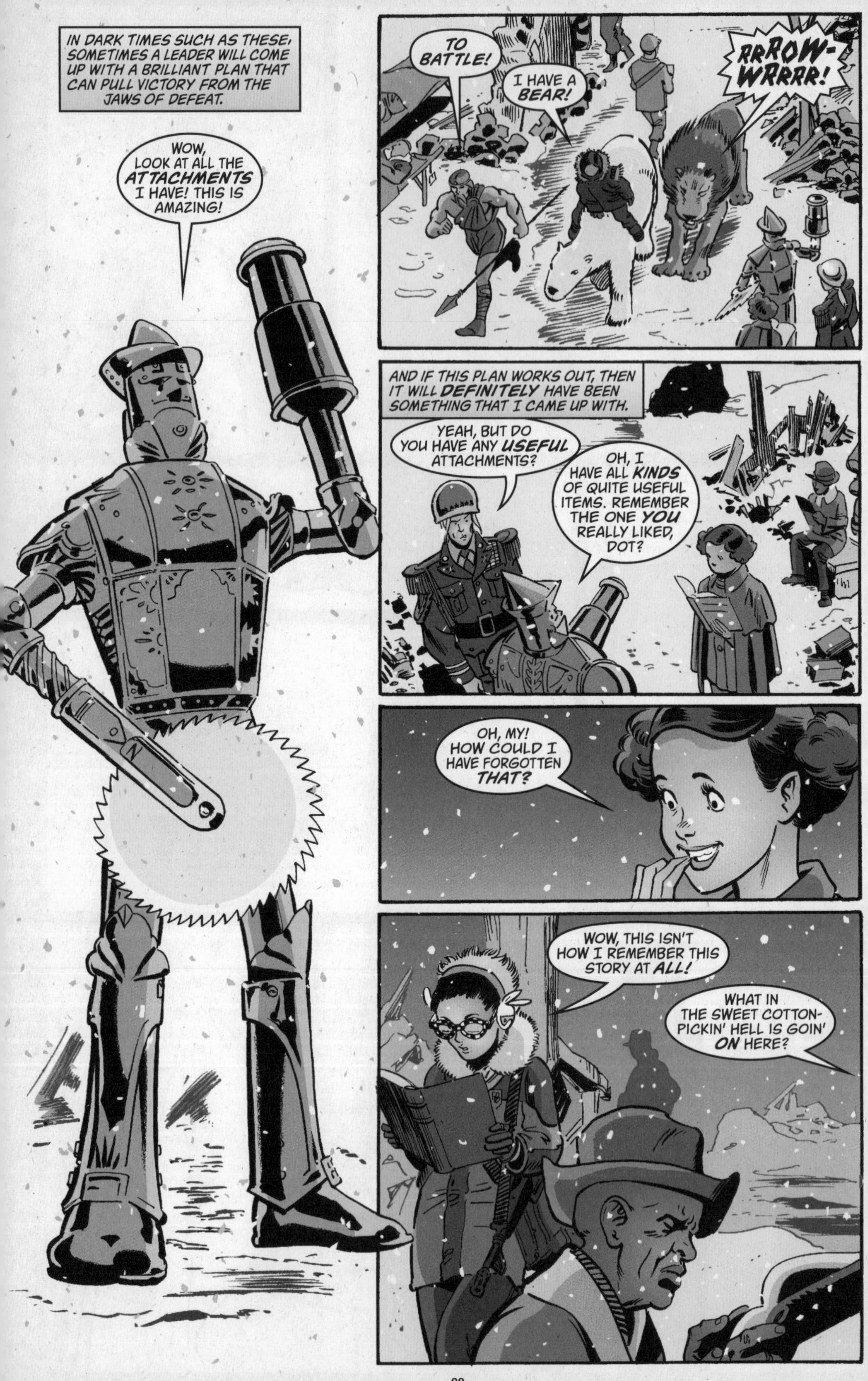
IN DARK TIMES SUCH AS THESE, SOMETIMES A LEADER WILL COME UP WITH A BRILLIANT PLAN THAT CAN PULL VICTORY FROM THE JAWS OF DEFEAT.
WOW, LOOK AT ALL THE ATTACHMENTS I HAVE! THIS IS AMAZING!
TO BATTLE!
I HAVE A BEAR!
RRROW-WRRRR!
AND IF THIS PLAN WORKS OUT, THEN IT WILL DEFINITELY HAVE BEEN SOMETHING THAT I CAME UP WITH.
YEAH, BUT DO YOU HAVE ANY USEFUL ATTACHMENTS?
OH, I HAVE ALL KINDS OF QUITE USEFUL ITEMS. REMEMBER THE ONE YOU REALLY LIKED, DOT?
OH, MY! HOW COULD I HAVE FORGOTTEN THAT?
WOW, THIS ISN'T HOW I REMEMBER THIS STORY AT ALL!
WHAT IN THE SWEET COTTON-PICKIN' HELL IS GOIN' ON HERE?

WELL? YOU MOOKS JUST GONNA STAND AROUND *GAWKIN'*, OR IS SOMEBODY GONNA TELL ME WHERE THE CRAP I *AM?*

UHM, IT SEEMS YOU'RE THE OTHER PIG--FROM THE *FOUR LITTLE PIGS.*

THE ONE WHO BUILT HIS HOUSE OUT OF... *CLOTH.*

YEAH, YEAH. "CARL," THEY SAID, "A *TENT* AIN'T GONNA KEEP OUT A BIG, BAD WOLF."

WHAT CAN I SAY? I MAY BE LAZY, BUT MY HOME WAS BUILT DAYS BEFORE ANY OF THE OTHERS.

HILLARY, WOULD YOU CARE TO EXPLAIN WHERE THIS *SWINE* CAME FROM?

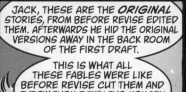

JACK, THESE ARE THE *ORIGINAL* STORIES, FROM BEFORE REVISE EDITED THEM. AFTERWARDS HE HID THE ORIGINAL VERSIONS AWAY IN THE BACK ROOM OF THE FIRST DRAFT.

THIS IS WHAT ALL THESE FABLES WERE LIKE BEFORE REVISE CUT THEM AND THREW THEM DOWN THE MEMORY HOLE. THE *BOOKS* ARE RESTORING THEM!

HEY, BABY. YOU MARRIED, OR *WHAT?*

GUYS-- BOOKBURNER'S CALLING FOR A *TRUCE.* HE WANTS TO *TALK.*

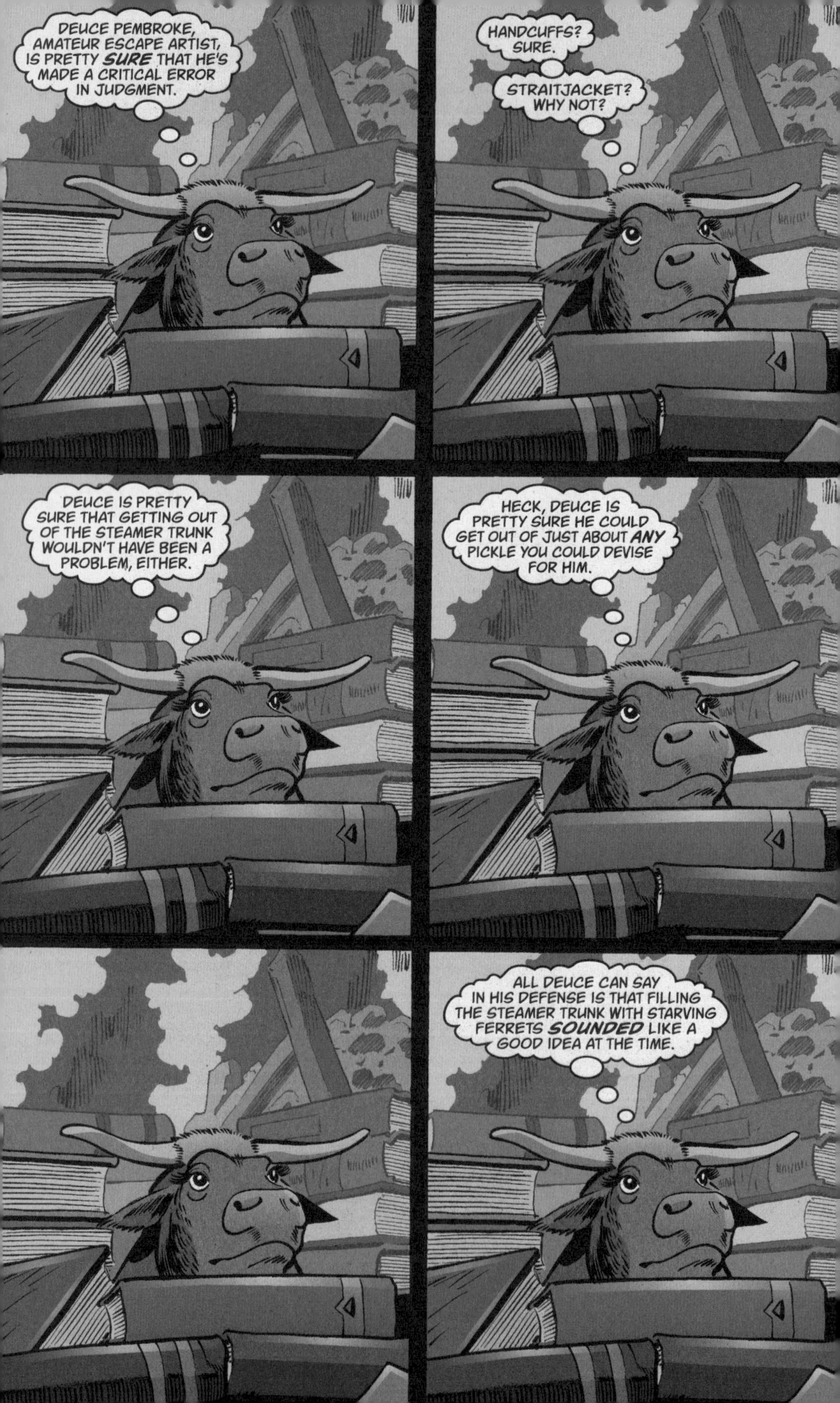

DEUCE PEMBROKE, AMATEUR ESCAPE ARTIST, IS PRETTY SURE THAT HE'S MADE A CRITICAL ERROR IN JUDGMENT.
HANDCUFFS? SURE.
STRAITJACKET? WHY NOT?
DEUCE IS PRETTY SURE THAT GETTING OUT OF THE STEAMER TRUNK WOULDN'T HAVE BEEN A PROBLEM, EITHER.
HECK, DEUCE IS PRETTY SURE HE COULD GET OUT OF JUST ABOUT ANY PICKLE YOU COULD DEVISE FOR HIM.
ALL DEUCE CAN SAY IN HIS DEFENSE IS THAT FILLING THE STEAMER TRUNK WITH STARVING FERRETS SOUNDED LIKE A GOOD IDEA AT THE TIME.

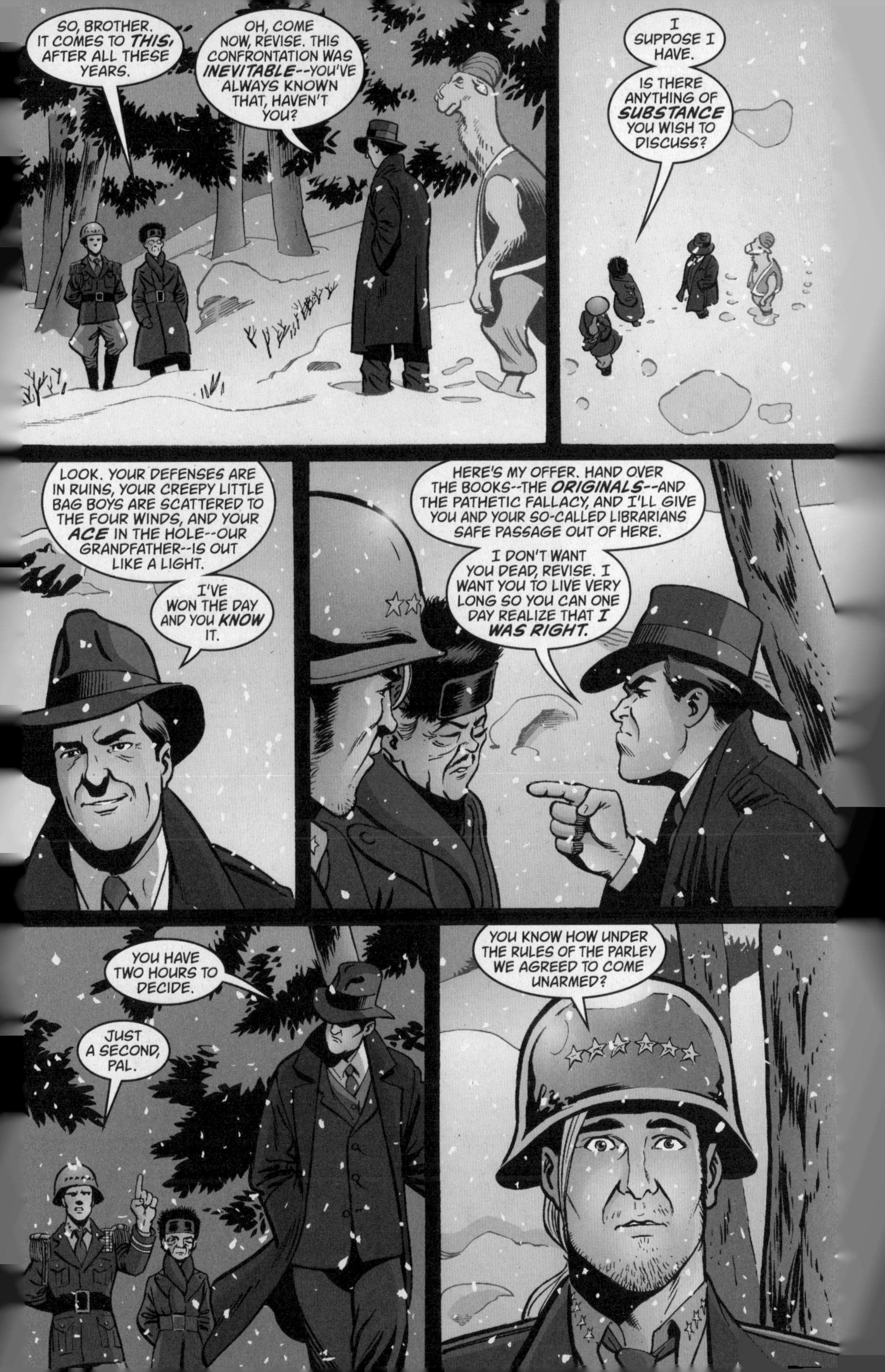
SO, BROTHER. IT COMES TO THIS, AFTER ALL THESE YEARS.
OH, COME NOW, REVISE. THIS CONFRONTATION WAS INEVITABLE--YOU'VE ALWAYS KNOWN THAT, HAVEN'T YOU?
I SUPPOSE I HAVE.
IS THERE ANYTHING OF SUBSTANCE YOU WISH TO DISCUSS?
LOOK. YOUR DEFENSES ARE IN RUINS, YOUR CREEPY LITTLE BAG BOYS ARE SCATTERED TO THE FOUR WINDS, AND YOUR ACE IN THE HOLE--OUR GRANDFATHER--IS OUT LIKE A LIGHT.
I'VE WON THE DAY AND YOU KNOW IT.
HERE'S MY OFFER. HAND OVER THE BOOKS--THE ORIGINALS--AND THE PATHETIC FALLACY, AND I'LL GIVE YOU AND YOUR SO-CALLED LIBRARIANS SAFE PASSAGE OUT OF HERE.
I DON'T WANT YOU DEAD, REVISE. I WANT YOU TO LIVE VERY LONG SO YOU CAN ONE DAY REALIZE THAT I WAS RIGHT.
YOU HAVE TWO HOURS TO DECIDE.
JUST A SECOND, PAL.
YOU KNOW HOW UNDER THE RULES OF THE PARLEY WE AGREED TO COME UNARMED?

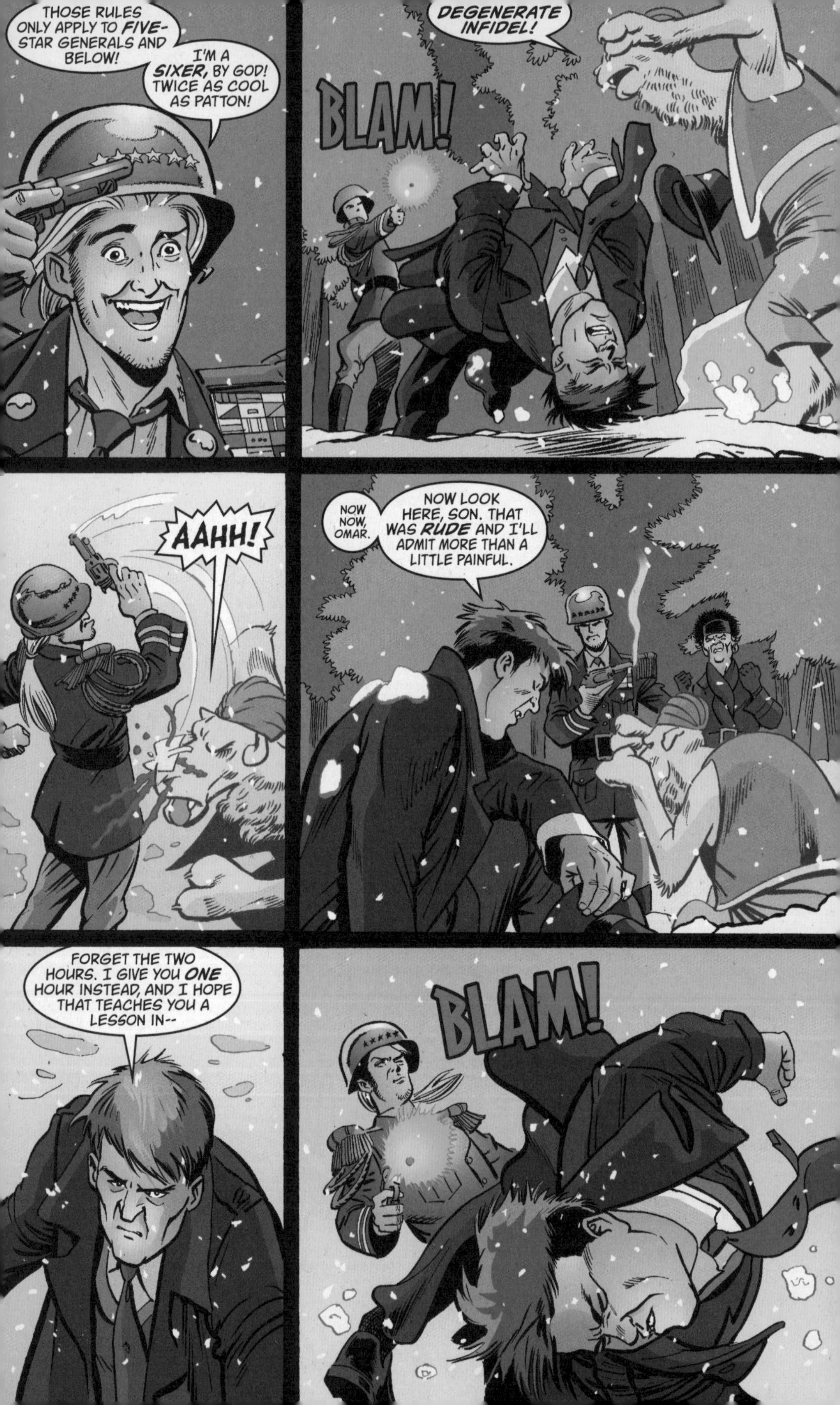
THOSE RULES ONLY APPLY TO FIVE-STAR GENERALS AND BELOW!
I'M A SIXER, BY GOD! TWICE AS COOL AS PATTON!
DEGENERATE INFIDEL!
BLAM!
AAHH!
NOW NOW, OMAR.
NOW LOOK HERE, SON. THAT WAS RUDE AND I'LL ADMIT MORE THAN A LITTLE PAINFUL.
FORGET THE TWO HOURS. I GIVE YOU ONE HOUR INSTEAD, AND I HOPE THAT TEACHES YOU A LESSON IN--
BLAM!

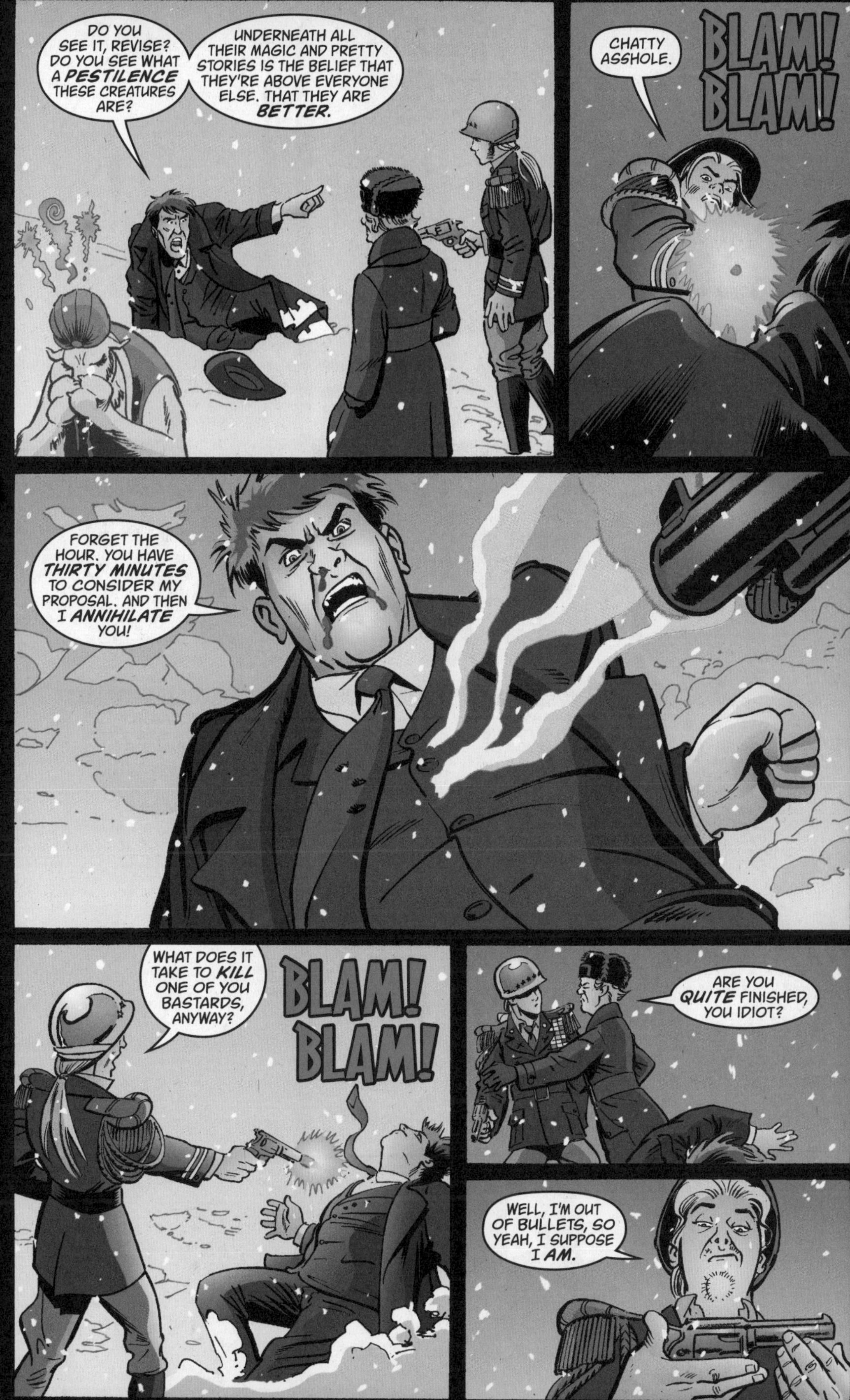
DO YOU SEE IT, REVISE? DO YOU SEE WHAT A PESTILENCE THESE CREATURES ARE?
UNDERNEATH ALL THEIR MAGIC AND PRETTY STORIES IS THE BELIEF THAT THEY'RE ABOVE EVERYONE ELSE. THAT THEY ARE BETTER.
CHATTY ASSHOLE.
BLAM! BLAM!
FORGET THE HOUR. YOU HAVE THIRTY MINUTES TO CONSIDER MY PROPOSAL. AND THEN I ANNIHILATE YOU!
WHAT DOES IT TAKE TO KILL ONE OF YOU BASTARDS, ANYWAY?
BLAM! BLAM!
ARE YOU QUITE FINISHED, YOU IDIOT?
WELL, I'M OUT OF BULLETS, SO YEAH, I SUPPOSE I AM.

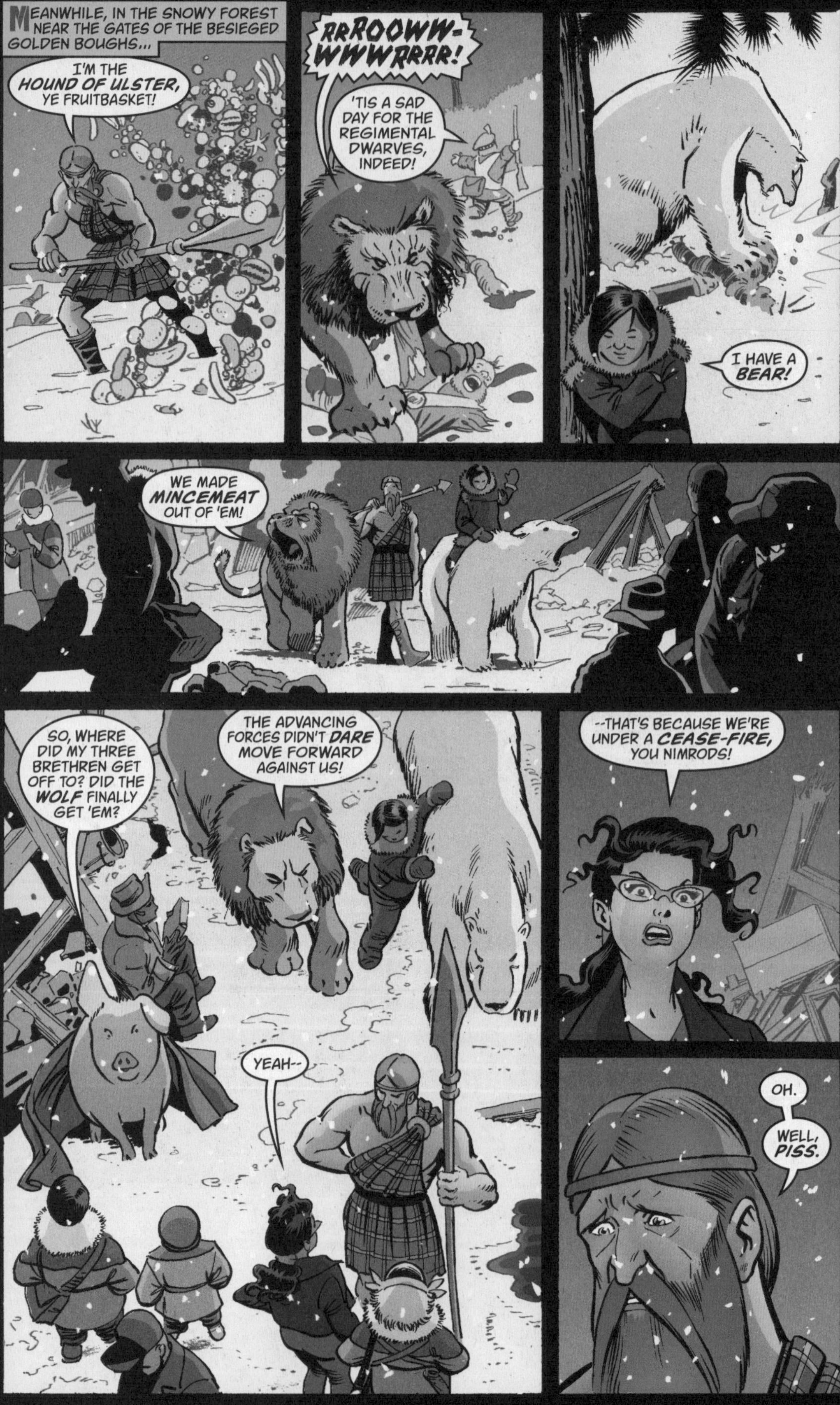
MEANWHILE, IN THE SNOWY FOREST NEAR THE GATES OF THE BESIEGED GOLDEN BOUGHS...
I'M THE HOUND OF ULSTER, YE FRUITBASKET!
RRROOWW-WWWRRRR!
'TIS A SAD DAY FOR THE REGIMENTAL DWARVES, INDEED!
I HAVE A BEAR!
WE MADE MINCEMEAT OUT OF 'EM!
SO, WHERE DID MY THREE BRETHREN GET OFF TO? DID THE WOLF FINALLY GET 'EM?
THE ADVANCING FORCES DIDN'T DARE MOVE FORWARD AGAINST US!
YEAH--
--THAT'S BECAUSE WE'RE UNDER A CEASE-FIRE, YOU NIMRODS!
OH.
WELL, PISS.

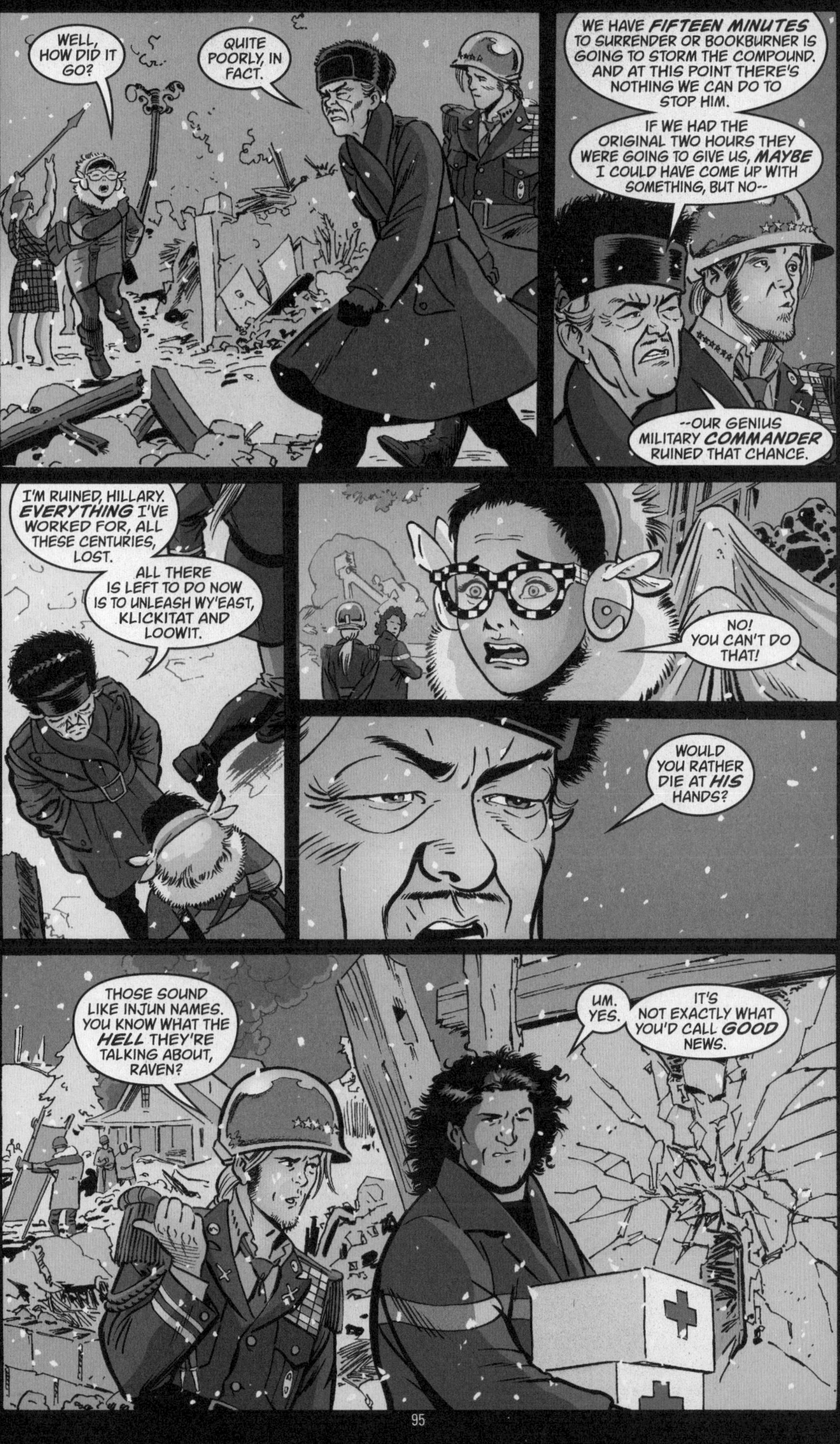
WELL, HOW DID IT GO?
QUITE POORLY, IN FACT.
WE HAVE FIFTEEN MINUTES TO SURRENDER OR BOOKBURNER IS GOING TO STORM THE COMPOUND. AND AT THIS POINT THERE'S NOTHING WE CAN DO TO STOP HIM.
IF WE HAD THE ORIGINAL TWO HOURS THEY WERE GOING TO GIVE US, MAYBE I COULD HAVE COME UP WITH SOMETHING, BUT NO--
--OUR GENIUS MILITARY COMMANDER RUINED THAT CHANCE.
I'M RUINED, HILLARY. EVERYTHING I'VE WORKED FOR, ALL THESE CENTURIES, LOST.
ALL THERE IS LEFT TO DO NOW IS TO UNLEASH WY'EAST, KLICKITAT AND LOOWIT.
NO! YOU CAN'T DO THAT!
WOULD YOU RATHER DIE AT HIS HANDS?
THOSE SOUND LIKE INJUN NAMES. YOU KNOW WHAT THE HELL THEY'RE TALKING ABOUT, RAVEN?
UM. YES.
IT'S NOT EXACTLY WHAT YOU'D CALL GOOD NEWS.

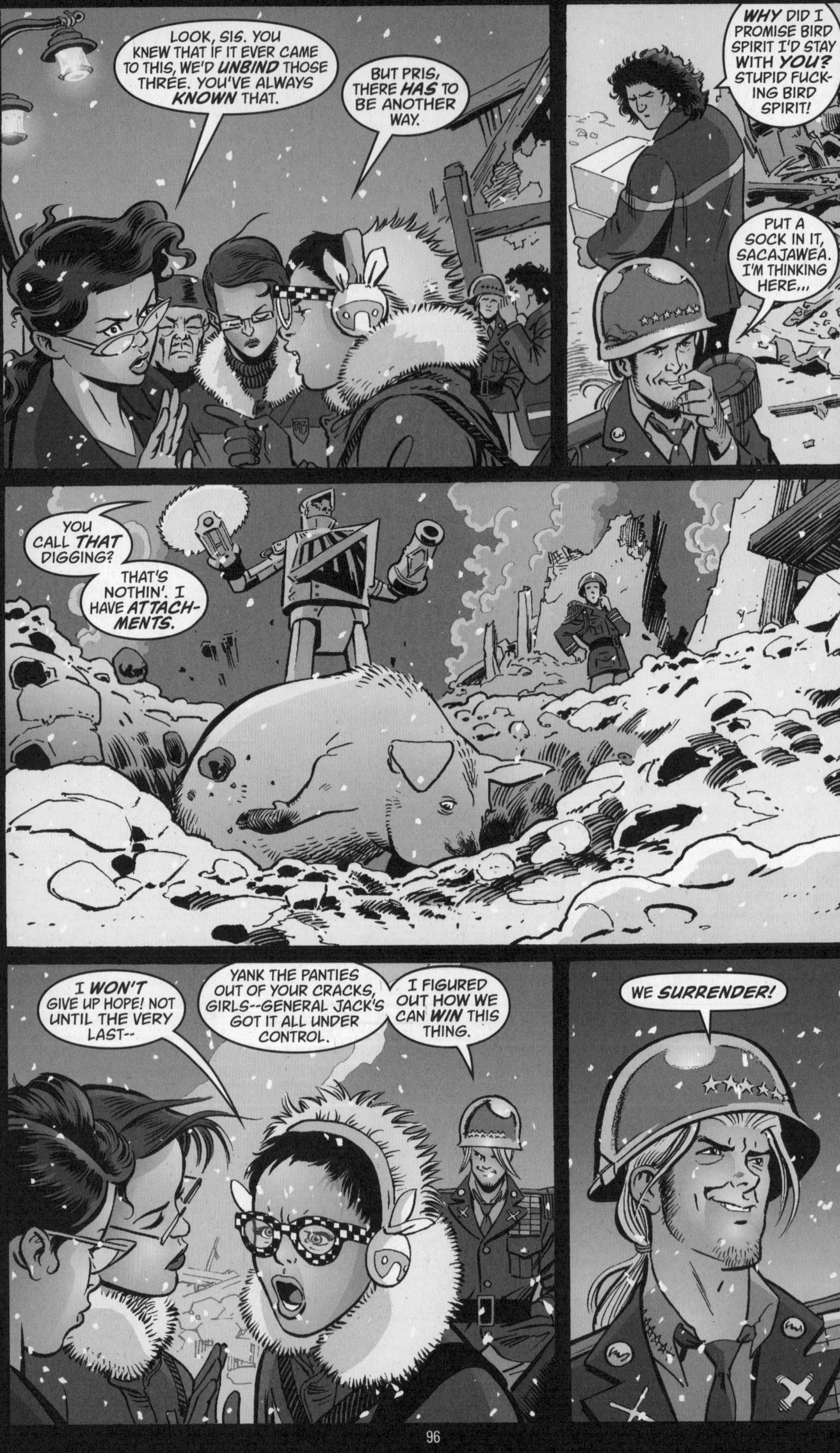
LOOK, SIS. YOU KNEW THAT IF IT EVER CAME TO THIS, WE'D UNBIND THOSE THREE. YOU'VE ALWAYS KNOWN THAT.
BUT PRIS, THERE HAS TO BE ANOTHER WAY.
WHY DID I PROMISE BIRD SPIRIT I'D STAY WITH YOU? STUPID FUCKING BIRD SPIRIT!
PUT A SOCK IN IT, SACAJAWEA. I'M THINKING HERE...
YOU CALL THAT DIGGING?
THAT'S NOTHIN'. I HAVE ATTACHMENTS.
I WON'T GIVE UP HOPE! NOT UNTIL THE VERY LAST--
YANK THE PANTIES OUT OF YOUR CRACKS, GIRLS--GENERAL JACK'S GOT IT ALL UNDER CONTROL.
I FIGURED OUT HOW WE CAN WIN THIS THING.
WE SURRENDER!

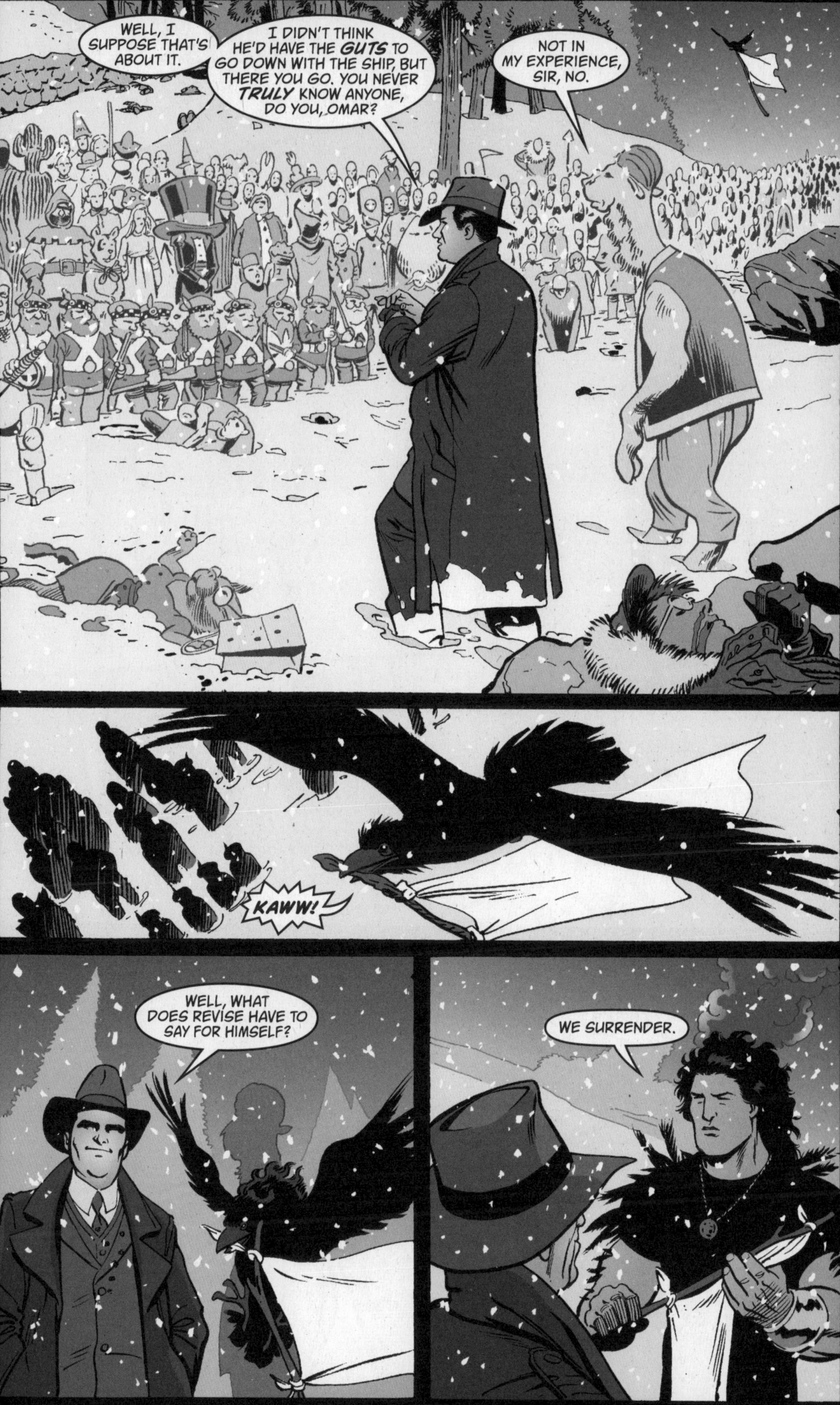
WELL, I SUPPOSE THAT'S ABOUT IT.
I DIDN'T THINK HE'D HAVE THE GUTS TO GO DOWN WITH THE SHIP, BUT THERE YOU GO. YOU NEVER TRULY KNOW ANYONE, DO YOU, OMAR?
NOT IN MY EXPERIENCE, SIR, NO.
KAWW!
WELL, WHAT DOES REVISE HAVE TO SAY FOR HIMSELF?
WE SURRENDER.

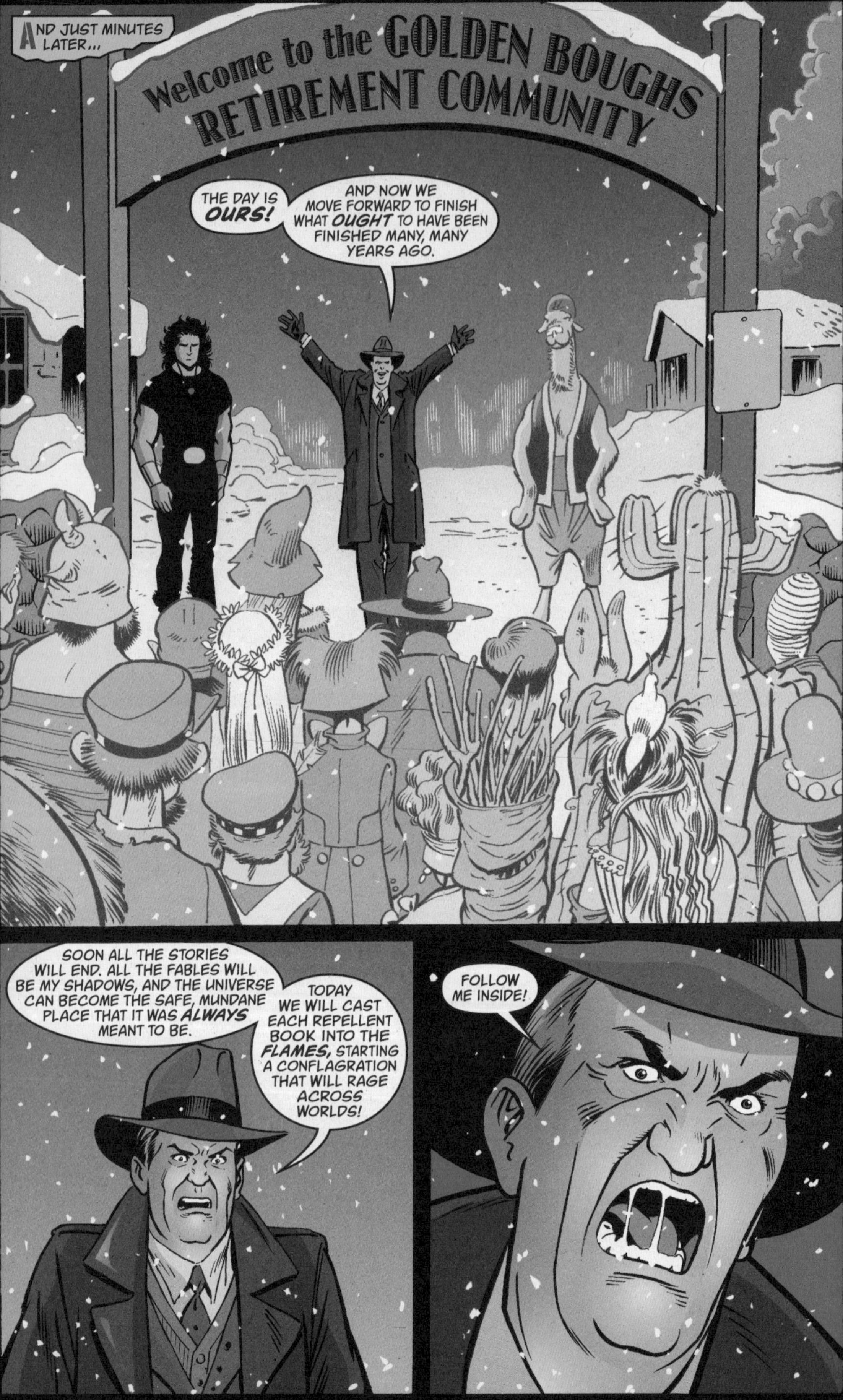
AND JUST MINUTES LATER...
Welcome to the GOLDEN BOUGHS RETIREMENT COMMUNITY
THE DAY IS OURS!
AND NOW WE MOVE FORWARD TO FINISH WHAT OUGHT TO HAVE BEEN FINISHED MANY, MANY YEARS AGO.
SOON ALL THE STORIES WILL END. ALL THE FABLES WILL BE MY SHADOWS, AND THE UNIVERSE CAN BECOME THE SAFE, MUNDANE PLACE THAT IT WAS ALWAYS MEANT TO BE.
TODAY WE WILL CAST EACH REPELLENT BOOK INTO THE FLAMES, STARTING A CONFLAGRATION THAT WILL RAGE ACROSS WORLDS!
FOLLOW ME INSIDE!

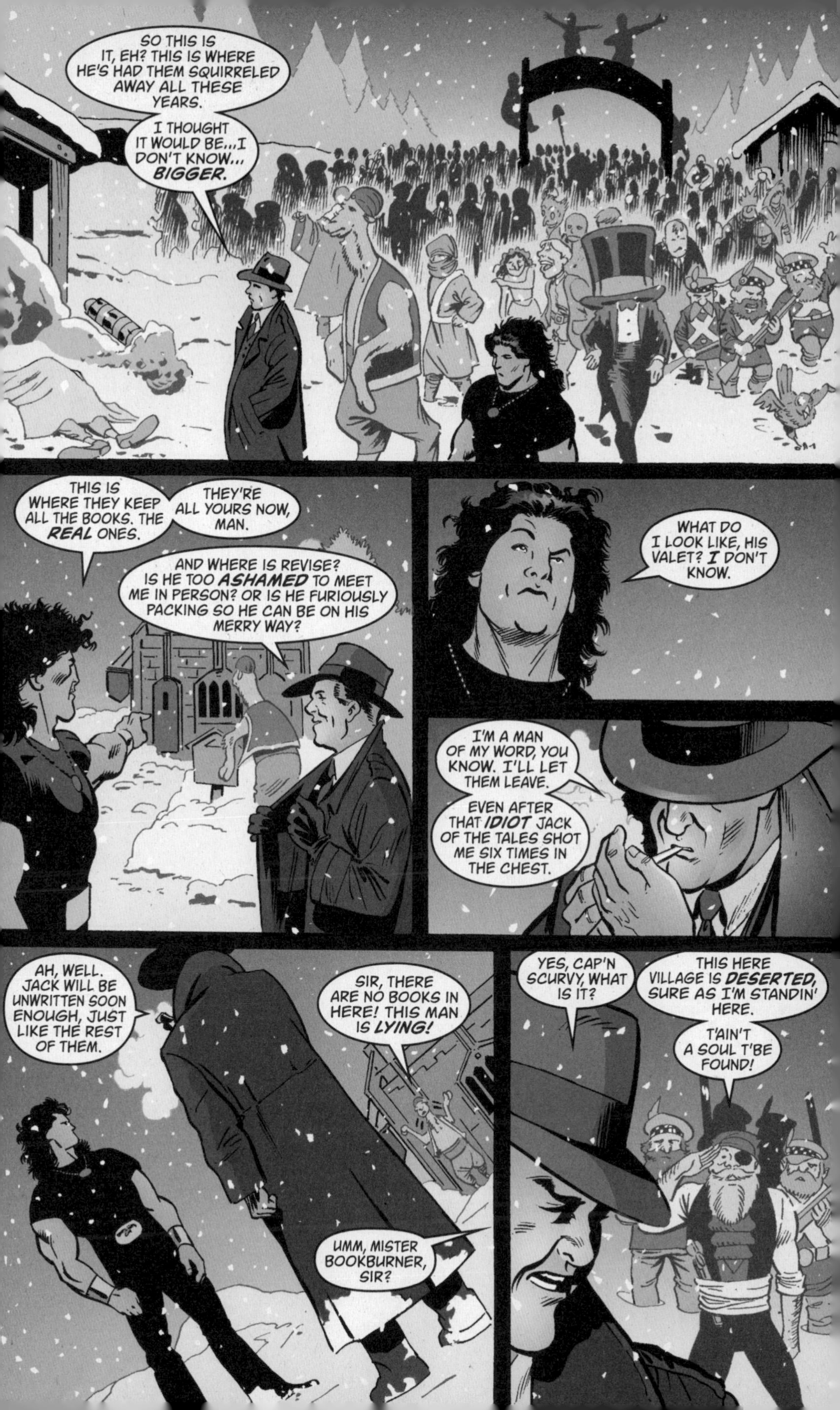
SO THIS IS IT, EH? THIS IS WHERE HE'S HAD THEM SQUIRRELED AWAY ALL THESE YEARS.
I THOUGHT IT WOULD BE...I DON'T KNOW... BIGGER.
THIS IS WHERE THEY KEEP ALL THE BOOKS. THE REAL ONES.
THEY'RE ALL YOURS NOW, MAN.
AND WHERE IS REVISE? IS HE TOO ASHAMED TO MEET ME IN PERSON? OR IS HE FURIOUSLY PACKING SO HE CAN BE ON HIS MERRY WAY?
WHAT DO I LOOK LIKE, HIS VALET? I DON'T KNOW.
I'M A MAN OF MY WORD, YOU KNOW. I'LL LET THEM LEAVE.
EVEN AFTER THAT IDIOT JACK OF THE TALES SHOT ME SIX TIMES IN THE CHEST.
AH, WELL. JACK WILL BE UNWRITTEN SOON ENOUGH, JUST LIKE THE REST OF THEM.
SIR, THERE ARE NO BOOKS IN HERE! THIS MAN IS LYING!
UMM, MISTER BOOKBURNER, SIR?
YES, CAP'N SCURVY, WHAT IS IT?
THIS HERE VILLAGE IS DESERTED, SURE AS I'M STANDIN' HERE.
T'AIN'T A SOUL T'BE FOUND!

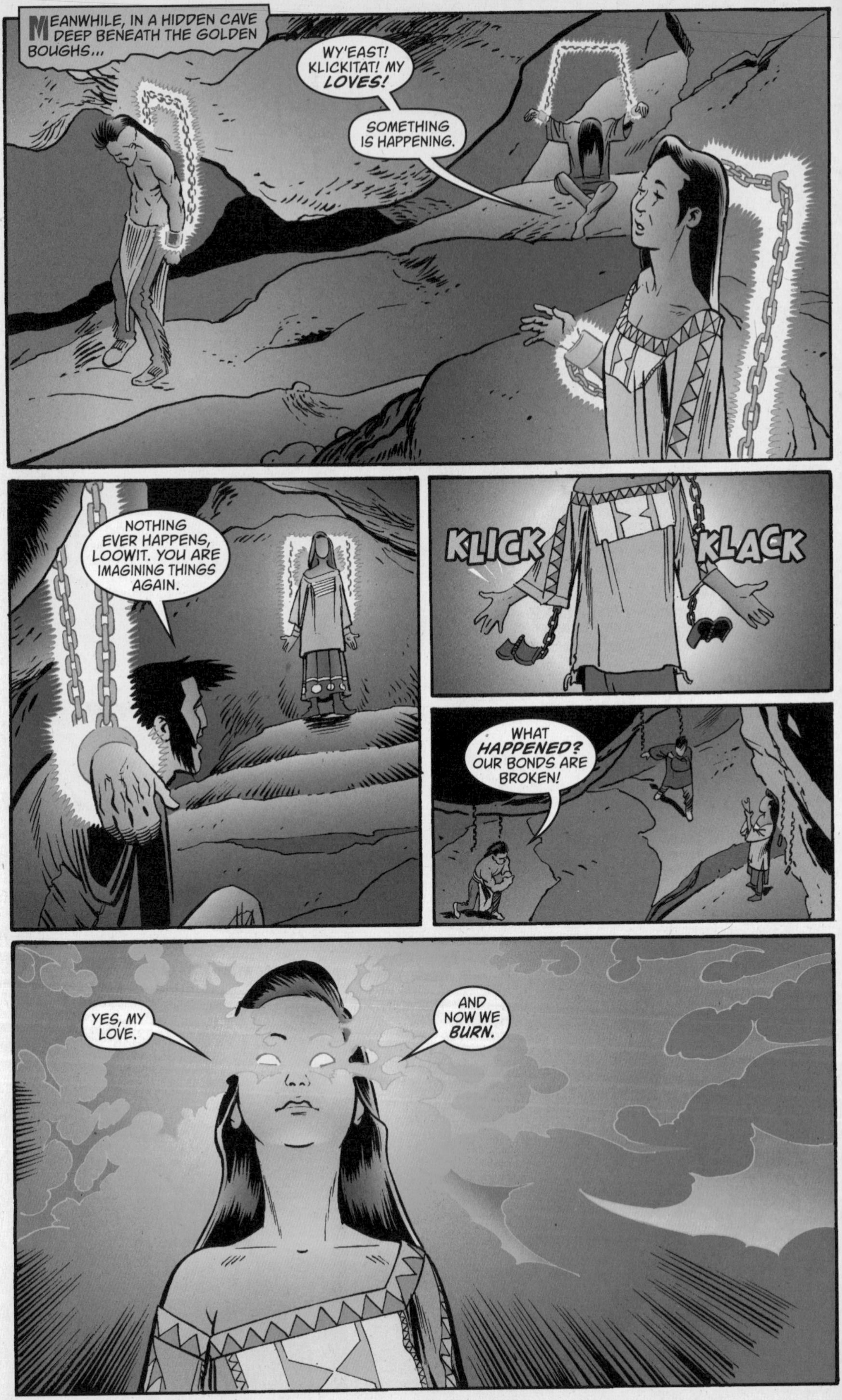
MEANWHILE, IN A HIDDEN CAVE DEEP BENEATH THE GOLDEN BOUGHS...
WY'EAST! KLICKITAT! MY LOVES!
SOMETHING IS HAPPENING.
NOTHING EVER HAPPENS, LOOWIT. YOU ARE IMAGINING THINGS AGAIN.
KLICK
KLACK
WHAT HAPPENED? OUR BONDS ARE BROKEN!
YES, MY LOVE.
AND NOW WE BURN.

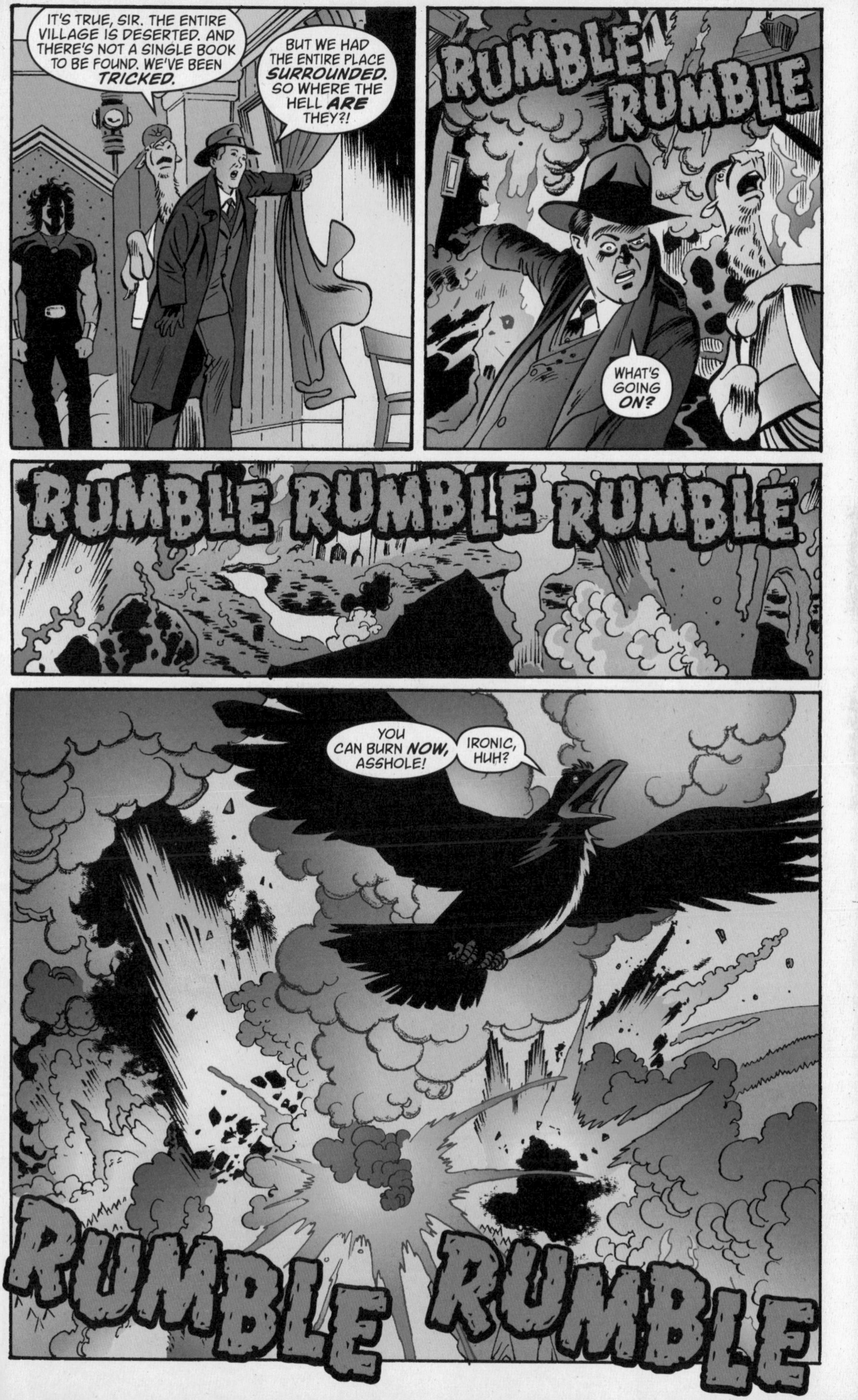

IT'S TRUE, SIR. THE ENTIRE VILLAGE IS DESERTED. AND THERE'S NOT A SINGLE BOOK TO BE FOUND. WE'VE BEEN **TRICKED**.
BUT WE HAD THE ENTIRE PLACE **SURROUNDED**. SO WHERE THE HELL **ARE** THEY?!
RUMBLE RUMBLE
WHAT'S GOING **ON**?
RUMBLE RUMBLE RUMBLE
YOU CAN BURN **NOW**, ASSHOLE!
IRONIC, HUH?
RUMBLE RUMBLE

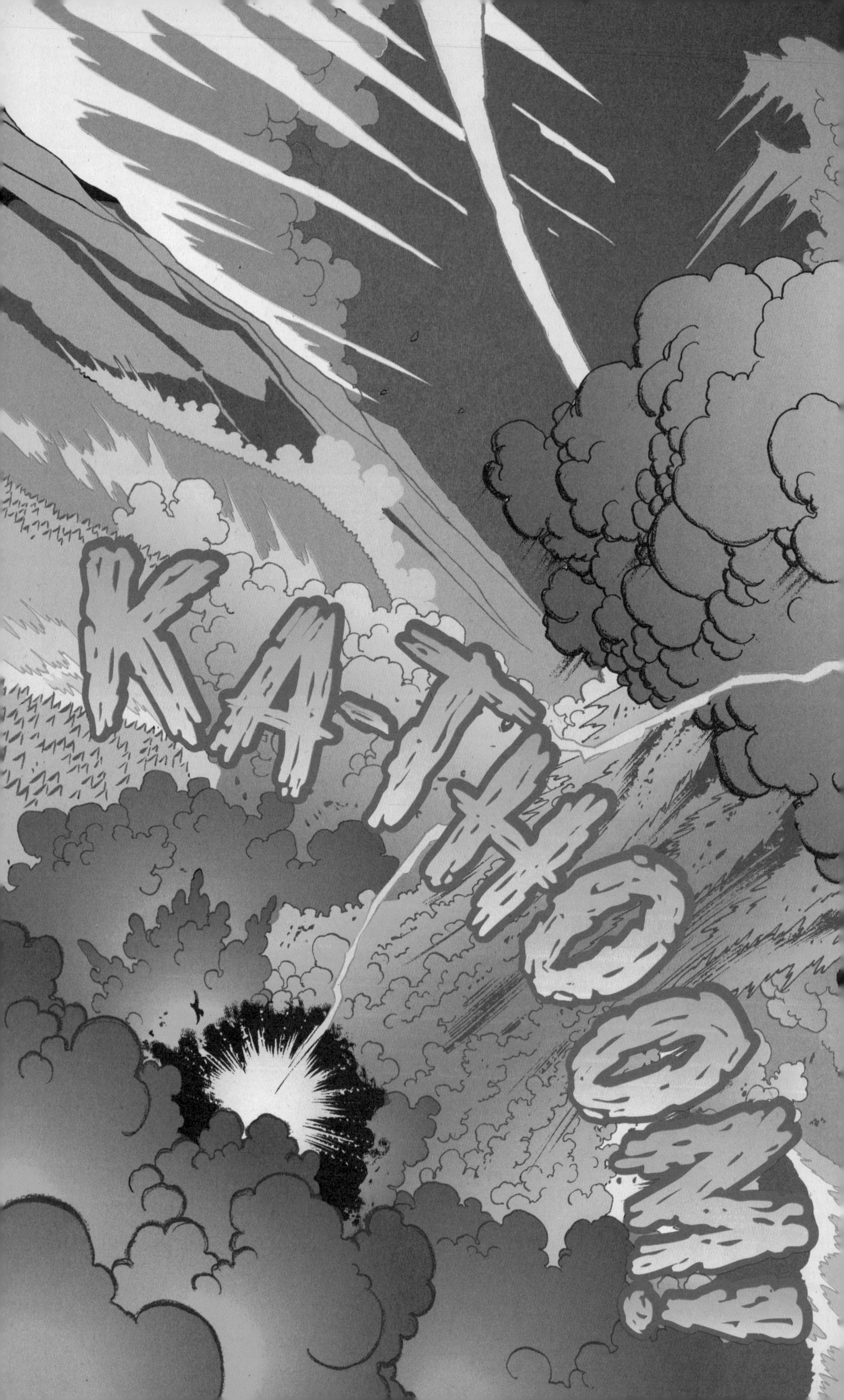
KA-THOOM!

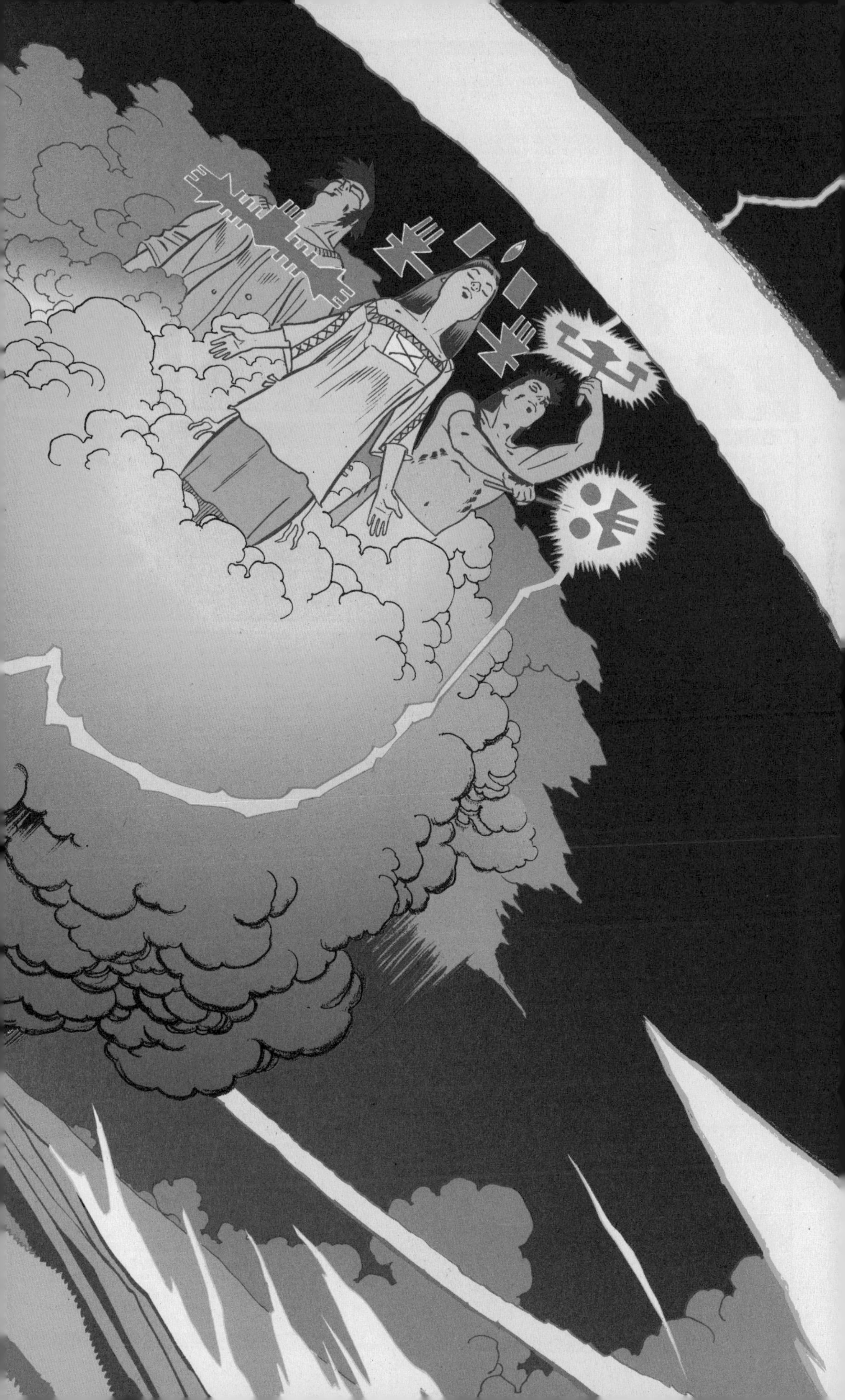

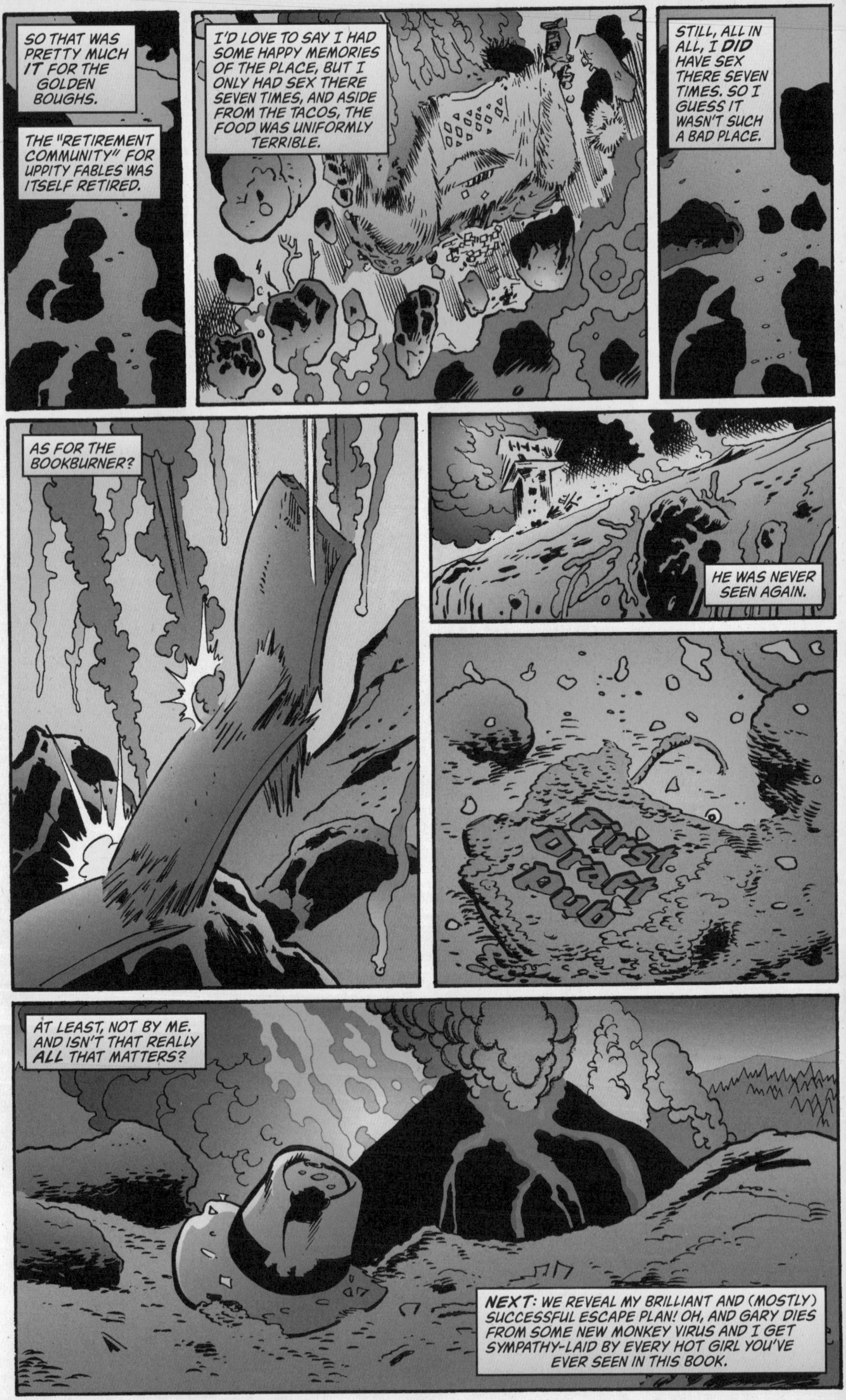
SO THAT WAS PRETTY MUCH IT FOR THE GOLDEN BOUGHS.
THE "RETIREMENT COMMUNITY" FOR UPPITY FABLES WAS ITSELF RETIRED.
I'D LOVE TO SAY I HAD SOME HAPPY MEMORIES OF THE PLACE, BUT I ONLY HAD SEX THERE SEVEN TIMES, AND ASIDE FROM THE TACOS, THE FOOD WAS UNIFORMLY TERRIBLE.
STILL, ALL IN ALL, I DID HAVE SEX THERE SEVEN TIMES. SO I GUESS IT WASN'T SUCH A BAD PLACE.
AS FOR THE BOOKBURNER?
HE WAS NEVER SEEN AGAIN.
First Draft Pub
AT LEAST, NOT BY ME. AND ISN'T THAT REALLY ALL THAT MATTERS?
NEXT: WE REVEAL MY BRILLIANT AND (MOSTLY) SUCCESSFUL ESCAPE PLAN! OH, AND GARY DIES FROM SOME NEW MONKEY VIRUS AND I GET SYMPATHY-LAID BY EVERY HOT GIRL YOU'VE EVER SEEN IN THIS BOOK.

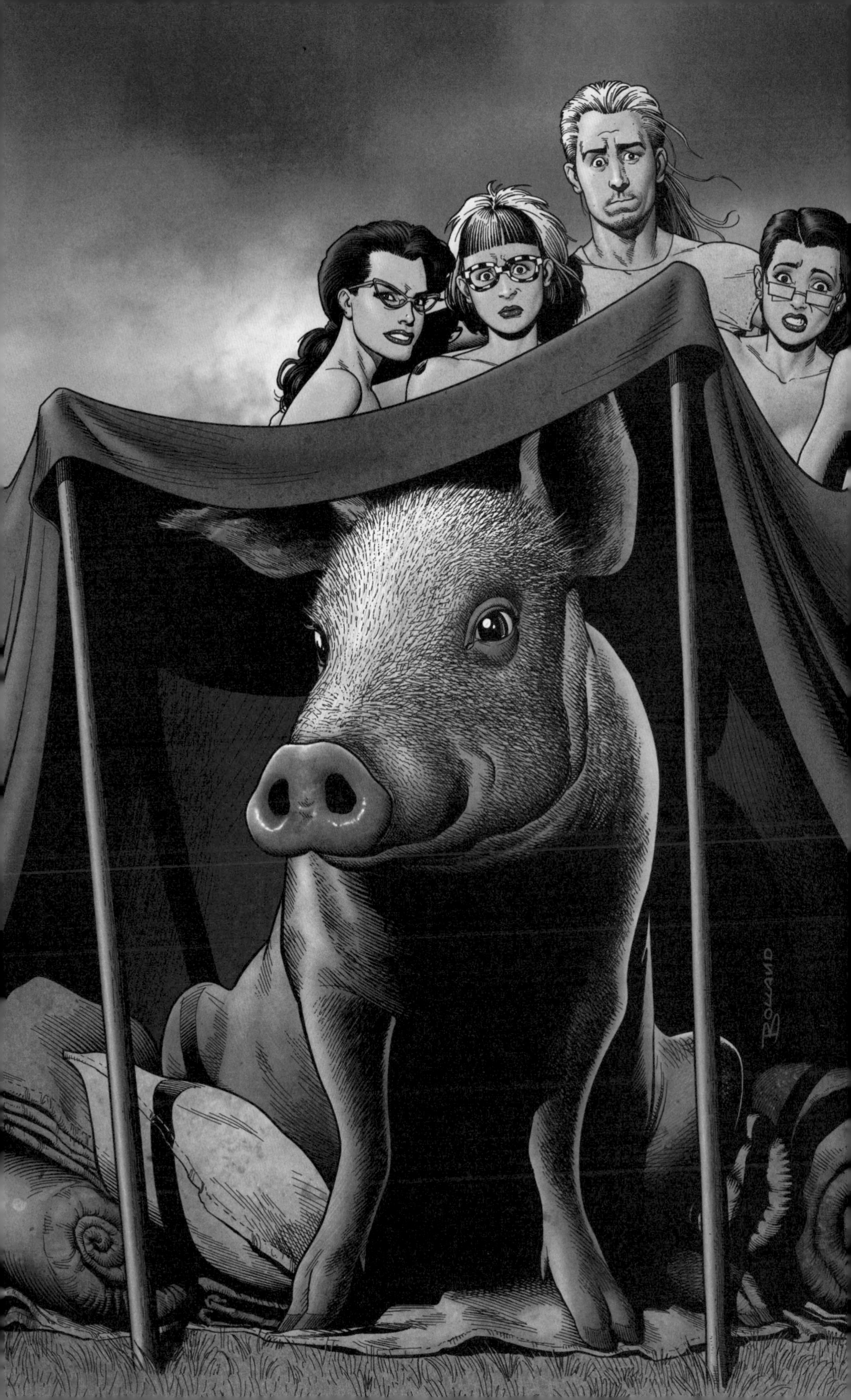
BOLLAND

*"My motto is, if I'm going down,
I'm damn sure going to take the other guy **with me**."*

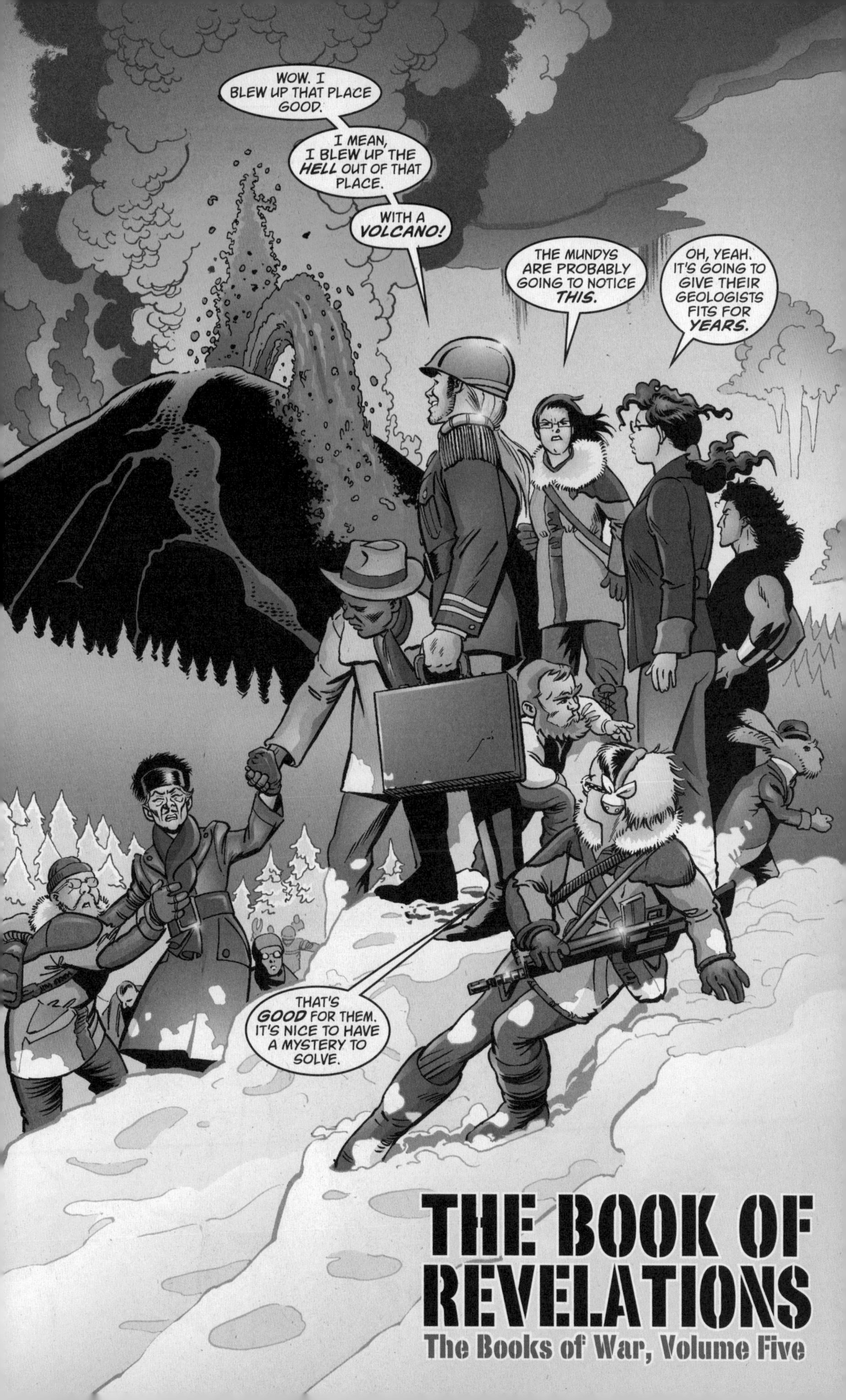
WOW. I BLEW UP THAT PLACE GOOD.
I MEAN, I BLEW UP THE HELL OUT OF THAT PLACE.
WITH A VOLCANO!
THE MUNDYS ARE PROBABLY GOING TO NOTICE THIS.
OH, YEAH. IT'S GOING TO GIVE THEIR GEOLOGISTS FITS FOR YEARS.
THAT'S GOOD FOR THEM. IT'S NICE TO HAVE A MYSTERY TO SOLVE.

THE BOOK OF REVELATIONS

The Books of War, Volume Five

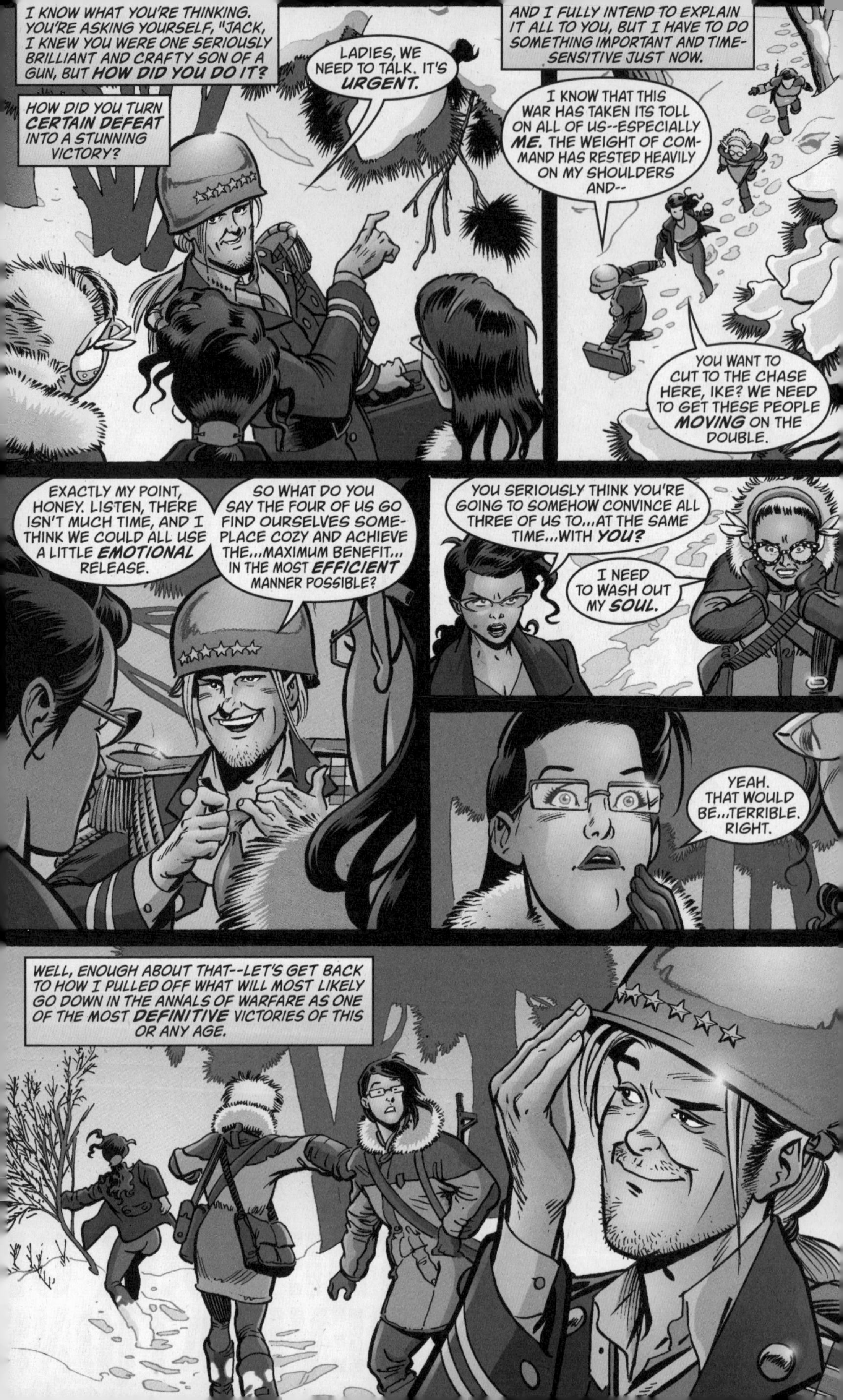

I KNOW WHAT YOU'RE THINKING. YOU'RE ASKING YOURSELF, "JACK, I KNEW YOU WERE ONE SERIOUSLY BRILLIANT AND CRAFTY SON OF A GUN, BUT HOW DID YOU DO IT?
HOW DID YOU TURN CERTAIN DEFEAT INTO A STUNNING VICTORY?
LADIES, WE NEED TO TALK. IT'S URGENT.
AND I FULLY INTEND TO EXPLAIN IT ALL TO YOU, BUT I HAVE TO DO SOMETHING IMPORTANT AND TIME-SENSITIVE JUST NOW.
I KNOW THAT THIS WAR HAS TAKEN ITS TOLL ON ALL OF US--ESPECIALLY ME. THE WEIGHT OF COMMAND HAS RESTED HEAVILY ON MY SHOULDERS AND--
YOU WANT TO CUT TO THE CHASE HERE, IKE? WE NEED TO GET THESE PEOPLE MOVING ON THE DOUBLE.
EXACTLY MY POINT, HONEY. LISTEN, THERE ISN'T MUCH TIME, AND I THINK WE COULD ALL USE A LITTLE EMOTIONAL RELEASE.
SO WHAT DO YOU SAY THE FOUR OF US GO FIND OURSELVES SOMEPLACE COZY AND ACHIEVE THE...MAXIMUM BENEFIT... IN THE MOST EFFICIENT MANNER POSSIBLE?
YOU SERIOUSLY THINK YOU'RE GOING TO SOMEHOW CONVINCE ALL THREE OF US TO...AT THE SAME TIME...WITH YOU?
I NEED TO WASH OUT MY SOUL.
YEAH. THAT WOULD BE...TERRIBLE. RIGHT.
WELL, ENOUGH ABOUT THAT--LET'S GET BACK TO HOW I PULLED OFF WHAT WILL MOST LIKELY GO DOWN IN THE ANNALS OF WARFARE AS ONE OF THE MOST DEFINITIVE VICTORIES OF THIS OR ANY AGE.

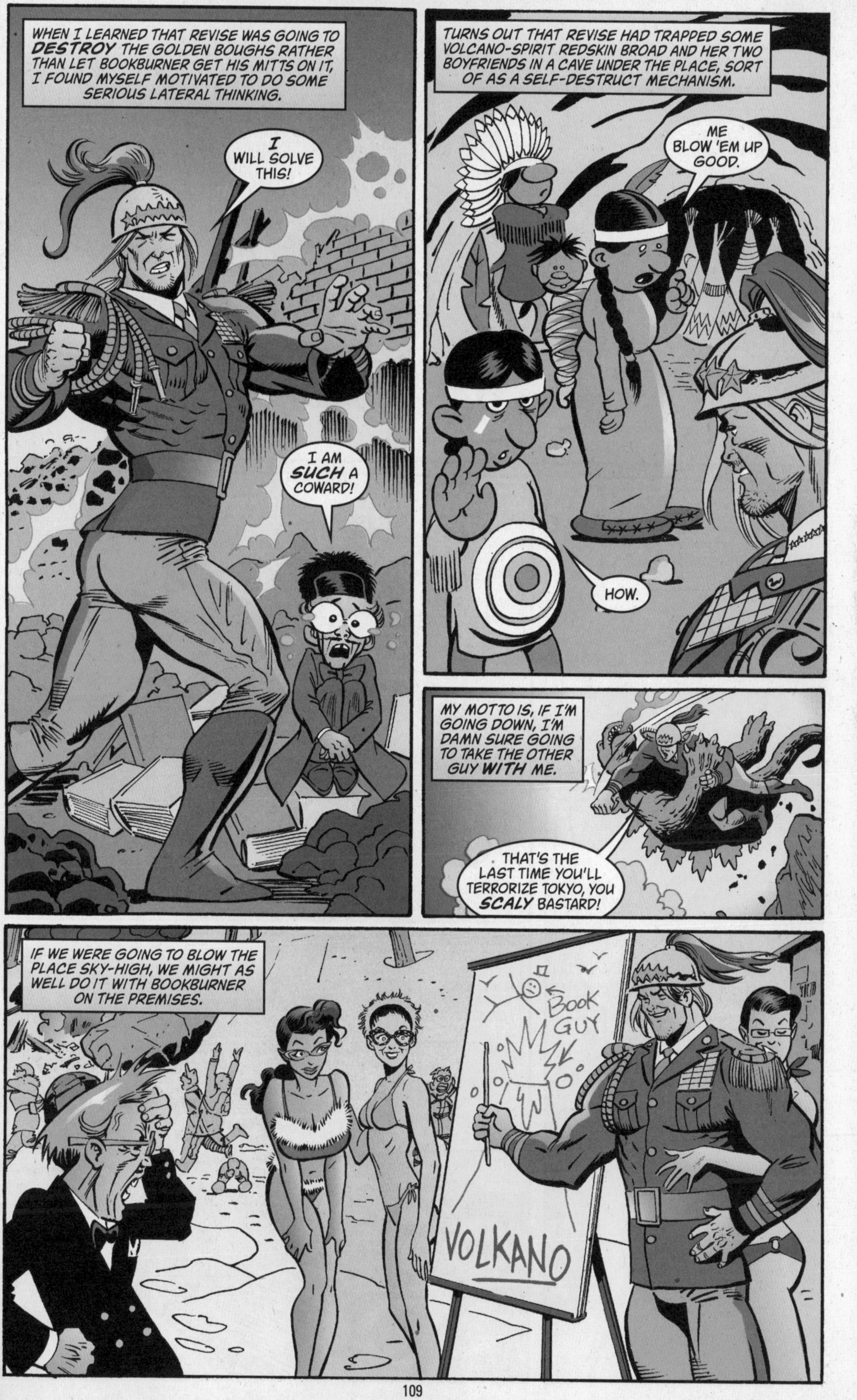
WHEN I LEARNED THAT REVISE WAS GOING TO DESTROY THE GOLDEN BOUGHS RATHER THAN LET BOOKBURNER GET HIS MITTS ON IT, I FOUND MYSELF MOTIVATED TO DO SOME SERIOUS LATERAL THINKING.
I WILL SOLVE THIS!
I AM SUCH A COWARD!
TURNS OUT THAT REVISE HAD TRAPPED SOME VOLCANO-SPIRIT REDSKIN BROAD AND HER TWO BOYFRIENDS IN A CAVE UNDER THE PLACE, SORT OF AS A SELF-DESTRUCT MECHANISM.
ME BLOW 'EM UP GOOD.
HOW.
MY MOTTO IS, IF I'M GOING DOWN, I'M DAMN SURE GOING TO TAKE THE OTHER GUY WITH ME.
THAT'S THE LAST TIME YOU'LL TERRORIZE TOKYO, YOU SCALY BASTARD!
IF WE WERE GOING TO BLOW THE PLACE SKY-HIGH, WE MIGHT AS WELL DO IT WITH BOOKBURNER ON THE PREMISES.
BOOK GUY
VOLKANO

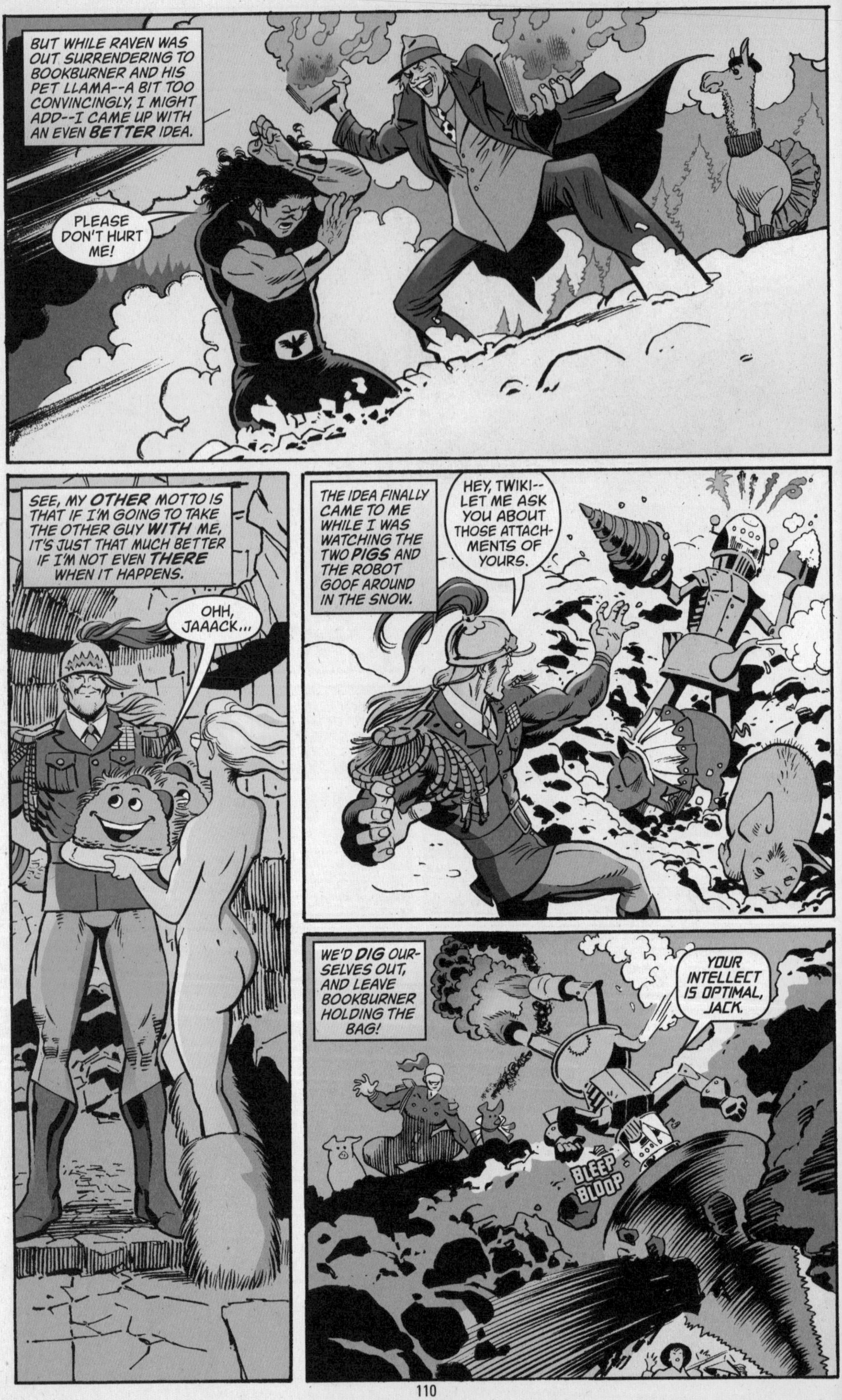
BUT WHILE RAVEN WAS OUT SURRENDERING TO BOOKBURNER AND HIS PET LLAMA--A BIT TOO CONVINCINGLY, I MIGHT ADD--I CAME UP WITH AN EVEN BETTER IDEA.
PLEASE DON'T HURT ME!
SEE, MY OTHER MOTTO IS THAT IF I'M GOING TO TAKE THE OTHER GUY WITH ME, IT'S JUST THAT MUCH BETTER IF I'M NOT EVEN THERE WHEN IT HAPPENS.
OHH, JAAACK...
THE IDEA FINALLY CAME TO ME WHILE I WAS WATCHING THE TWO PIGS AND THE ROBOT GOOF AROUND IN THE SNOW.
HEY, TWIKI-- LET ME ASK YOU ABOUT THOSE ATTACHMENTS OF YOURS.
WE'D DIG OURSELVES OUT, AND LEAVE BOOKBURNER HOLDING THE BAG!
YOUR INTELLECT IS OPTIMAL, JACK.
BLEEP BLOOP

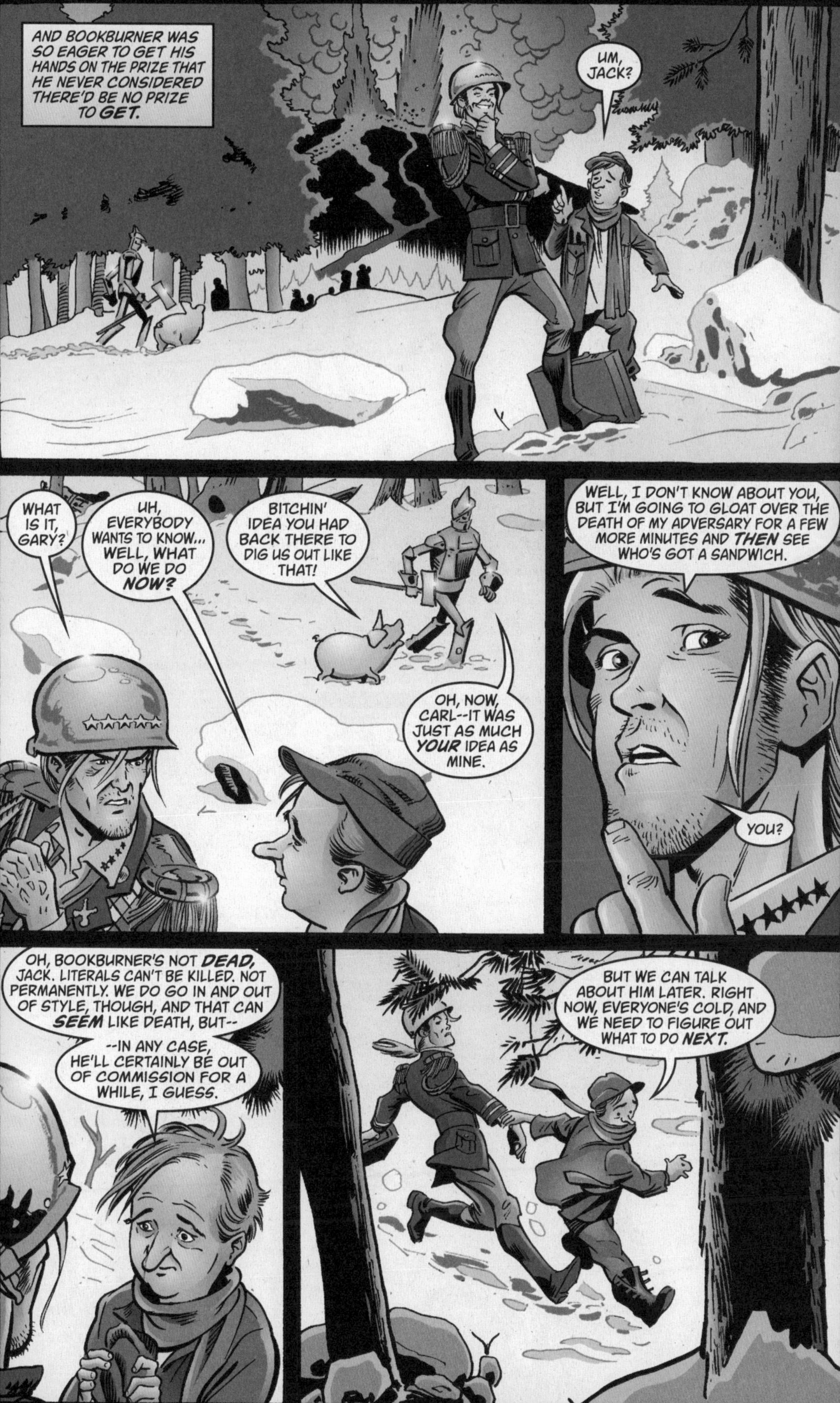
AND BOOKBURNER WAS SO EAGER TO GET HIS HANDS ON THE PRIZE THAT HE NEVER CONSIDERED THERE'D BE NO PRIZE TO *GET*.
UM, JACK?
WHAT IS IT, GARY?
UH, EVERYBODY WANTS TO KNOW... WELL, WHAT DO WE DO *NOW?*
BITCHIN' IDEA YOU HAD BACK THERE TO DIG US OUT LIKE THAT!
OH, NOW, CARL--IT WAS JUST AS MUCH *YOUR* IDEA AS MINE.
WELL, I DON'T KNOW ABOUT YOU, BUT I'M GOING TO GLOAT OVER THE DEATH OF MY ADVERSARY FOR A FEW MORE MINUTES AND *THEN* SEE WHO'S GOT A SANDWICH.
YOU?
OH, BOOKBURNER'S NOT *DEAD*, JACK. LITERALS CAN'T BE KILLED. NOT PERMANENTLY. WE DO GO IN AND OUT OF STYLE, THOUGH, AND THAT CAN *SEEM* LIKE DEATH, BUT--
--IN ANY CASE, HE'LL CERTAINLY BE OUT OF COMMISSION FOR A WHILE, I GUESS.
BUT WE CAN TALK ABOUT HIM LATER. RIGHT NOW, EVERYONE'S COLD, AND WE NEED TO FIGURE OUT WHAT TO DO *NEXT*.

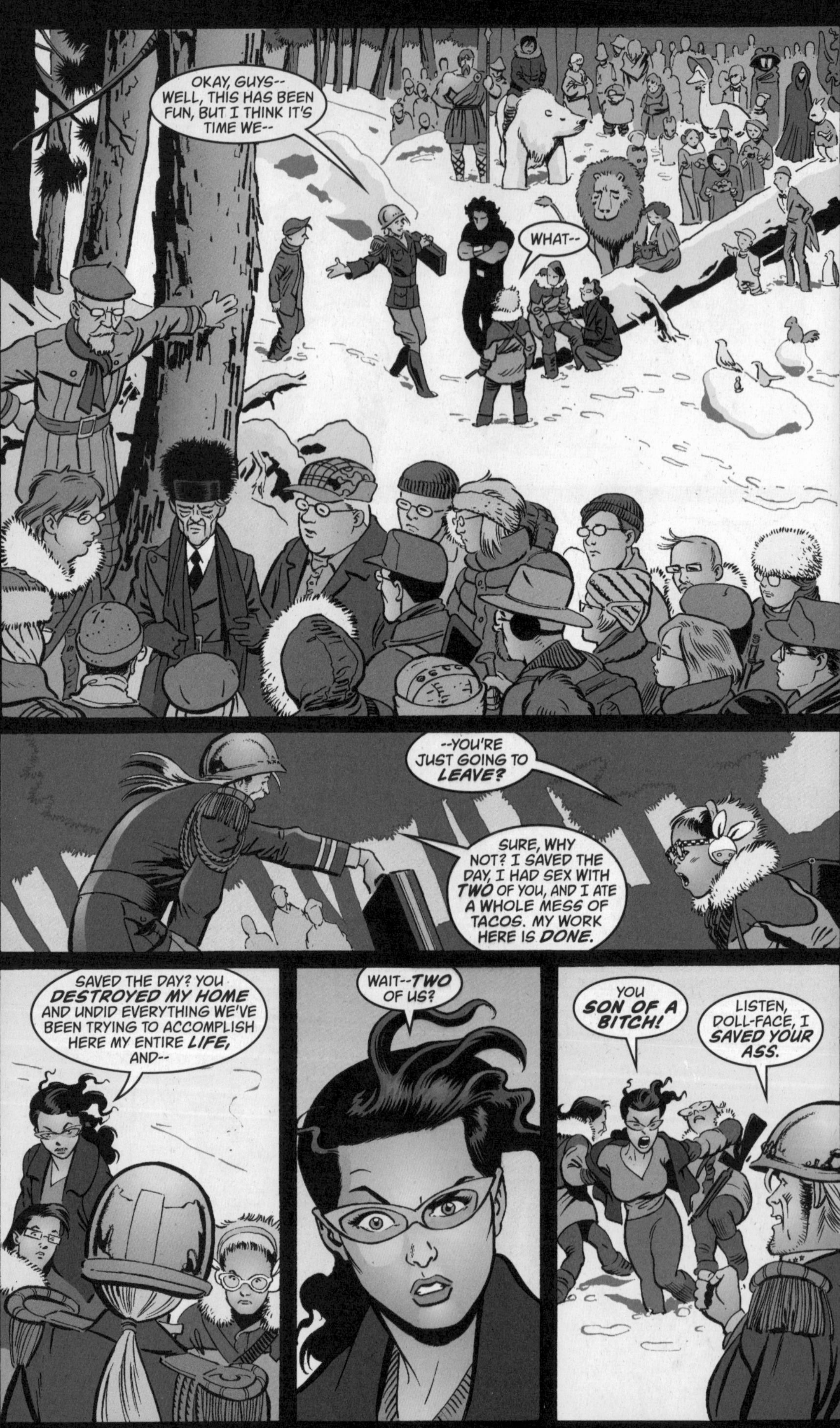
OKAY, GUYS-- WELL, THIS HAS BEEN FUN, BUT I THINK IT'S TIME WE--
WHAT--
--YOU'RE JUST GOING TO LEAVE?
SURE, WHY NOT? I SAVED THE DAY, I HAD SEX WITH TWO OF YOU, AND I ATE A WHOLE MESS OF TACOS. MY WORK HERE IS DONE.
SAVED THE DAY? YOU DESTROYED MY HOME AND UNDID EVERYTHING WE'VE BEEN TRYING TO ACCOMPLISH HERE MY ENTIRE LIFE, AND--
WAIT--TWO OF US?
YOU SON OF A BITCH!
LISTEN, DOLL-FACE, I SAVED YOUR ASS.

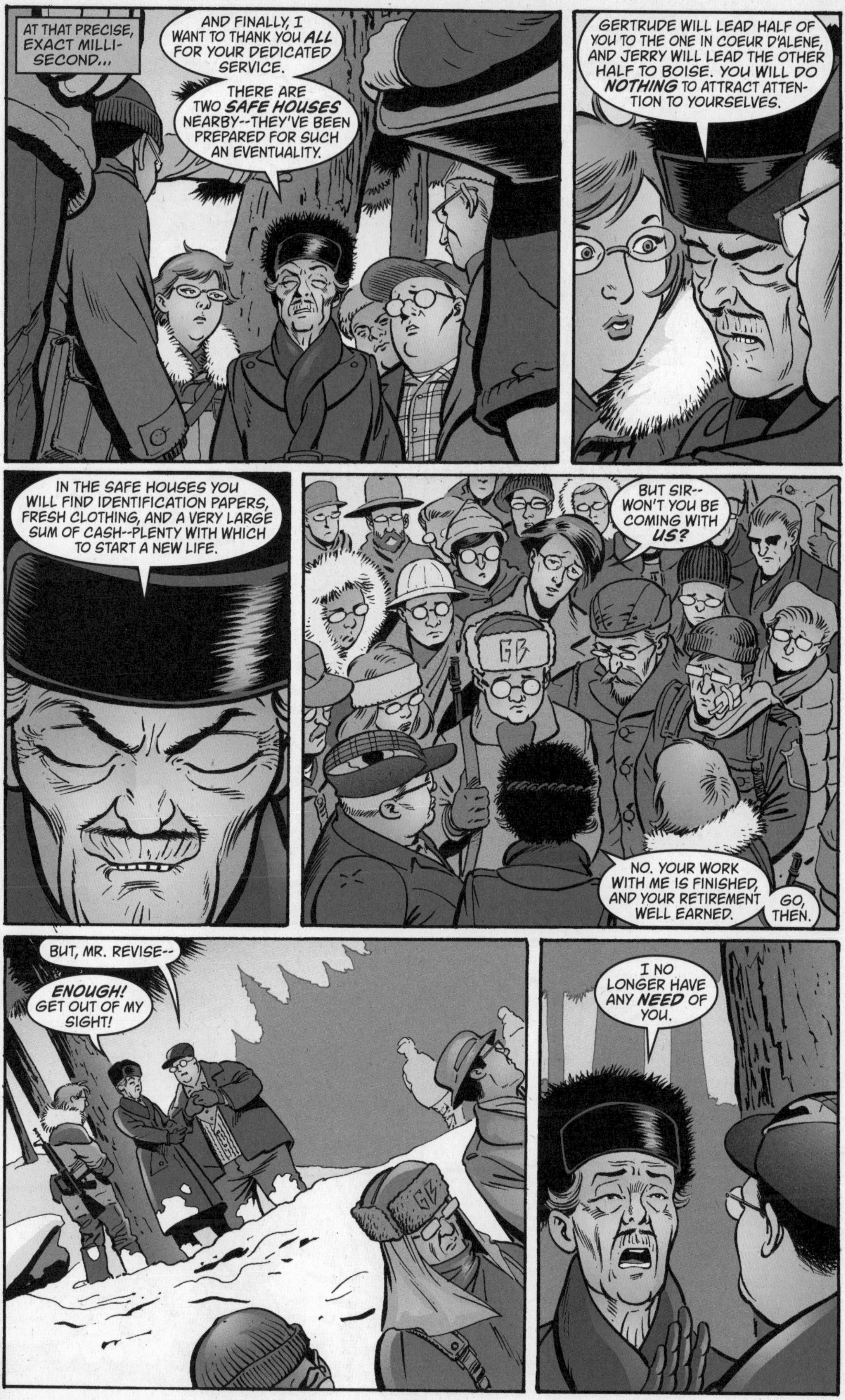

AT THAT PRECISE, EXACT MILLI-SECOND...
AND FINALLY, I WANT TO THANK YOU ALL FOR YOUR DEDICATED SERVICE.
THERE ARE TWO SAFE HOUSES NEARBY--THEY'VE BEEN PREPARED FOR SUCH AN EVENTUALITY.
GERTRUDE WILL LEAD HALF OF YOU TO THE ONE IN COEUR D'ALENE, AND JERRY WILL LEAD THE OTHER HALF TO BOISE. YOU WILL DO NOTHING TO ATTRACT ATTENTION TO YOURSELVES.
IN THE SAFE HOUSES YOU WILL FIND IDENTIFICATION PAPERS, FRESH CLOTHING, AND A VERY LARGE SUM OF CASH--PLENTY WITH WHICH TO START A NEW LIFE.
BUT SIR--WON'T YOU BE COMING WITH US?
GB
NO. YOUR WORK WITH ME IS FINISHED, AND YOUR RETIREMENT WELL EARNED.
GO, THEN.
BUT, MR. REVISE--
ENOUGH! GET OUT OF MY SIGHT!
GB
I NO LONGER HAVE ANY NEED OF YOU.

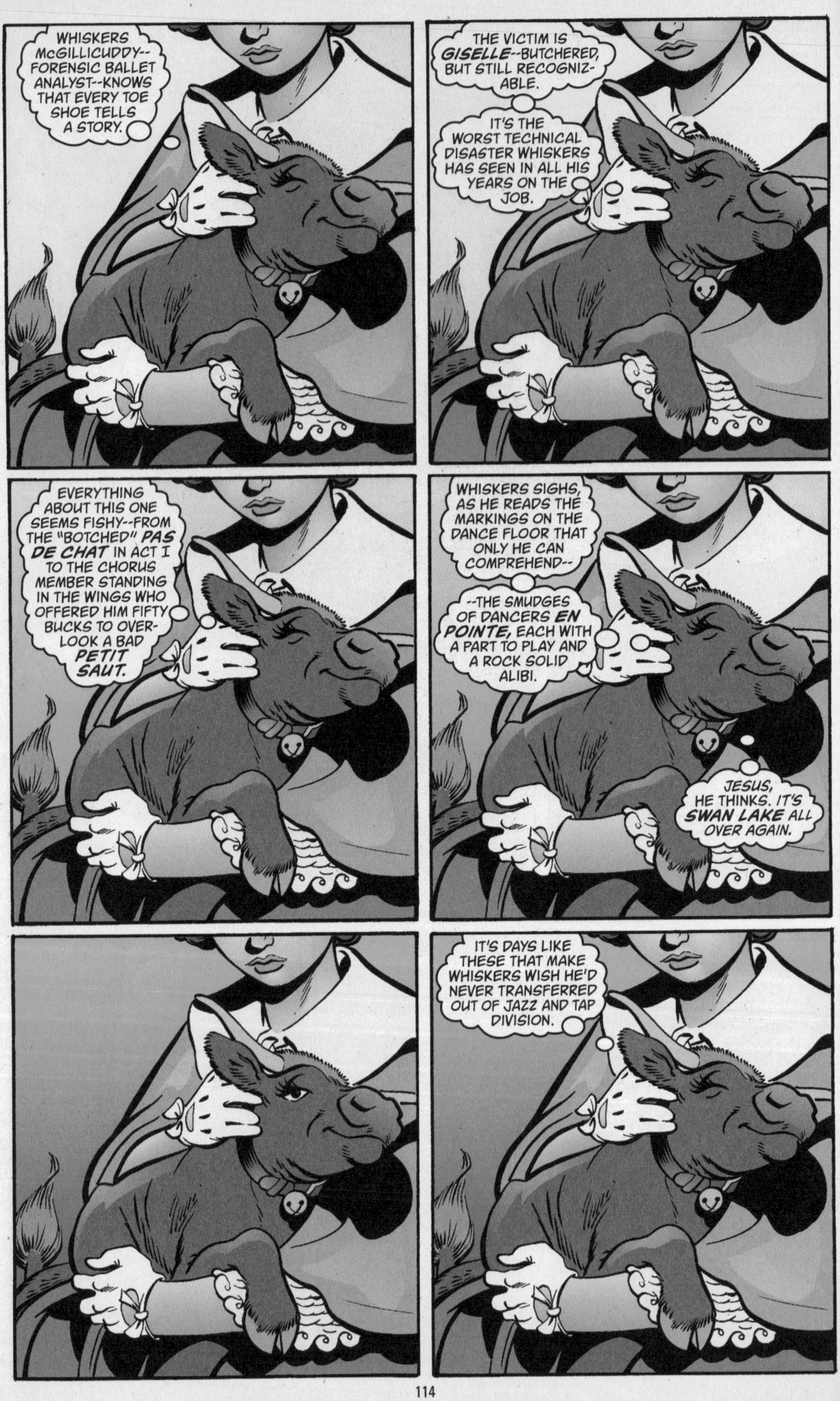
WHISKERS McGILLICUDDY--FORENSIC BALLET ANALYST--KNOWS THAT EVERY TOE SHOE TELLS A STORY.
THE VICTIM IS GISELLE--BUTCHERED, BUT STILL RECOGNIZ-ABLE.
IT'S THE WORST TECHNICAL DISASTER WHISKERS HAS SEEN IN ALL HIS YEARS ON THE JOB.
EVERYTHING ABOUT THIS ONE SEEMS FISHY--FROM THE "BOTCHED" PAS DE CHAT IN ACT I TO THE CHORUS MEMBER STANDING IN THE WINGS WHO OFFERED HIM FIFTY BUCKS TO OVER-LOOK A BAD PETIT SAUT.
WHISKERS SIGHS, AS HE READS THE MARKINGS ON THE DANCE FLOOR THAT ONLY HE CAN COMPREHEND--
--THE SMUDGES OF DANCERS EN POINTE, EACH WITH A PART TO PLAY AND A ROCK SOLID ALIBI.
JESUS, HE THINKS. IT'S SWAN LAKE ALL OVER AGAIN.
IT'S DAYS LIKE THESE THAT MAKE WHISKERS WISH HE'D NEVER TRANSFERRED OUT OF JAZZ AND TAP DIVISION.

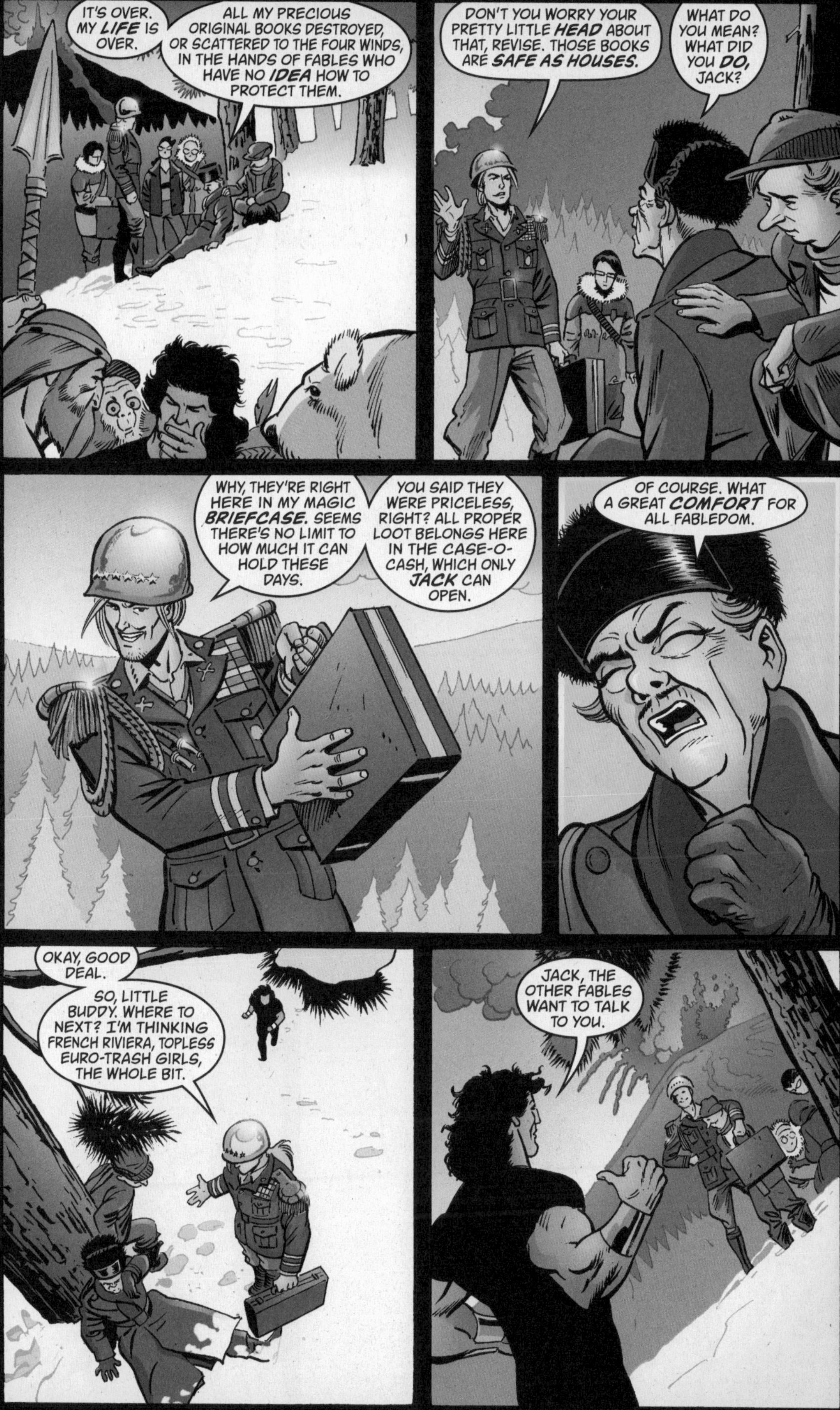

IT'S OVER. MY LIFE IS OVER.
ALL MY PRECIOUS ORIGINAL BOOKS DESTROYED, OR SCATTERED TO THE FOUR WINDS, IN THE HANDS OF FABLES WHO HAVE NO IDEA HOW TO PROTECT THEM.
DON'T YOU WORRY YOUR PRETTY LITTLE HEAD ABOUT THAT, REVISE. THOSE BOOKS ARE SAFE AS HOUSES.
WHAT DO YOU MEAN? WHAT DID YOU DO, JACK?
WHY, THEY'RE RIGHT HERE IN MY MAGIC BRIEFCASE. SEEMS THERE'S NO LIMIT TO HOW MUCH IT CAN HOLD THESE DAYS.
YOU SAID THEY WERE PRICELESS, RIGHT? ALL PROPER LOOT BELONGS HERE IN THE CASE-O-CASH, WHICH ONLY JACK CAN OPEN.
OF COURSE. WHAT A GREAT COMFORT FOR ALL FABLEDOM.
OKAY, GOOD DEAL.
SO, LITTLE BUDDY. WHERE TO NEXT? I'M THINKING FRENCH RIVIERA, TOPLESS EURO-TRASH GIRLS, THE WHOLE BIT.
JACK, THE OTHER FABLES WANT TO TALK TO YOU.

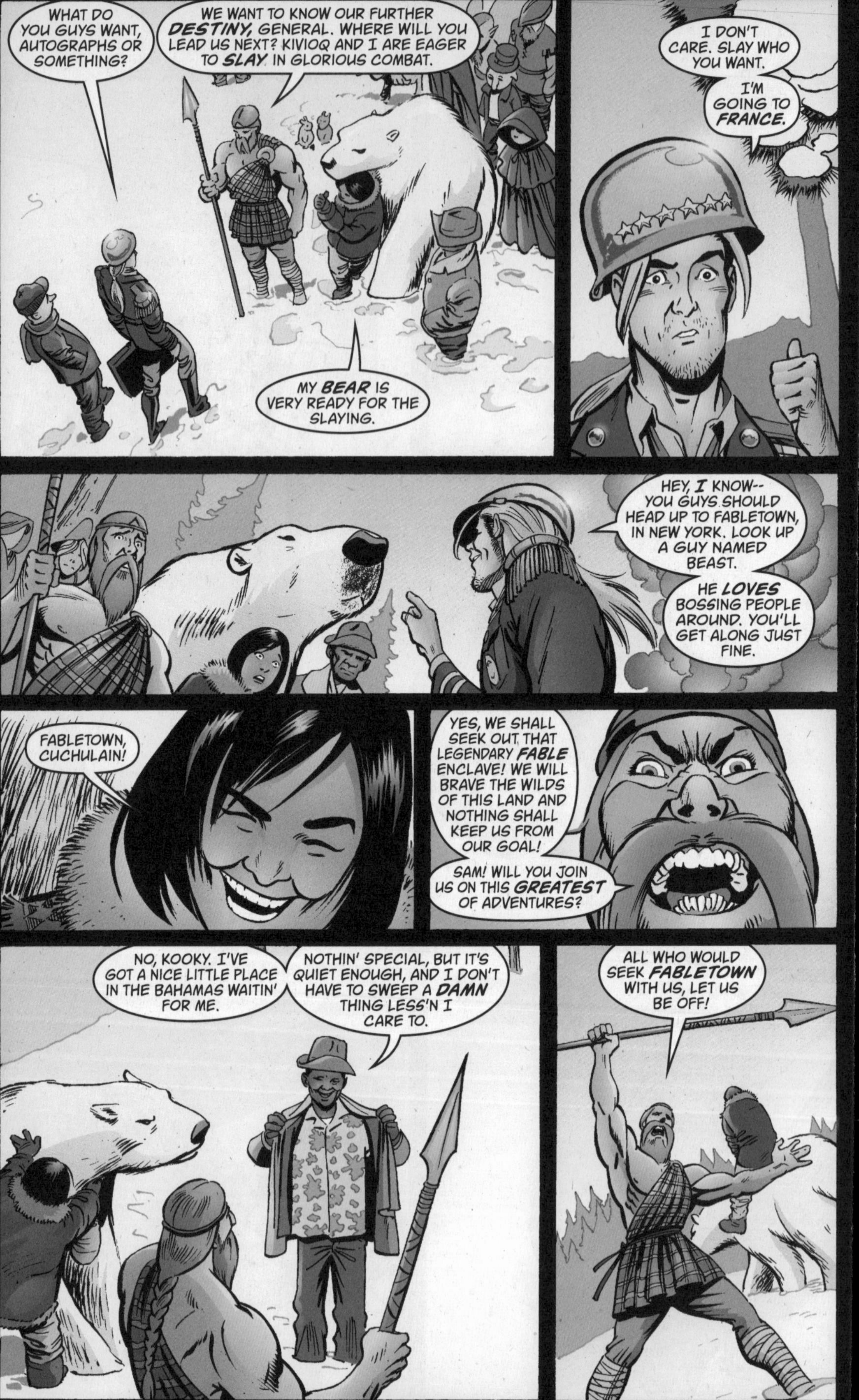
WHAT DO YOU GUYS WANT, AUTOGRAPHS OR SOMETHING?
WE WANT TO KNOW OUR FURTHER DESTINY, GENERAL. WHERE WILL YOU LEAD US NEXT? KIVIOQ AND I ARE EAGER TO SLAY IN GLORIOUS COMBAT.
MY BEAR IS VERY READY FOR THE SLAYING.
I DON'T CARE. SLAY WHO YOU WANT.
I'M GOING TO FRANCE.
HEY, I KNOW-- YOU GUYS SHOULD HEAD UP TO FABLETOWN, IN NEW YORK. LOOK UP A GUY NAMED BEAST.
HE LOVES BOSSING PEOPLE AROUND. YOU'LL GET ALONG JUST FINE.
FABLETOWN, CUCHULAIN!
YES, WE SHALL SEEK OUT THAT LEGENDARY FABLE ENCLAVE! WE WILL BRAVE THE WILDS OF THIS LAND AND NOTHING SHALL KEEP US FROM OUR GOAL!
SAM! WILL YOU JOIN US ON THIS GREATEST OF ADVENTURES?
NO, KOOKY. I'VE GOT A NICE LITTLE PLACE IN THE BAHAMAS WAITIN' FOR ME.
NOTHIN' SPECIAL, BUT IT'S QUIET ENOUGH, AND I DON'T HAVE TO SWEEP A DAMN THING LESS'N I CARE TO.
ALL WHO WOULD SEEK FABLETOWN WITH US, LET US BE OFF!

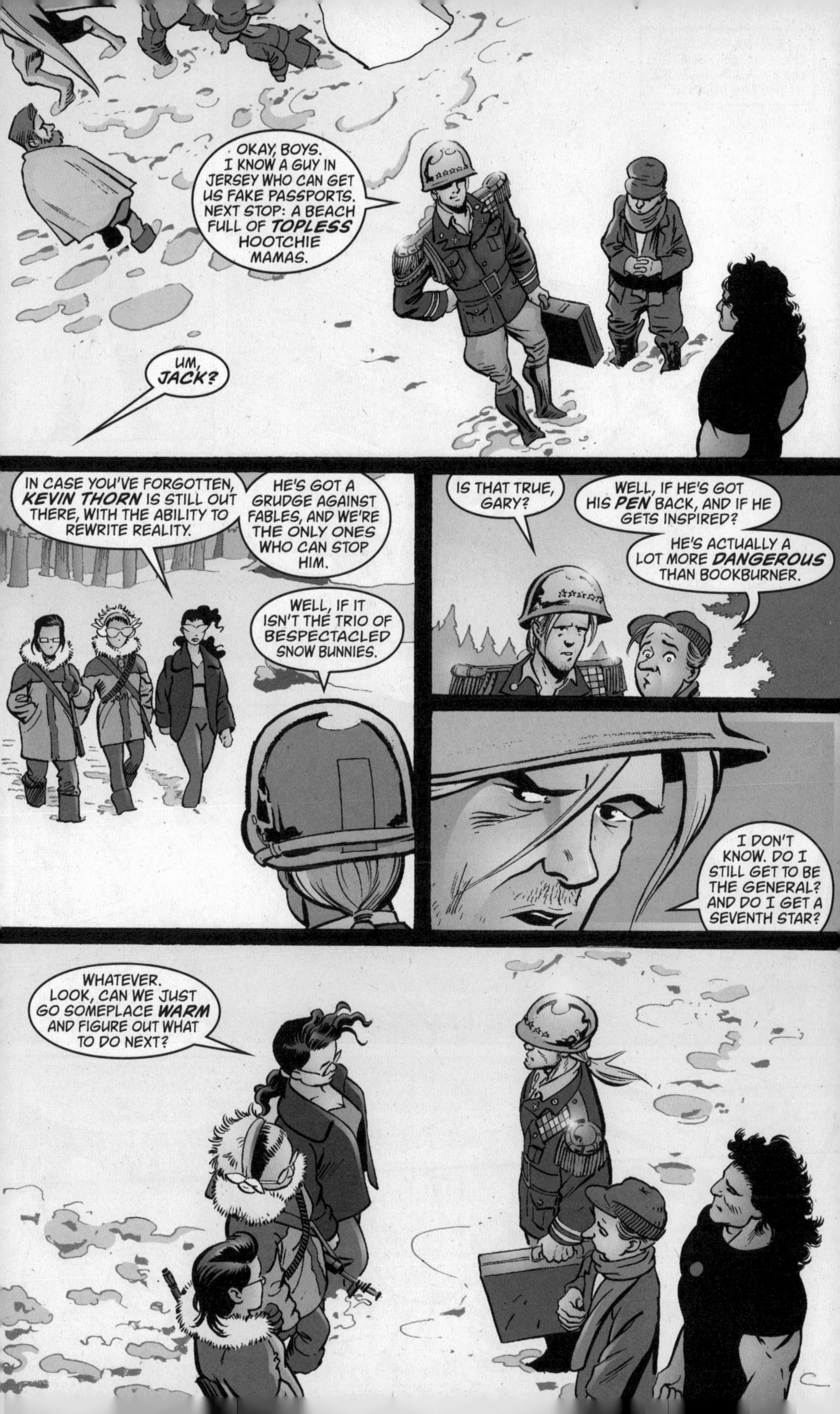

OKAY, BOYS. I KNOW A GUY IN JERSEY WHO CAN GET US FAKE PASSPORTS. NEXT STOP: A BEACH FULL OF TOPLESS HOOTCHIE MAMAS.
UM, JACK?
IN CASE YOU'VE FORGOTTEN, KEVIN THORN IS STILL OUT THERE, WITH THE ABILITY TO REWRITE REALITY.
HE'S GOT A GRUDGE AGAINST FABLES, AND WE'RE THE ONLY ONES WHO CAN STOP HIM.
WELL, IF IT ISN'T THE TRIO OF BESPECTACLED SNOW BUNNIES.
IS THAT TRUE, GARY?
WELL, IF HE'S GOT HIS PEN BACK, AND IF HE GETS INSPIRED?
HE'S ACTUALLY A LOT MORE DANGEROUS THAN BOOKBURNER.
I DON'T KNOW. DO I STILL GET TO BE THE GENERAL? AND DO I GET A SEVENTH STAR?
WHATEVER. LOOK, CAN WE JUST GO SOMEPLACE WARM AND FIGURE OUT WHAT TO DO NEXT?

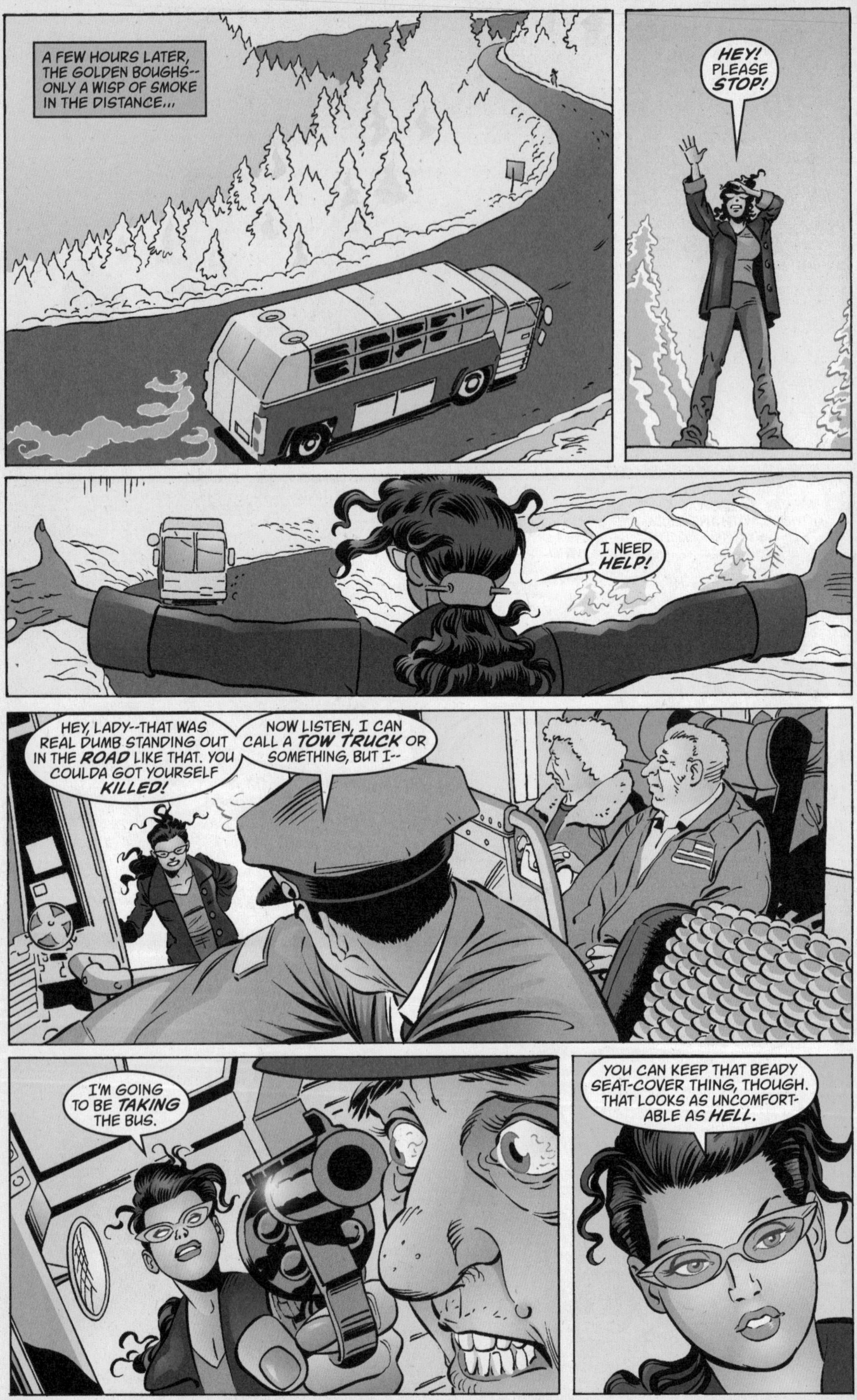
A FEW HOURS LATER, THE GOLDEN BOUGHS--ONLY A WISP OF SMOKE IN THE DISTANCE...
HEY! PLEASE STOP!
I NEED HELP!
HEY, LADY--THAT WAS REAL DUMB STANDING OUT IN THE ROAD LIKE THAT. YOU COULDA GOT YOURSELF KILLED!
NOW LISTEN, I CAN CALL A TOW TRUCK OR SOMETHING, BUT I--
I'M GOING TO BE TAKING THE BUS.
YOU CAN KEEP THAT BEADY SEAT-COVER THING, THOUGH. THAT LOOKS AS UNCOMFORTABLE AS HELL.

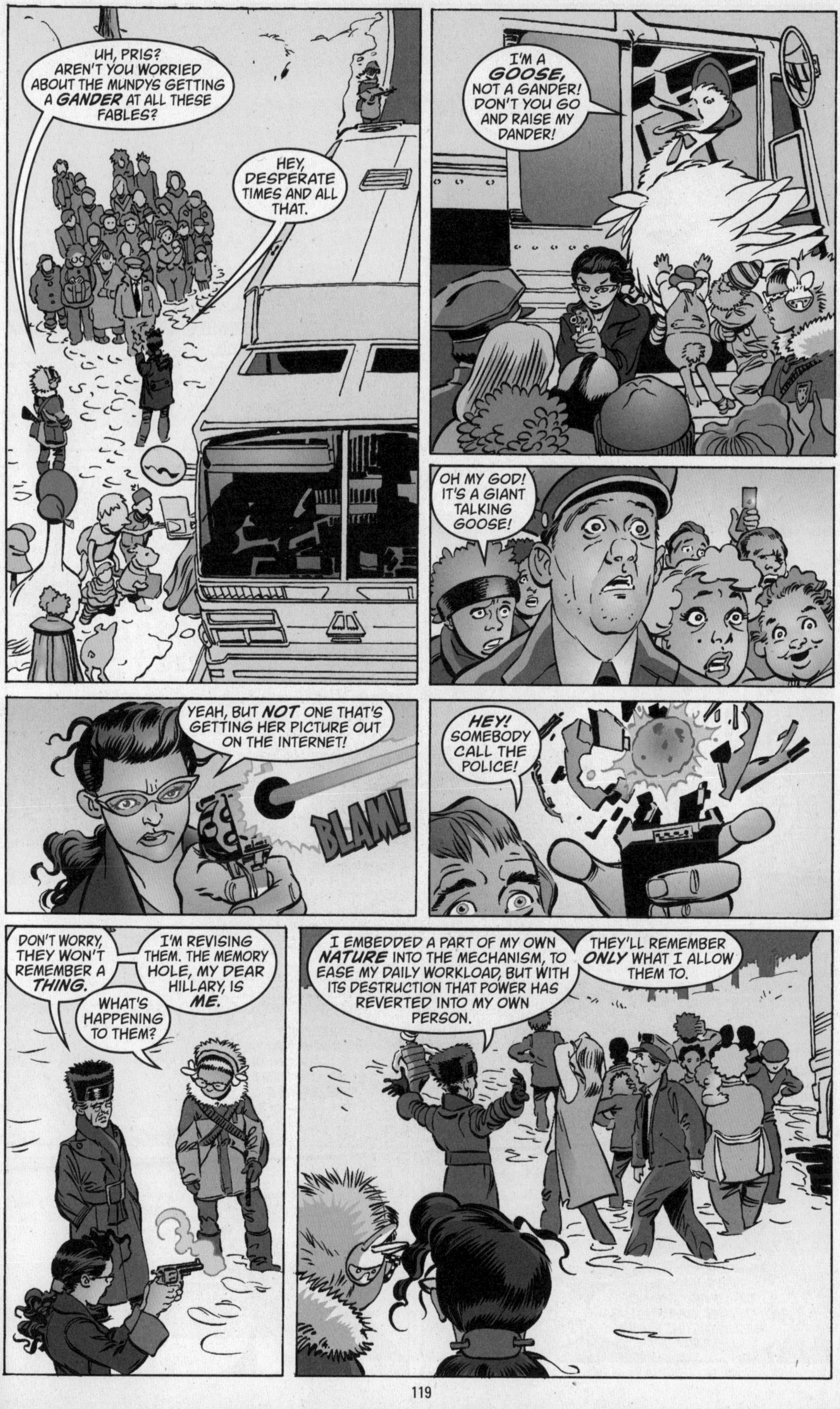
UH, PRIS? AREN'T YOU WORRIED ABOUT THE MUNDYS GETTING A GANDER AT ALL THESE FABLES?
HEY, DESPERATE TIMES AND ALL THAT.
I'M A GOOSE, NOT A GANDER! DON'T YOU GO AND RAISE MY DANDER!
OH MY GOD! IT'S A GIANT TALKING GOOSE!
YEAH, BUT NOT ONE THAT'S GETTING HER PICTURE OUT ON THE INTERNET!
BLAM!
HEY! SOMEBODY CALL THE POLICE!
DON'T WORRY, THEY WON'T REMEMBER A THING.
WHAT'S HAPPENING TO THEM?
I'M REVISING THEM. THE MEMORY HOLE, MY DEAR HILLARY, IS ME.
I EMBEDDED A PART OF MY OWN NATURE INTO THE MECHANISM, TO EASE MY DAILY WORKLOAD, BUT WITH ITS DESTRUCTION THAT POWER HAS REVERTED INTO MY OWN PERSON.
THEY'LL REMEMBER ONLY WHAT I ALLOW THEM TO.

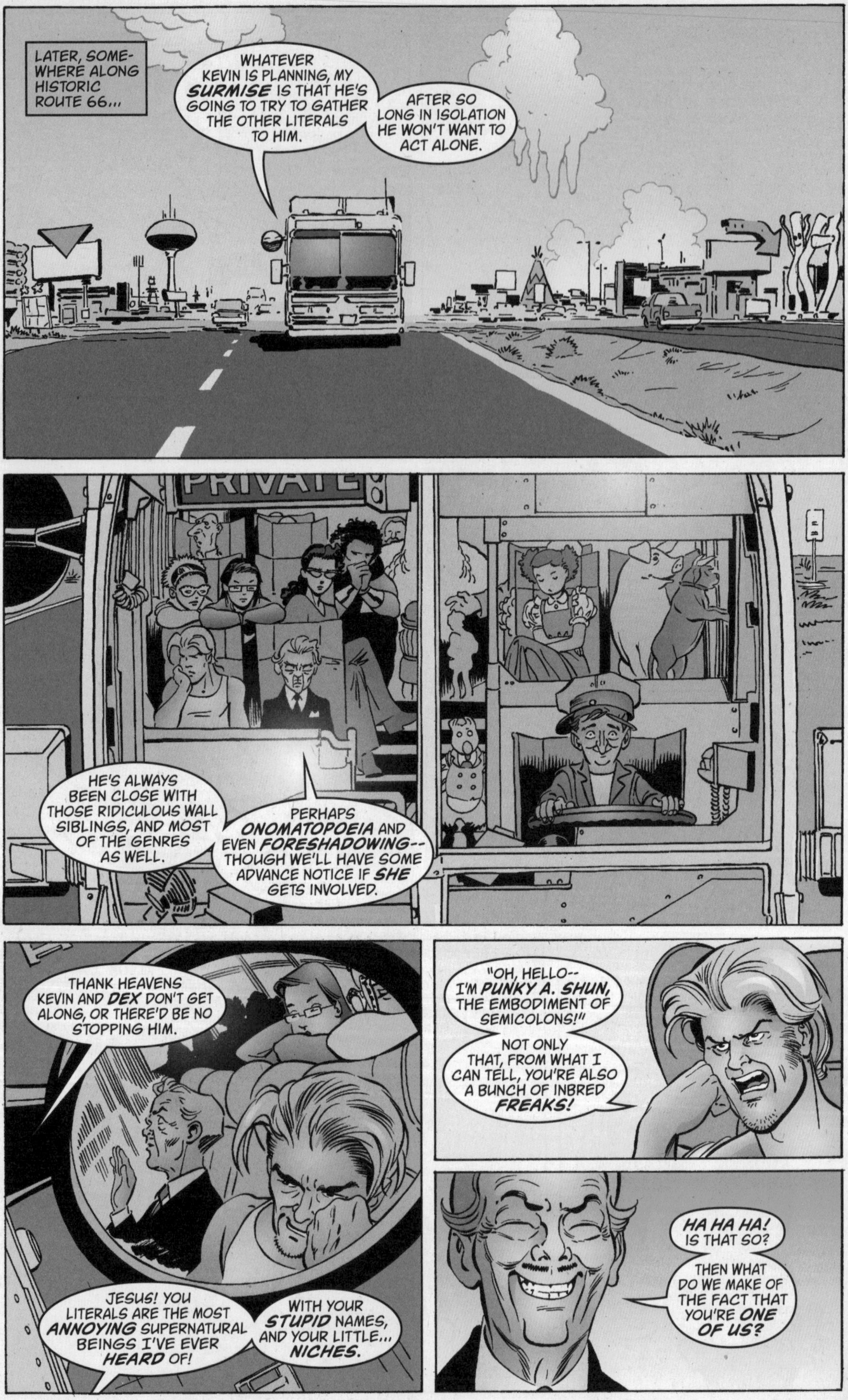
LATER, SOMEWHERE ALONG HISTORIC ROUTE 66...
WHATEVER KEVIN IS PLANNING, MY SURMISE IS THAT HE'S GOING TO TRY TO GATHER THE OTHER LITERALS TO HIM.
AFTER SO LONG IN ISOLATION HE WON'T WANT TO ACT ALONE.
PRIVATE
HE'S ALWAYS BEEN CLOSE WITH THOSE RIDICULOUS WALL SIBLINGS, AND MOST OF THE GENRES AS WELL.
PERHAPS ONOMATOPOEIA AND EVEN FORESHADOWING-- THOUGH WE'LL HAVE SOME ADVANCE NOTICE IF SHE GETS INVOLVED.
THANK HEAVENS KEVIN AND DEX DON'T GET ALONG, OR THERE'D BE NO STOPPING HIM.
JESUS! YOU LITERALS ARE THE MOST ANNOYING SUPERNATURAL BEINGS I'VE EVER HEARD OF!
WITH YOUR STUPID NAMES, AND YOUR LITTLE... NICHES.
"OH, HELLO-- I'M PUNKY A. SHUN, THE EMBODIMENT OF SEMICOLONS!"
NOT ONLY THAT, FROM WHAT I CAN TELL, YOU'RE ALSO A BUNCH OF INBRED FREAKS!
HA HA HA! IS THAT SO?
THEN WHAT DO WE MAKE OF THE FACT THAT YOU'RE ONE OF US?

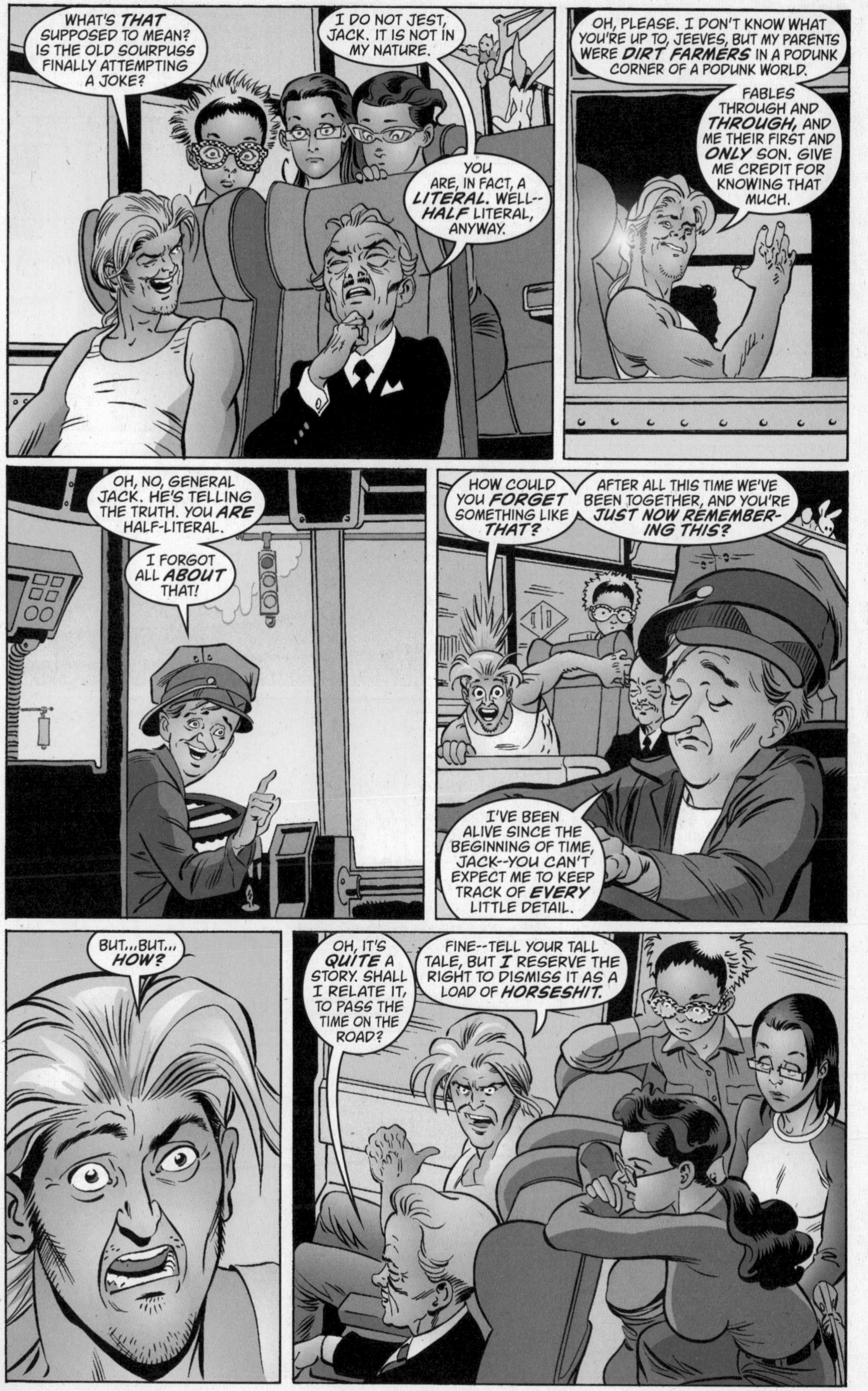
WHAT'S THAT SUPPOSED TO MEAN? IS THE OLD SOURPUSS FINALLY ATTEMPTING A JOKE?
I DO NOT JEST, JACK. IT IS NOT IN MY NATURE.
YOU ARE, IN FACT, A LITERAL. WELL-- HALF LITERAL, ANYWAY.
OH, PLEASE. I DON'T KNOW WHAT YOU'RE UP TO, JEEVES, BUT MY PARENTS WERE DIRT FARMERS IN A PODUNK CORNER OF A PODUNK WORLD.
FABLES THROUGH AND THROUGH, AND ME THEIR FIRST AND ONLY SON. GIVE ME CREDIT FOR KNOWING THAT MUCH.
OH, NO, GENERAL JACK. HE'S TELLING THE TRUTH. YOU ARE HALF-LITERAL.
I FORGOT ALL ABOUT THAT!
HOW COULD YOU FORGET SOMETHING LIKE THAT?
AFTER ALL THIS TIME WE'VE BEEN TOGETHER, AND YOU'RE JUST NOW REMEMBER-ING THIS?
I'VE BEEN ALIVE SINCE THE BEGINNING OF TIME, JACK--YOU CAN'T EXPECT ME TO KEEP TRACK OF EVERY LITTLE DETAIL.
BUT...BUT... HOW?
OH, IT'S QUITE A STORY. SHALL I RELATE IT, TO PASS THE TIME ON THE ROAD?
FINE--TELL YOUR TALL TALE, BUT I RESERVE THE RIGHT TO DISMISS IT AS A LOAD OF HORSESHIT.

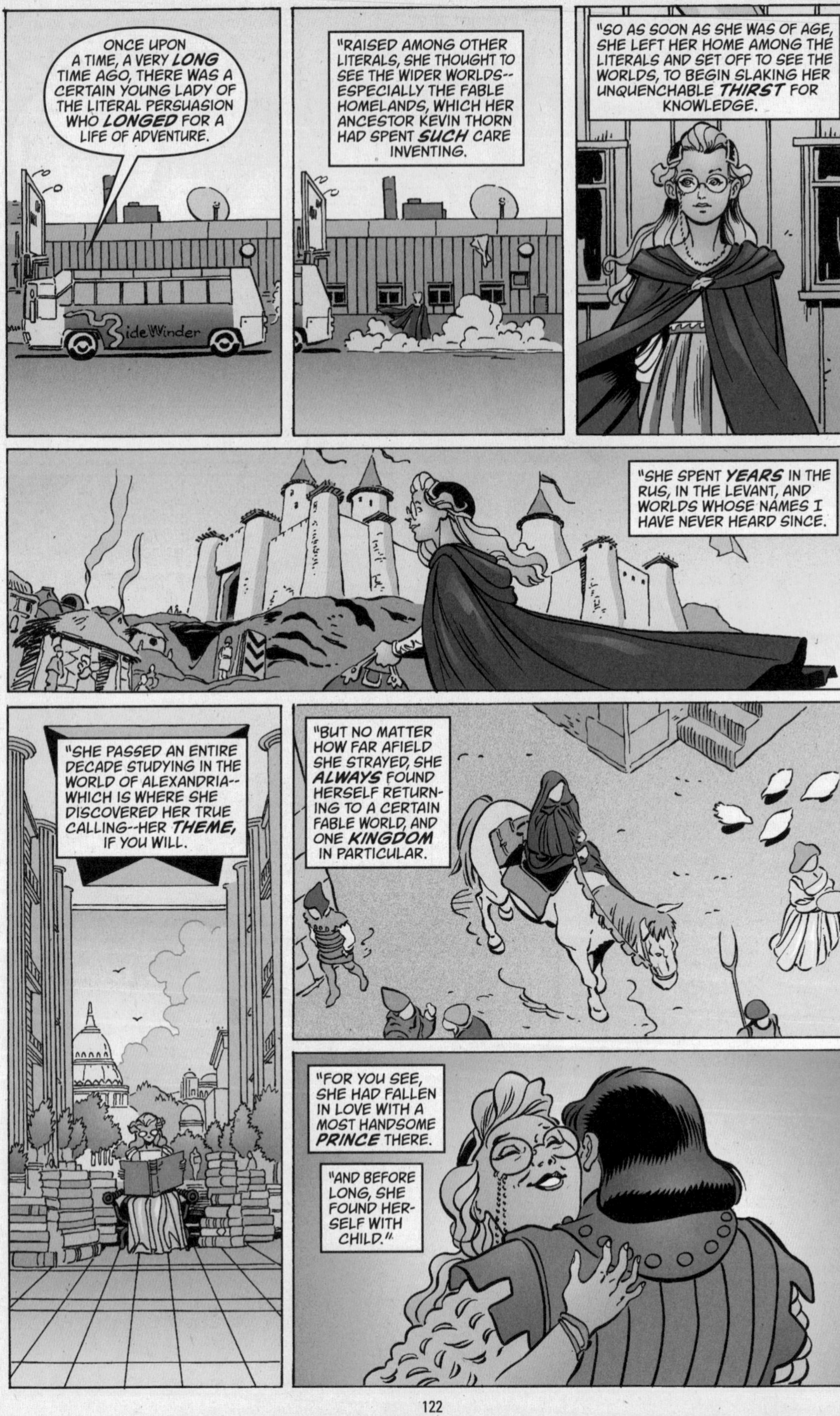
ONCE UPON A TIME, A VERY LONG TIME AGO, THERE WAS A CERTAIN YOUNG LADY OF THE LITERAL PERSUASION WHO LONGED FOR A LIFE OF ADVENTURE.
SideWinder
"RAISED AMONG OTHER LITERALS, SHE THOUGHT TO SEE THE WIDER WORLDS-- ESPECIALLY THE FABLE HOMELANDS, WHICH HER ANCESTOR KEVIN THORN HAD SPENT SUCH CARE INVENTING.
"SO AS SOON AS SHE WAS OF AGE, SHE LEFT HER HOME AMONG THE LITERALS AND SET OFF TO SEE THE WORLDS, TO BEGIN SLAKING HER UNQUENCHABLE THIRST FOR KNOWLEDGE.
"SHE SPENT YEARS IN THE RUS, IN THE LEVANT, AND WORLDS WHOSE NAMES I HAVE NEVER HEARD SINCE.
"SHE PASSED AN ENTIRE DECADE STUDYING IN THE WORLD OF ALEXANDRIA-- WHICH IS WHERE SHE DISCOVERED HER TRUE CALLING--HER THEME, IF YOU WILL.
"BUT NO MATTER HOW FAR AFIELD SHE STRAYED, SHE ALWAYS FOUND HERSELF RETURNING TO A CERTAIN FABLE WORLD, AND ONE KINGDOM IN PARTICULAR.
"FOR YOU SEE, SHE HAD FALLEN IN LOVE WITH A MOST HANDSOME PRINCE THERE.
"AND BEFORE LONG, SHE FOUND HERSELF WITH CHILD."

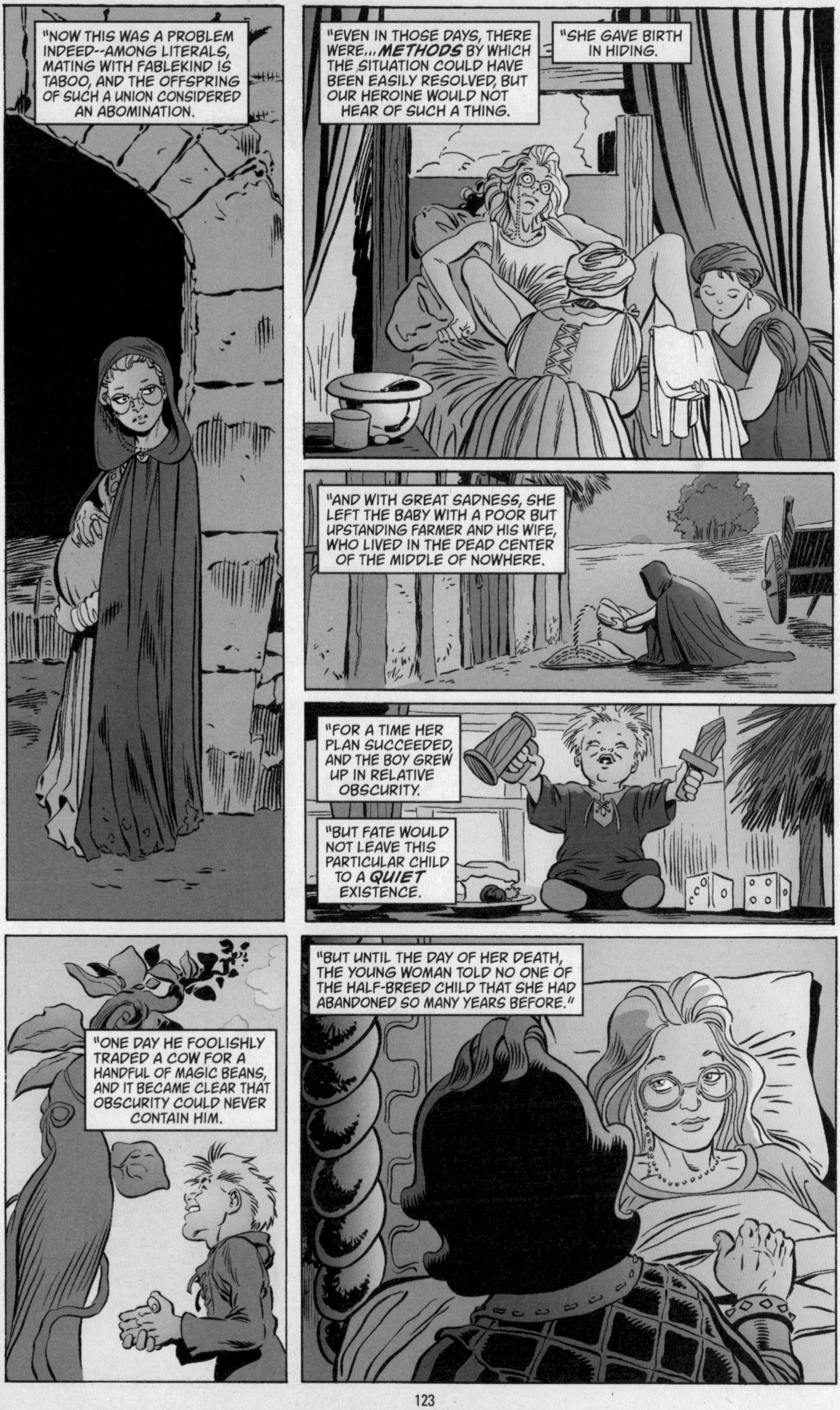
"NOW THIS WAS A PROBLEM INDEED--AMONG LITERALS, MATING WITH FABLEKIND IS TABOO, AND THE OFFSPRING OF SUCH A UNION CONSIDERED AN ABOMINATION.
"EVEN IN THOSE DAYS, THERE WERE... METHODS BY WHICH THE SITUATION COULD HAVE BEEN EASILY RESOLVED, BUT OUR HEROINE WOULD NOT HEAR OF SUCH A THING.
"SHE GAVE BIRTH IN HIDING.
"AND WITH GREAT SADNESS, SHE LEFT THE BABY WITH A POOR BUT UPSTANDING FARMER AND HIS WIFE, WHO LIVED IN THE DEAD CENTER OF THE MIDDLE OF NOWHERE.
"FOR A TIME HER PLAN SUCCEEDED, AND THE BOY GREW UP IN RELATIVE OBSCURITY.
"BUT FATE WOULD NOT LEAVE THIS PARTICULAR CHILD TO A QUIET EXISTENCE.
"ONE DAY HE FOOLISHLY TRADED A COW FOR A HANDFUL OF MAGIC BEANS, AND IT BECAME CLEAR THAT OBSCURITY COULD NEVER CONTAIN HIM.
"BUT UNTIL THE DAY OF HER DEATH, THE YOUNG WOMAN TOLD NO ONE OF THE HALF-BREED CHILD THAT SHE HAD ABANDONED SO MANY YEARS BEFORE."

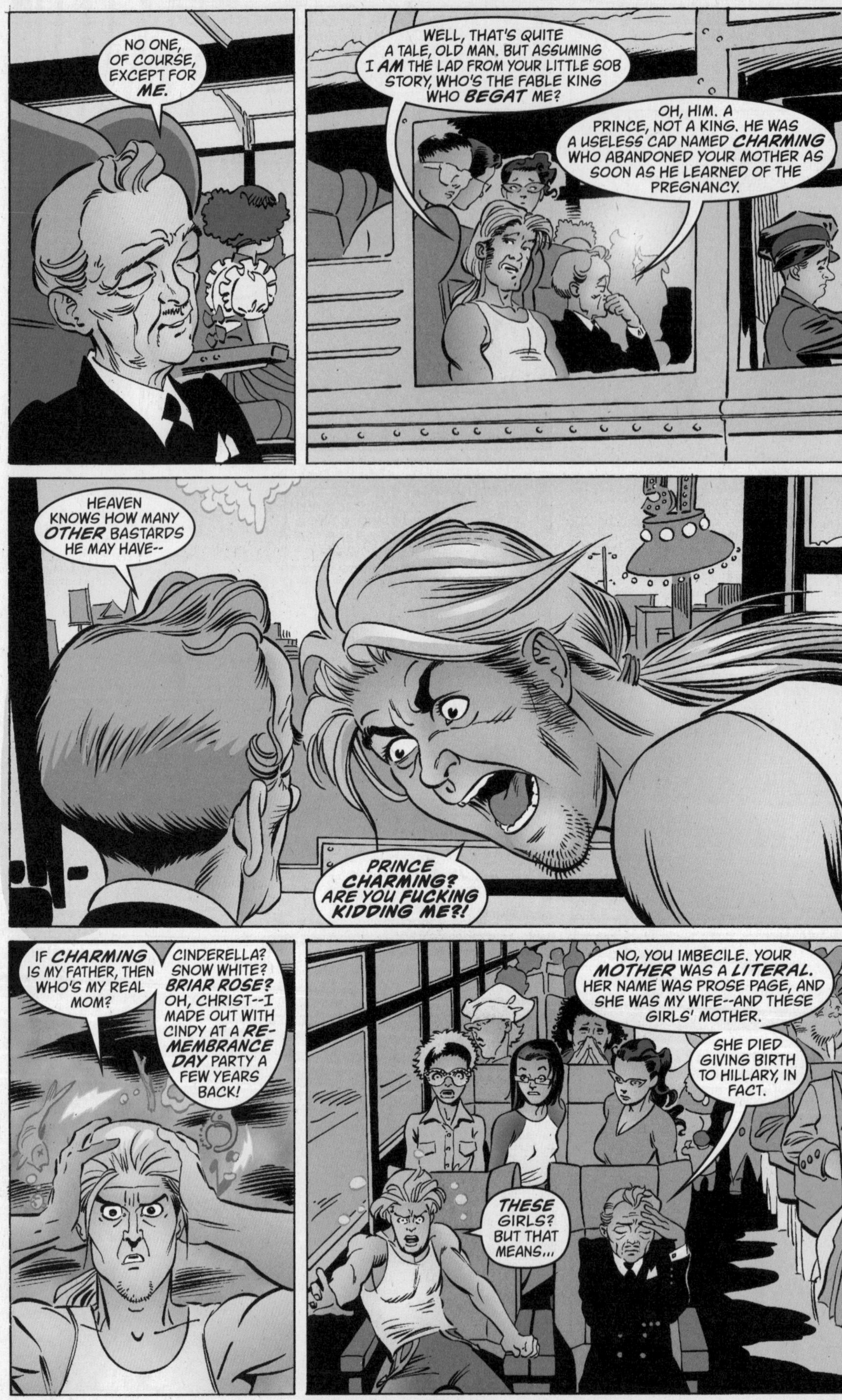
NO ONE, OF COURSE, EXCEPT FOR ME.
WELL, THAT'S QUITE A TALE, OLD MAN. BUT ASSUMING I AM THE LAD FROM YOUR LITTLE SOB STORY, WHO'S THE FABLE KING WHO BEGAT ME?
OH, HIM. A PRINCE, NOT A KING. HE WAS A USELESS CAD NAMED CHARMING WHO ABANDONED YOUR MOTHER AS SOON AS HE LEARNED OF THE PREGNANCY.
HEAVEN KNOWS HOW MANY OTHER BASTARDS HE MAY HAVE--
PRINCE CHARMING? ARE YOU FUCKING KIDDING ME?!
IF CHARMING IS MY FATHER, THEN WHO'S MY REAL MOM?
CINDERELLA? SNOW WHITE? BRIAR ROSE? OH, CHRIST--I MADE OUT WITH CINDY AT A RE-MEMBRANCE DAY PARTY A FEW YEARS BACK!
NO, YOU IMBECILE. YOUR MOTHER WAS A LITERAL. HER NAME WAS PROSE PAGE, AND SHE WAS MY WIFE--AND THESE GIRLS' MOTHER.
SHE DIED GIVING BIRTH TO HILLARY, IN FACT.
THESE GIRLS? BUT THAT MEANS...

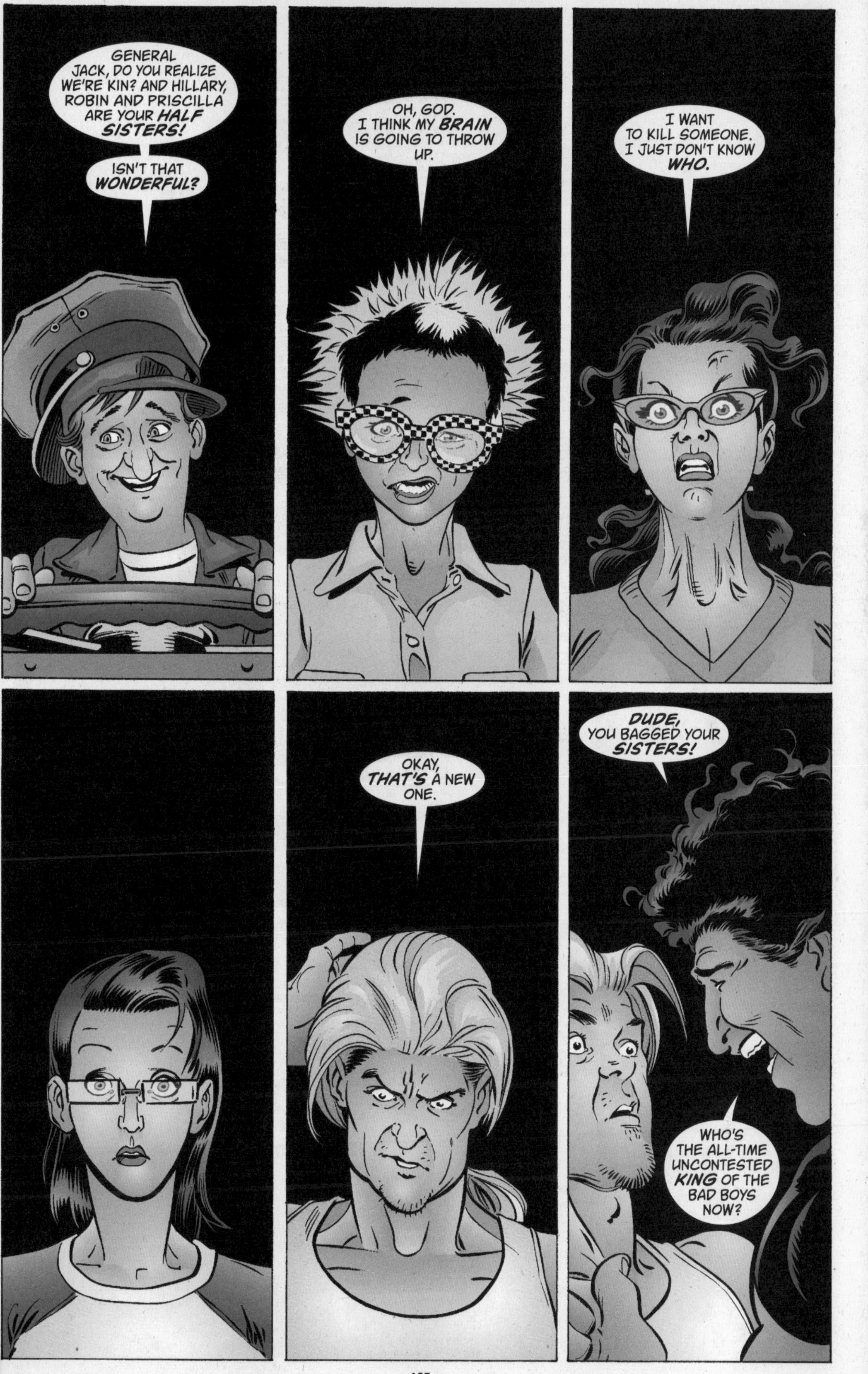
GENERAL JACK, DO YOU REALIZE WE'RE KIN? AND HILLARY, ROBIN AND PRISCILLA ARE YOUR HALF SISTERS!
ISN'T THAT WONDERFUL?
OH, GOD. I THINK MY BRAIN IS GOING TO THROW UP.
I WANT TO KILL SOMEONE. I JUST DON'T KNOW WHO.
OKAY, THAT'S A NEW ONE.
DUDE, YOU BAGGED YOUR SISTERS!
WHO'S THE ALL-TIME UNCONTESTED KING OF THE BAD BOYS NOW?

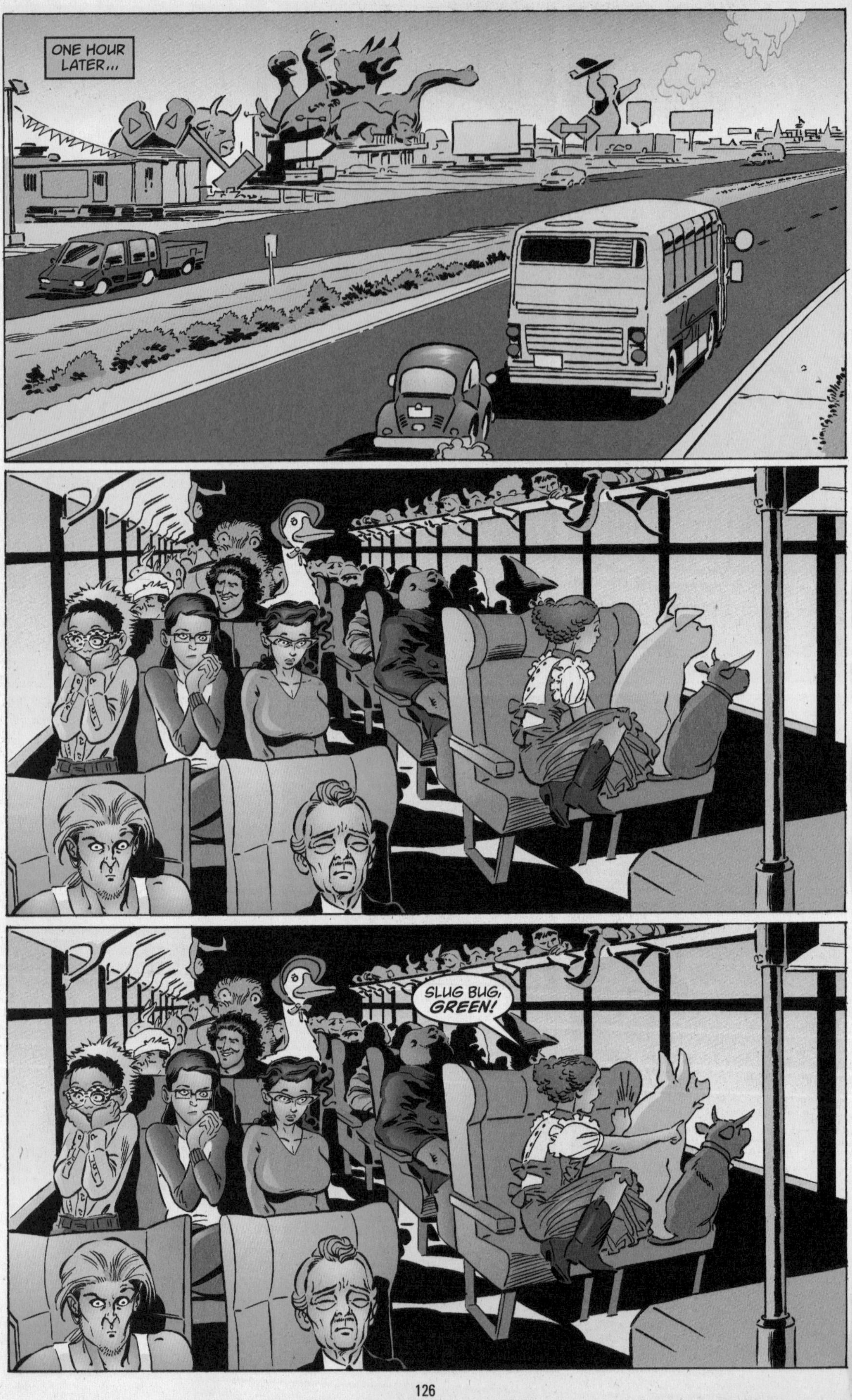
ONE HOUR LATER...
SLUG BUG, GREEN!

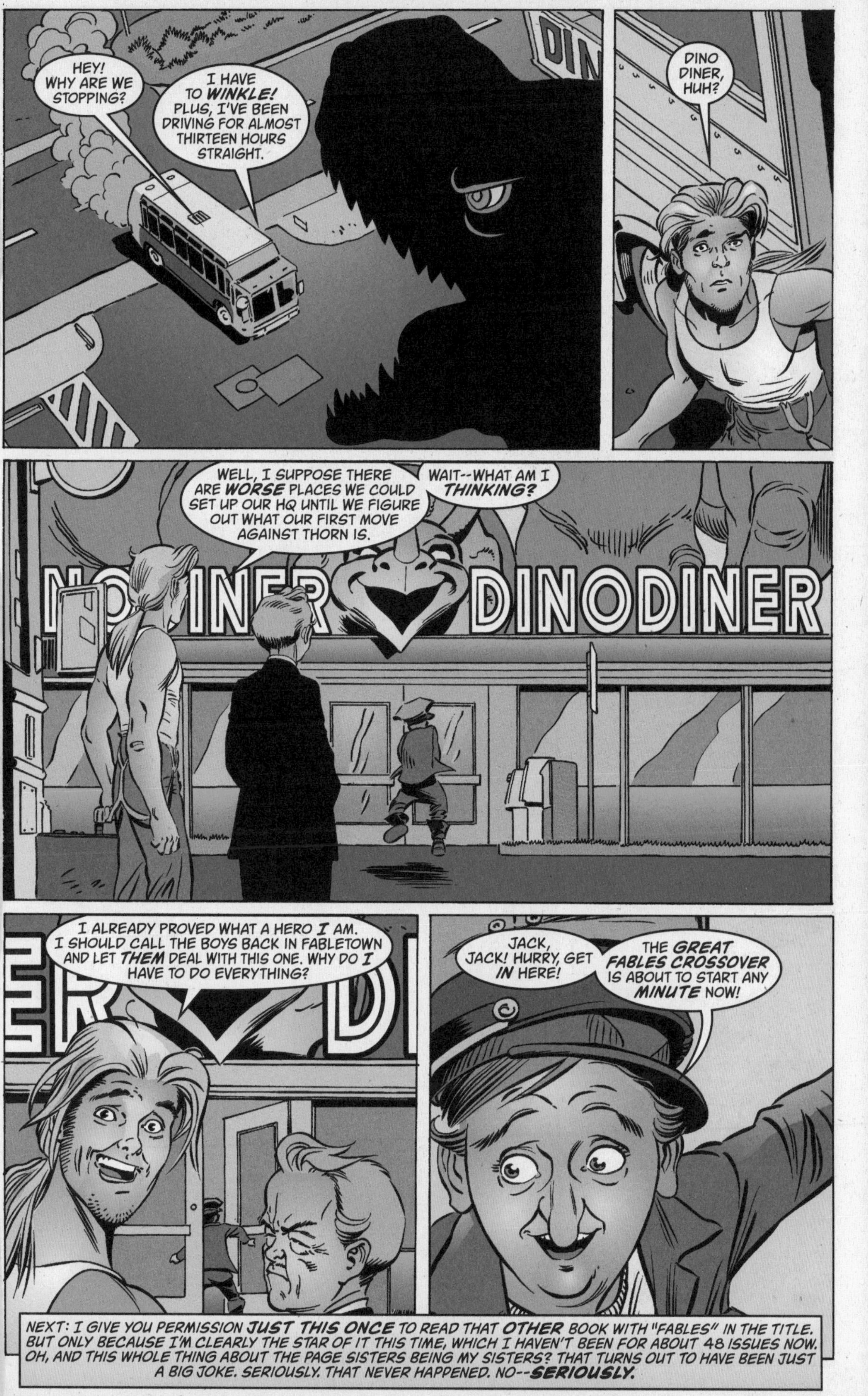
HEY! WHY ARE WE STOPPING?
I HAVE TO WINKLE! PLUS, I'VE BEEN DRIVING FOR ALMOST THIRTEEN HOURS STRAIGHT.
DINO DINER, HUH?
WELL, I SUPPOSE THERE ARE WORSE PLACES WE COULD SET UP OUR HQ UNTIL WE FIGURE OUT WHAT OUR FIRST MOVE AGAINST THORN IS.
WAIT--WHAT AM I THINKING?
DINODINER
I ALREADY PROVED WHAT A HERO I AM. I SHOULD CALL THE BOYS BACK IN FABLETOWN AND LET THEM DEAL WITH THIS ONE. WHY DO I HAVE TO DO EVERYTHING?
JACK, JACK! HURRY, GET IN HERE!
THE GREAT FABLES CROSSOVER IS ABOUT TO START ANY MINUTE NOW!
NEXT: I GIVE YOU PERMISSION JUST THIS ONCE TO READ THAT OTHER BOOK WITH "FABLES" IN THE TITLE. BUT ONLY BECAUSE I'M CLEARLY THE STAR OF IT THIS TIME, WHICH I HAVEN'T BEEN FOR ABOUT 48 ISSUES NOW. OH, AND THIS WHOLE THING ABOUT THE PAGE SISTERS BEING MY SISTERS? THAT TURNS OUT TO HAVE BEEN JUST A BIG JOKE. SERIOUSLY. THAT NEVER HAPPENED. NO--SERIOUSLY.

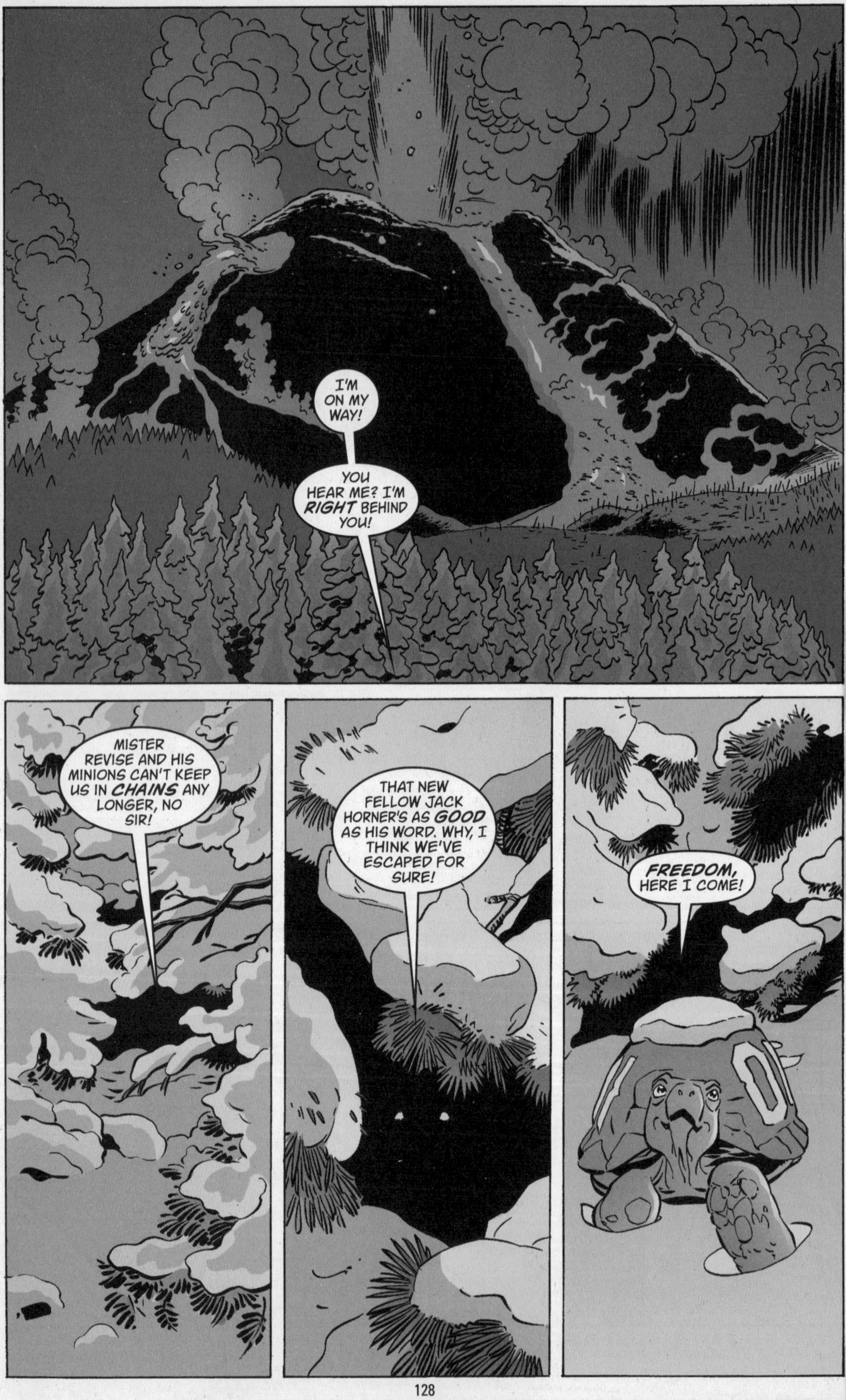
I'M ON MY WAY!
YOU HEAR ME? I'M RIGHT BEHIND YOU!
MISTER REVISE AND HIS MINIONS CAN'T KEEP US IN CHAINS ANY LONGER, NO SIR!
THAT NEW FELLOW JACK HORNER'S AS GOOD AS HIS WORD. WHY, I THINK WE'VE ESCAPED FOR SURE!
FREEDOM, HERE I COME!